DISCARD

OEMCO

Brodart
12/14/88
$31.50

# Inquisition and Society in Early Modern Europe

# Inquisition and Society in Early Modern Europe

Edited and translated by
Stephen Haliczer

Barnes & Noble Books
Totowa, New Jersey

© 1987 Stephen Haliczer
First published in the USA 1987 by
Barnes & Noble Books,
81 Adams Drive,
Totowa, New Jersey, 07512
Printed in Great Britain

**Library of Congress Cataloging-in-Publication Data**

Inquisition and society in early modern Europe.
    1. Inquisition — Europe. 2. Europe — Church history.
I. Haliczer, Stephen, 1942-
BX1712.I576  1987  272'.2    86-26493
ISBN 0-389-20700-4

# Contents

For Deborah and Elena

# Acknowledgements

I should like to thank Karen Blaser of word processing service at Northern Illinois University for her work in typing the index. I am also very grateful to my wife, Deborah Haliczer for her support throughout the entire project and help in designing the index.

# Introduction

Sixtus IV's bull of 1 November 1478 inaugurated the 'modern' Inquisition, one of Western Europe's most durable and most controversial institutions. Condemned by its enemies for 'committing the most repulsive crimes under cover of religion', it was seen by its supporters as the indispensable bulwark of Catholic orthodoxy and public morality.[1]

First established in the Crown of Castile in order to 'officialise' and channel Old Christian hostility to the converted Jews, the Spanish Inquisition quickly spread to the Kingdom of Aragon and later to the Spanish dependencies in Italy and the New World. Although it is virtually impossible to arrive at an exact figure for its overall activity, a recent study of the case summaries which the provincial tribunals began sending the Supreme Council in the mid-sixteenth century places at 49,092 the number of cases tried by the Spanish Inquisition between 1540 and 1700.[2]

During the early and least well documented period of its activity (before 1530), the Spanish Inquisition concentrated its attention mainly on the converted Jews. Later, after this primary material had been exhausted and the major centres of crypto-Jewish activity destroyed, the tribunal turned its attention to the Old Christian population. Here the major focus was mainly on the remoulding of popular culture along the lines dictated at the Council of Trent, as a way of both innoculating the popular masses against the threat of Protestantism and eliminating attitudes and opinions hostile to the church and Catholic orthodoxy.

The Portuguese Inquisition was the second of the great Mediterranean tribunals to be established. For almost its entire history, from the first *auto-de-fe* of 1540 until the reforms instituted by the Marquis of Pombal in 1751, the tribunal was concerned almost entirely with the converted Jews or Cristãos novos. A survey made for the Portuguese government estimated the overall activity of the

1

three Portuguese tribunals (Lisbon, Coimbra, Evora) at 23,068 penanced between 1540 and 1732.[3] The vast majority of these individuals were Cristãos novos, even though by the late seventeenth century the Portuguese Inquisition was punishing increasing numbers of Old Christians for superstition, witchcraft, bigamy, blasphemy and other offences.[4]

The Roman Inquisition, which was established by Pope Paul III in 1542, was a direct consequence of the failure of Charles V's efforts to reconcile Catholics and Protestants at the Regensburg reunion conference of the previous year. The calling of the Council of Trent which was designed to define Catholic orthodoxy and draw the line against Protestantism meant a sharp polarisation of the religious situation in Italy, where moderate reformers like Cardinals Giovanni Morone and Reginald Pole had sought to find a middle ground between the Catholic and Protestant positions. Even though both Morone and Pole had served briefly on the Congregation of the Inquisition, Morone was later (1557) arrested by that body.

Storm clouds were also gathering over the Protestant conventicles which had brought nobles and commoners together in many parts of Italy but particularly at Venice where Andrea di Antonio Da Ponte, brother of a future Doge, was an important leader. Da Ponte and others fled Italy in the 1560s just ahead of the Inquisition but this still left a considerable number of Protestants or neo-Protestants from both the aristocracy and the popular classes to face inquisitorial persecution during the rest of the sixteenth century.[5] The Roman Inquisition was also concerned with popular culture since popular attitudes towards important tenets of the Catholic faith and towards the church itself were far from satisfactory. Like its counterpart in Spain, and for many of the same reasons, the Roman Inquisition sought to remould popular culture in accordance with the post-Tridentine religious ideal.

This book of essays by leading Inquisition scholars is designed to present the areas of concern that were common to all of the great Mediterranean tribunals: Judaising and Protestantism, popular culture and the control of thought and expression. In Part I, the essays by Stephen Haliczer and Nicolas Davidson deal with the Inquisition and the problem of the converted Jews in Spain, Portugal and Italy, while the essay by Jaime Contreras discusses the challenge of Protestantism in Spain. In Part II, the Inquisition's confrontation with popular culture is analysed in the work of Sara Nalle, Mary Elizabeth Perry, Jean-Pierre DeDieu and Mary

O'Neil, while Protestantism among Venetian artisans is the subject of the essay by John Martin. The Inquisition's impact on cultural and intellectual life is addressed by Virgilio Pinto Crespo in Part III.

The growing interest in the Inquisition on both sides of the Atlantic has been reflected in the publication of a number of important scholarly monographs, while the general public's fascination with the Inquisition has been demonstrated by the success of two recent public exhibitions, in Madrid (1982) and at the Newberry Library in Chicago (1985). The presentation of the work of leading experts on the Inquisition is, therefore, especially timely and it is hoped that these essays will contribute to dispelling some of the myths, misinformation and sectarian prejudices that still obscure its image.

## Notes

1. Antonio Puigblanch, *The Inquisition Unmasked* (2 vols, Baldwin, Cradock & Joy, London, 1816), vol. 1, p. 131.
2. Jaime Contreras, 'Las causas de fe en la Inquisición española. 1540-1700. Análisis de una estadistica', paper presented at the Interdisciplinary Symposium on the Medieval and Modern Inquisition (Copenhagen, 5-9 September 1978), p. 17.
3. J. Lucio D'Acevedo, *Historia dos Christãos Novos Portugueses* (Livraria Classica, Lisbon, 1977), p. 337.
4. Michael Geddes, 'A View of the Inquisition of Portugal: With a List of the Prisoners Which Came Out of the Inquisition of Lisbon in an Act of Faith Celebrated Anno 1682', in *Miscellaneous Tracts* (A. & J. Churchill, 1702), pp. 433, 442.
5. Paul F. Grendler, *The Roman Inquisition and the Venetian Press* (Princeton University Press, Princeton, NJ, 1977), pp. 134-8.

# Part I
# The Inquisition and Religious Heresy

# 1

# The First Holocaust: The Inquisition and the Converted Jews of Spain and Portugal

*Stephen Haliczer*

A series of discriminatory measures adopted at the Fourth Lateran Council of 1215 ushered in a period of growing difficulty for the Jews of Western Europe.[1] At the Council of Narbonne of 1235, Jews were forced to wear a distinguishing yellow patch on their clothing. In 1290 they were expelled from England, and in France public hostility towards them resulted in successive expulsions and pogroms.[2] Spain was the only major European country which retained a high degree of tolerance for the Jewish community, largely because the Jews provided essential services and skills in what was, for a long time, a frontier society with vast under-populated regions.

By the fourteenth century, however, the reconquest had accomplished its main objectives, the Christian population had risen dramatically in frontier regions and both Jews and Mudejares (Moors living under Christian rule) began to suffer discrimination. In the case of the Mudejares of Valencia, this involved being pushed out of the major towns and the fertile *huerta* regions along the coast and into the barren, mountainous regions of the interior.[3] In the case of the Jews, something very similar happened. Beginning in the 1340s rabble-rousing and antisemitic preachers like Hernán Martinez began attacking the Jews openly in their sermons and inciting mobs against them. By mid-century, *'convivencia'*, once so widely accepted in Spain, became a bone of contention in the struggle between Pedro I and his half-brother Henry of Trastamara for the Castilian throne. The civil war that ended with Pedro's death was marked by brutal attacks on Jewish communities and even though Henry I attempted to return to the Crown's former policy of supporting the independent existence of Jewish communities, the old tolerance could no longer be re-established. In 1391, a series of pogroms devastated the Jewish ghettos over much of Spain.[4] Like the Mudejares, the Jews were pushed out of the major towns into the countryside where economic opportunities were fewer.[5] But, unlike the Mudejares, whose influence virtually disappeared from the Valencian towns, the decline of urban Jewry left behind a new group: the *conversos*.

Of course, there had always been a few Jews who had converted to Christianity. It was in order to protect these people from the hostility of Old Christians that a law of the Partidas ordered Christians not to call such persons 'turncoats', 'Marranos' and other names.[6] Salamon ha Levi, chief rabbi of the flourishing Jewish community of Burgos, was just such a person, having converted to Christianity one year before the outbreak of the 1391 pogroms.[7] But, after 1391, something that had only affected a small minority became a mass phenomenon as the mobs had forced thousands of Jews to convert. The 1391 pogroms, moreover, were followed by the missionary campaigns of the Dominican Vicente Ferrer which touched off antisemitic rioting in 1412-14, the disputation at Tortosa (1413-14) and the forced conversion of the large Jewish community on Mallorca in 1435.[8]

Like the Agermanados of the 1520s who forceably converted the Mudejares of Valencia, the popular masses who rose to attack the Jewish ghettos in 1391 hoped that by shattering the Jewish community they would deprive the social elite of a powerful tool of oppression, since the Jews had played a major role in tax and revenue collection for crown, church and nobility.[9] As it turned out, converted Jews merely replaced Jews as tax-farmers and money-lenders while their conversion provided a passport to Christian society which they could now fully enter, having shed the legal disabilities that they had had as Jews. This was the position taken by both church and crown, and with such powerful support, the conversos proceeded to prosper economically and occupy powerful positions in city councils and in the royal administration itself.

Within a few decades of the 1391 pogroms, therefore, the Old Christians found themselves confronted with a new and ambitious group whose intelligence and ability allowed them to shoulder aside the traditional Old Christian urban elites and make rapid progress in every area of Spanish life. But if christianisation could open paths to upward social mobility to the conversos, dechristianisation was a way of closing them. By the middle of the fifteenth century, Old Christian writers stressed the insincerity of the converted and the same charges of ritual murders and implacable hostility towards Christians were being levied against the conversos as were formerly levied against the Jews. The infamous libel of the Niño de la

Guardia, which has been been roundly discredited but is still accepted as valid by such apologists for the Inquisition as Tarsicio de Azcona, was an accusation of the ritual crucifixion of a Christian child as part of a religious ceremony in a synagogue and involved both Jews and conversos.[10]

Even more disquieting for those conversos who hoped for peaceful integration into Old Christian society was the growing evidence of overt racialism in Spanish society. Legal exclusion of conversos from craft guilds and from city councils was becoming common by the middle of the fifteenth century and was frequently accompanied by violent attacks on the homes and persons of conversos.[11] This was followed in the 1470s by a series of violent popular uprisings against conversos that came dangerously close to degenerating into attacks on the authority of the crown itself, especially since the mobs concentrated their fire on conversos who collected royal taxes.[12]

When Ferdinand and Isabella came to the throne in 1475, they were acutely aware that the power and independence of the Castilian monarchy could not be re-established without forging a strong relationship with the towns. Confronted by a rebellion that had the active or tacit support of many of Castile's great magnates, they moved quickly to capitalise on the anti-aristocratic Hermandad movement which had mobilised urban militias in support of the monarchy during the aristocratic conspiracies of the previous reign.[13] Moreover, in what was to become a pattern of their administration, they 'officialised' the urban militia movement, making the frequently ineffective leagues of cities of the 1460s into an arm of the state with its own central council.[14]

In helping Ferdinand and Isabella institute the Santa Hermandad (Holy Brotherhood), however, the Castilian towns got more than they bargained for: a national organisation that saddled them with heavy taxes until 1498.[15] The same miscalculation was made by those members of the converso elite who, like Alonso Díaz de Montalvo, attacked the Jews and called for the establishment of an Inquisition. They felt that discriminatory measures taken against the Jews and a tribunal that would punish backsliders in the converso community would help to accomplish their goal of full integration. They, too, got more than they bargained for.

The Catholic Sovereigns eagerly embraced the idea of an Inquisition which should be, like the Santa Hermandad, a national, not episcopal, institution and involve strong state control complete with an Inquisitor-General nominated by the crown and a central governing council (the Suprema, established in 1483). By 'officialising' the persecution of the conversos, Ferdinand and Isabella gained support among the popular masses and the old Christian clergy while at the same time greatly increasing the power of the state by establishing an institution that, at least theoretically, was unconstrained by considerations of social status, wealth or political influence.

Placed under the control of fanatical theologians who were frequently Dominican monks, this 'first Inquisition' concentrated its fire overwhelmingly against the converted Jews. The tribunal that was established in Ciudad Real in November 1483, for example, decimated the converso community in that town and then moved on to the much larger city of Toledo in 1485.[16] From 1485 to 1500 more than 99 per cent of its cases concerned the converted Jews. In 1490 alone, 433 persons were penanced or relaxed.[17] In Valencia, between 1484 and 1530, 91 per cent of the accused were conversos and between 1488 and 1505, 1,191 of the 1,199 persons reconciled by the Barcelona tribunal were conversos.[18]

These early tribunals also had a penchant for handing out harsh punishments. Of the 1,997 persons penanced by the tribunal of Valencia between 1484 and 1530, 909 or 45.5 per cent were given death sentences and of these 754 were actually executed. In some tribunals, the percentage of death sentences was even higher, with the short-lived tribunals of Avila and Guadalupe condemning 58.1 per cent and 82.2 per cent, respectively.[19]

By the late 1540s and as early as the 1530s in some tribunals, this 'first Inquisition', characterised by highly autonomous regional tribunals, frequent violations of procedure and an obsession with Judaisers, was coming to an end.[20] The violent persecution of the late fifteenth and early sixteenth centuries had destroyed the centres of Crypto-Judaism in Spain.

By the end of the sixteenth century, there was a powerful movement to abolish or modify the purity of blood statutes and Fray Agustin Salucio, an opponent of the statutes, could justify his position by arguing that 'in general' the conversos were 'christians at heart'.[21] At the same time, the excesses of such local inquisitors as Diego Rodriguez Lucero in Cordoba or Juan González de Munibrega in Valencia led to greatly increased interference by the Suprema in the affairs of local tribunals.[22] As a result of this intervention, procedure was regularised and made uniform for all tribunals and the Suprema made it a practice to review cases on a regular basis. The judicial autonomy of local tribunals was curbed even further by forcing them to refer to the Suprema before torturing a suspect and by requesting the submission of sentences for review by the Suprema in a variety of cases.[23]

The result of these trends was a sharp decline in the number of conversos tried by most Spanish tribunals. Between 1540 and 1559, for example, Judaisers comprised a mere 5.9 per cent of the 29,584 accused before all tribunals while in Zaragoza they were only 4 per cent of the 481 cases.[24] This lull in the Spanish Inquisition's persecution of the converted Jews was to end only when a large influx of Portuguese New Christians provided a rich new crop of denunciations for Crypto-Judaism.

The sudden forced conversion of all Portuguese Jews in 1497 created a massive New Christian class which differed radically from the conversos of Spain. As Josef Hayim Yerushalmi has observed, the Portuguese New Christians were spared 'the demoralizing intracommunal and intrafamilial ruptures which conversion had inflicted upon Spanish Jewry'.[25] As a result, Portuguese New Christians were able to maintain a degree of cohesiveness and a level of Judaic culture that could not be achieved by the Spanish conversos. Moreover, by forbidding any judicial inquiry into evidence of Judaising for 20 years from 30 May 1497 and extending the exemption to 1534, King Manoel unwittingly helped preserve that communal solidarity by freeing the New Christians from any fear of persecution for a considerable period of time after their conversion.

One result of this remarkable situation was the tenacious resistance offered by the New Christians to João III's efforts to establish a Spanish-style Inquisition. This campaign of resistance involved a great expenditure of funds that must have been raised by broadly-based subscriptions from the New Christian community. Even after the establishment of an Inquisition on the Spanish model on 17 July 1547, that resistance continued and almost certainly restrained the activity of the early Portuguese Inquisition. In the 33 years between 1547 and 1580 when Portugal passed under Spanish control, we have evidence of only 34 *autos-de-fe* with 1,998 individuals punished and 220 death sentences.[26]

By this time, however, a virulent form of antisemitism had taken possession of the popular masses, most of the clergy and an important part of the aristocracy. Violently antisemitic works like João de Barros's attack on the Talmud or the *Breve Discurso contra a heretica perfidia do Judaismo* by Vicente de Costa Mattos poured from the printing presses in a country where such works had once been conspicuous by their absence.[27] Adding to the pressure, bishops' juntas and the popular estate in the Cortes repeatedly demanded the virtual exclusion of New Christians from honourable offices, trades and professions.[28]

Around the time of Cardinal Henry's (Portugal's first Inquisitor-General) death on 14 January 1580, therefore, the Inquisition had acquired such strong popular support that nothing could prevent it from unleashing a terrible wave of persecution. Between 1581 and 1600 the three Portuguese tribunals (Lisbon, Coimbra and Evora) held 50 *autos-de-fe* at which more than 2,979 persons were penanced and 221 death sentences were handed down.[29] One result of this massive persecution was the exodus of large numbers of New Christians who established communities in southwestern France (especially Bordeaux and Bayonne), the Papal States, Amsterdam, Turkey and Greece.[30]

Given the sharp upswing in the activity of the Portuguese tribunals, it is little wonder that many New Christians looked longingly across the border where the Spanish Inquisition had largely ceased persecuting the conversos. But there were other, perhaps even more compelling reasons for the influx of Portuguese New Christians into Spain during the late sixteenth and early seventeenth centuries. By the 1580s a powerful group of mainly New Christian financiers had emerged and had come to dominate Portuguese long-distance trade. Largely avoiding the pepper trade where excessive royal regulation and Dutch competition reduced potential profits, these merchants dealt in pearls, precious stones, porcelains and other commodities. Using the profits from the Asiatic trade, the New Christian merchants developed the sugar industry of Brazil and invaded Spanish America using their superior access to the products of Northern Europe (through the Sephardic Jews of Amsterdam) and Asia to compete with the Seville trade monopoly. As a result, the *asiento* system whereby mainly Genoese syndicates of bankers would advance funds to the crown and be repaid with American silver brought in through Seville was becoming undermined as the New Christians drew more and more silver to Lisbon.[31]

The growing wealth of the New Christians had not escaped the notice of the penurious Spanish government of Philip III. Disregarding the objectives of the Portuguese hierarchy, the government obtained a papal pardon for which the New Christians paid 1,860,000 ducats into the royal treasury as well as substantial bribes to the Duke of Lerma and other government officials.[32] This was followed in 1606 by the lifting of all restrictions on New Christian travel. Even though the crown re-imposed the travel restrictions in 1619, the stage had been set for a new chapter in the relationship between the Spanish Monarchy and the Portuguese New Christians.

Under Philip IV and his reform-minded chief minister, the count-duke of Olivares, limitations were placed on the 'purity of blood' genealogical examinations that had made it so difficult for those of Judaic ancestry to enter university colleges, military orders and other honourable corporations, and the government began to lend a sympathetic ear to the proposals of the New Christians.[33] The latter had become increasingly interested in entering the legal and heavily protected Seville American trade as Dutch and English freebooters made the unescorted illegal trade increasingly dangerous. For its part, the Spanish government realised that it would need the financial services of the New Christians if it was to be successful in defending the empire. In order to bring the New Christians into imperial finance, Philip IV granted them complete freedom to travel anywhere in the empire as well as naturalisations to participate in the Seville American trade.[34] New Christian participation in that trade proved highly beneficial to Spain by guaranteeing its survival after the disastrous loss of the entire treasure fleet to the Dutch in September 1628.[35]

New Christian bankers also became key players in the crown's system of international payments. Between 1626 and 1640 their share of the *asiento* contracts rose from 5 per cent to more than 50 per cent, making possible a remarkable revival in Spain's military fortunes between 1631 and 1640.[36]

In spite of the manifest utility of the Portuguese and the improvement in the crown's financial position (including dramatically lower interest rates) that their participation in the *asientos* had brought about, they had many enemies. Apart from the Portuguese clergy, these included the municipal councils and merchant corporations of Spain who were ousted from lucrative revenue and customs collection positions by the New Christians, bureaucrats who were angry over the special taxes on official salaries and pensions imposed by the Olivares regime, and the merchants of Seville, Lima and Mexico who had suffered because of competition from the New Christians.[37]

Because of its special responsibility for the preservation of Roman Catholicism, the Inquisition was in the best position to strike at the New Christians who, in many instances, had preserved their Judaic culture and were in close commercial contract with the Portuguese Jews of Amsterdam, Hamburg and Italy.[38] In Portugal, the three tribunals continued their high level of activity, handing down 391 death sentences (230 were actually burned) and punishing 4,995 other individuals between 1620 and 1640.[39] In Spain, despite government pressure for moderation, the Inquisition remained highly suspicious of the Portuguese. The Holy Office had helped to sabotage the 1606 act guaranteeing the new Christians freedom of movement by alleging that they only wished to leave the Iberian Peninsula in order to revert to Judaism abroad.[40] The Suprema also ordered the provincial tribunals to maintain a special series of books to record denunciations of New Christians even after the liberal former royal confessor Don Antonio de Sotomayor had been appointed Inquisitor-General in 1632.[41]

As a consequence of these and other measures, Judaisers once again figured prominently among those brought to trial by the Spanish Inquisition. Before 1560 and 1614 the 1,759 Judaisers made up only 5.5 per cent of the 29,584 cases tried by the Holy Office but between 1615 and 1700 there were 3,171 persons tried for Judaising, more than 20 per cent of the 15,326 cases tried during that period.[42]

Of course, some tribunals were hardly affected by this phenomenon. In Toledo, Judaisers comprised 44.3 per cent of the accused while in Zaragoza only 3.1 per cent of cases involved Judaising. The tribunal of Valencia, which was similary remote from the areas of heavy New Christian penetration, had only 15 such cases.[43]

The Inquisition also struck at the New Christians in Peru (1634), and Cartagena de Indias (1636) and against the wealthy and influential Portuguese merchants in Mexico.[44] Beginning in 1642, the Mexican Holy Office carried out a series of *autos* culminating in the great *auto general* of 11 April 1649 at which there were 109 penitents, all but one convicted of Judaising. At this auto, 13 persons were executed but only one, the impenitent Thomas Treviño de Sobremonte, was burned alive, the others having been garrotted before being consigned to the flames.[45]

In Portugal, after the decree of 6 February 1649 by which João IV eliminated confiscation of property by the Inquisition in return for the financial support that led to the recovery of Pernambuco from the Dutch, the Inquisition revenged itself on the New Christians by unleashing a veritable reign of terror. Between 1651 and

1673 the three tribunals penanced 473 persons and handed down 243 death sentences.[46] In 1656, the Inquisition even went so far as formally to excommunicate all those who had had anything to do with the act against confiscations, including the king himself.[47]

New Christian resistance continued strong, however, and resulted in a suspension of inquisitorial activity by Pope Clement X which lasted from 1674 to 1681.[48] In 1682, the Portuguese Inquisition resumed operations with a grand *auto-de-fe* held in Lisbon at which 76 of the 105 penitents were New Christians and 4 were burnt.[49] This was just two years after the *auto-de-fe* held in Madrid before Charles III and his entire court, where 20 of the 21 condemned to death were Portuguese New Christians who, before they died, heard themselves denounced from the pulpit as 'perfidious Jews . . . God's worst enemies'.[50]

After a reduction in activity between 1682 and 1700, the Portuguese tribunals displayed a last burst of energy during the first two decades of the eighteenth century. This wave of persecution was so ferocious that it virtually depopulated certain villages and was blamed for the decline of economic life in large parts of central and northern Portugal.[51]

In Spain, the furious persecution of the late seventeenth century continued into the 1720s in spite of the change of dynasty from Hapsburg to Bourbon and Philip V's obvious distaste for the Holy Office.[52] Between 1721 and 1725, 902 Judaisers were penanced and 160 were executed.[53] After 1725, however, the number of cases declined rapidly. The last case tried by the Toledo tribunal occurred in 1756 and, of the more than 5,000 cases coming before all tribunals between 1780 and 1820, only 16 involved Judaising.[54]

For their part, the Portuguese tribunals remained active through the middle of the century, even though many New Christians had married into Old Christian families, but with the coming of Jose I (1750-77) and his chief minister, Sebastiao Jose De Carvalho e Melo, later created Marquis de Pombal, the days of the Inquisition's political power were numbered. As minister-dictator during Jose's reign, Pombal sought to subordinate the country's leading institutions to the monarchy and build up the national economy and colonial trade. In order to do this, it was essential to stop the unbridled depredations of the Holy Office and end discrimination against the New Christians who still played a vital role in the colonial economy and Portuguese overseas trade. As a first step, Pombal ordered the records of all 'purity of blood' investigations destroyed in 1768 and, in 1771, the Inquisition was made into just another royal tribunal with the use of torture sharply restricted, secret proceedings abolished and executions prohibited without special royal permission.[55] By the late eighteenth century, inquisitorial persecution of the New Christians had largely died out and the Portuguese Inquisition concentrated its efforts on such crimes as blasphemy, bigamy, solicitation and witchcraft. Nevertheless, the Portuguese Inquisition had left a remarkable and chilling record of persecution. Of the 23,068 individuals penanced between 1536 and 1732, nine-tenths were New Christian Judaisers.[56]

The demise of formal persecution, however, did not mean the end of anti-semitism or Crypto-Judaism in the Iberian Peninsula. Even after Pombal's reforms, Portuguese New Christians continued to flee Portugal to join the Jewish Communities in Bordeaux, Salonika and other places.[57] Only in 1865 was 'purity of blood' removed as a requirement for holding public office in Spain while throughout the nineteenth and twentieth centuries the Catholic right-wing tended to identify the Jew with anything that seemed to threaten the values of traditional Spain.[58]

Tantalizingly, as recent investigations have shown, vestiges of Crypto-Judaism can still be found in rural Spain and Portugal.[59] The more than 300-year effort to eradicate Judaism as a cultural as well as a religious force in the Iberian Peninsula appears to have been at least a partial failure.

## Notes

1. Francisco Martin Hernández, 'La Inquisición en España antes de los Reyes Catolicos', in Joaquín Pérez Villanueva (ed.), *La Inquisición Española: nueva vision, nuevos horizontes* (Siglo Vientiuno, Madrid, 1980), p. 22.

2. Philippe Wolff, 'The 1391 Pogrom in Spain. Social Crisis or Not?', *Past and Present, 50* (Feb. 1971), p. 5.

3. Henri Lapeyre, *La Géograpie de l'Espagne morisque* (SEVPEN, Paris, 1959), pp. 27-8.

4. In Ciudad Real, for example, the riots devastated the Jewish quarter while the main synagogue was turned into a Dominican monastery. Haim Beinart, *Conversos on Trial* (The Magnes Press, Jerusalem, 1981), pp. 49-50.

5. Angus MacKay, 'Popular Movements and Pogroms in Fifteenth Century Castile', *Past and Present, 55* (1972), pp. 38-9.

6. Martin Hernández, 'La Inquisición en España', p. 26. For the origins of the insulting term 'Marrano' which has unfortunately been picked up by modern historiography, see I.S. Revah, 'Les Marranes', *Revue des Etudes Juives, 108* (1959-60), p. 30.

7. Luciano Serrano, *Los Conversos D. Pablo de Santa Maria D. Alfonso de Cartegena* (SCIS, Madrid, 1942), pp. 21-2.

8. Revah, 'Les Marranes, pp. 31-2.

9. For the revolt of the Germanías see Ricardo García Cárcel, *Las Germanías de Valencia* (Ediciones Península, Barcelona, 1975).

10. Tarsício de Azcona, *Isabel la Católica* (Biblioteca de Autores Christianos, Madrid, 1964), p. 638. Azcona is generous enough to admit that the ritual sacrifice of Christian children was not an annual event in the synagogues.

11. Henry Kamen, *Inquisition and Society in Spain* (Weidenfeld & Nicolson, London, 1985), p. 25. The first racist law in Spain was the Sentencia Estatuto which declared all conversos suspect of apostasy and therefore incapable of holding public office. Revah, 'Les Marranes', p. 33.

12.¹ MacKay, 'Popular Movements', pp. 60-3.

13. Azcona, *Isabel la Católica*, pp. 98-9.

14. Marvin Lunenfeld, *The Council of the Santa Hermandad* (University of Miami Press, Coral Gables, Florida, 1970), p. 76.

15. Ibid., p. 73.

16. Beinart, *Conversos*, pp. 89-100.

17. Jean-Pierre Dedieu, 'Les Quatre temps de l'Inquisition', in Bartolomé Bennassar (ed.), *L'Inquisition espagnole* (Hachette, Paris, 1979), p. 20.

18. Ricardo García Cárcel, *Orígines de la Inquisición Española* (Ediciones Península, Barcelona, 1976), p. 170.

19. DeDieu, 'Les Quatre temps', p. 34.

20. For a discussion of procedural irregularities see Henry Charles Lea, *A History of the Inquisition of Spain* (4 vols, Macmillan, New York, 1906-7), vol. 3, pp. 211-13.

21. Revah, 'Les Marranes', p. 38.

22. Lea, *A History*, vol. 1, pp. 191-210. For the activities of Juan de Munibrega see Archivo Histórico Nacional (hereafter AHN), 29 May 1528, leg. 170, no. 1, 30 July, 18 February 1540, leg. 542, no. 1, exp. 6 and 16 October 1543, leg. 542, no. 1 exp. 26.

23. Lea, *A History*, vol. 2, pp. 180-1.

24. De Dieu, 'Les Quatre temps', pp. 29-30.

25. Yosef Hayim Yerushalmi, 'Prolegomenon' to Alexandre Herculano, *History of the Origin and Establishment of the Inquisition of Portugal* (KTAV Publishing House, New York, 1971), p. 38.

26. Lea, *A History*, vol. 3, p. 259.

27. Ibid., pp. 272-3.

28. J. Lucio D'Acevedo, *Historia dos Christãos Novos Portugueses* (Livraria Classica, Lisbon, 1922), pp. 148-9, 159, 199-215.

29. Lea, *A History*, vol. 3, pp. 265-6.

30. Revah, 'Les Marranes,' pp. 66-7.

31. James Boyajian, *Portuguese Bankers at the Court of Spain 1626-1650* (Rutgers University Press, New Brunswick, NJ, 1983), pp. 8-13.

32. Lea, *A History*, vol. 3, p. 267.

33. Boyajian, *Portuguese Bankers*, p. 18.

34. Kamen, *Inquisition and Society*, p. 225.

35. Boyajian, *Portuguese Bankers*, p. 40.

36. Ibid., p. 44.

37. Ibid., pp. 104, 107-8.

38. Ibid., pp. 73-85, 175.

39. Lea, *A History*, vol. 3, p. 273.

40. AHN, *Inquisición*, 6 July 1619, lib. 497, fols 300-300v.

41. AHN, *Inquisición*, 8 June 1638, lib. 926, fols 178-179v, 182, 182v.

42. Jaime Contreras, 'Las Causas de fe en la Inquisición española: 1540-1700. Análisis de una estadistica', papers presented at the Interdisciplinary Symposium on the Medieval and Modern Inquisition (Copenhagen, 5-9 September 1978), pp. 26-48.

43. Ibid., p. 50; DeDieu, 'Les Quatre temps', p. 31. I am referring to my own analysis of the case summaries for the figure on the activity of the Valencia tribunal during this period.

44. Boyajian, *Portuguese Bankers*, pp. 122-7.

45. Henry Charles Lea, *The Inquisition in the Spanish Dependencies* (Macmillan, New York, 1908), pp. 230-1. The inquisitorial official who wrote the account of this *auto* declared that Treviño must have been 'invaded by a legion of devils' to cause him to be so obstinate in his desire to die as a Jew. *Auto general de la fe celebrado en la muy noble y muy leal ciudad de Mexico 11 de Abril de 1649* (Antonio Calderon, Mexico City, 1649), fol. 233.

46. Acevedo, *Historia dos Christãos Novos*, pp. 251-61.

47. Lea, *A History*, vol. 3, p. 282.

48. Lea, *A History*, vol. 3, pp. 288-9.

49. Michael Geddes, 'A View of the Inquisition of Portugal: with a list of the Prisoners Which Came out of the Inquisition of Lisbon, in an Act of Faith Celebrated anno 1682', in *Miscellaneous Tracts* (A. & J. Churchill, 1702), pp. 417-48.

50. Joseph del Olmo, *Relación historica del auto general de fe que se celebró en Madrid en presencia de sus magestades el dia 30 de Junio de 1680* (Roque Rico de Miranda, Madrid, 1680), fols. 159-60;.

51. Acevedo, *Historia dos Christãos Novos*, pp. 332-5.

52. Kamen, *Inquisition and Society*, p. 233.

53. Ibid., p. 234.

54. Lea, *A History*, vol. 3, pp. 310-11.

55. Acevedo, *Historia dos Christãos Novos*, pp. 352-5.

56. Ibid., p. 237.

57. Revah, 'Les Marranes', p. 52.

58. Kamen, *Inquisition and Society*, pp. 235-6; Stephen Haliczer, 'La Inquisición como mito y como histroria: su abolición y el desarrollo de la ideologia política española', in Angel Alcalá (ed.), *Inquisición española y mentalidad inquisitorial* (Ariel, Barcelona, 1984), pp. 503-7.

59. José Jimenez Lozano, 'Supervivencia de cultemas islamohebraicos en la sociedad española o el fracaso historico de la Inquisición', in Alcalá (ed.), *Inquisición española*, pp. 355-70; Yerushalmi, 'Prolegomenon,' p. 55.

# 2

# The Inquisition and the Italian Jews

*Nicolas Davidson*

*'Ye shall have one manner of law, as well for the stranger as
for one of your own country'* (Leviticus 24:22)

In 1524, Lorenzo Lotto completed a remarkable fresco cycle in the
chapel of the Villa Suardi at Trescore, some 14km northeast of
Bergamo. On the north wall he painted a figure of Christ, facing
the onlooker with arms outstretched; the fingers of His hands are
extended, and grow into branches, which rise to form a row of large
circles enclosing the figures of 20 Christian saints. Above Christ's
head is inscribed a verse from St John's Gospel: 'I am the Vine,
ye are the branches.' At each end of the wall, Lotto painted an
additional group of men who, with knives in their hands, are fall-
ing to the ground from ladders resting against the branches of the
vine. Each man has been labelled with the name of an enemy of
Catholic doctrine. These men, it seems, had tried to climb
into the vine by the ladders, but have now been thrown down by
the Saints. 'I am the vine, and my Father is the husbandman
. . . Abide in me, and I in you. As the branch cannot bear fruit
of itself, except it abide in the vine; no more can ye, except ye abide
in me.'[1]

At an elementary level, the interpretation of these scenes is fairly
straightforward. The church, protected by the saints and strong in
its Catholic faith, will repel the assaults of all its enemies. The
significance of the cycle for the historian of the Inquisition is that
the enemies of the church in the group at the east end of the wall
are labelled 'Arianus', the Arian, 'Sabellianus', the Sabellian, and
'Judeus', the Jew. The Jew, like the ancient heretic, is seen as an
enemy of Catholic doctrine. This idea of the Jew as an enemy of
Christ can be paralleled in sixteenth-century Italian written sources
as well. In 1590, for example, Lodovico Carabello, a Franciscan
then living in Udine, protested against the 'practice of Jews and
Pharisees, who have always been accustomed to snap at the reputation of Christ'.[2]

These two examples could be used as evidence of a widespread hostility to the Jews in early modern Italy. But if such antagonism really existed, we should expect to find the Inquisition throughout the peninsula acting regularly against Judaism, for, as an anonymous denunciation reminded the Venetian tribunal in 1555, its duty was 'to cleanse this city of the enemies of our faith'.[3] So how widespread was such antisemitism in this period? And how systematically did the Inquisition persecute the Jews of Italy?

## I

The Cardinal Inquisitors in Rome once defined the function of the Holy Office as ensuring that 'the sacrosanct Catholic faith is preserved, immaculate and pure, from every heretical contagion'.[4] Its most immediate concern was to protect individuals from error. As Archbishop Girolamo Matteucci of Sarno wrote in 1588, 'the Holy Office devotes itself only to the health and the winning of souls';[5] its duty was to bring those in error back to the truth. The laity, and even governments, generally accepted this. In 1595, a group of Venetian legal advisers acknowledged in a report to the Doge that the Inquisitor's task was to investigate anyone suspected of heresy; 'and having found him to be a heretic, he may persuade him, and correct him, and give him that beneficial medicine and penance which will enable him to return to the flock of the faithful'.[6]

This image of the Inquisitor as a spiritual physician was very common;[7] and the Inquisitors themselves certainly believed their charge was to prescribe the most appropriate remedy for each case that came before them. According to the author of one seventeenth-century Inquisitor's manual, they were to proceed 'in accordance with the merit of the evidence, the words uttered, and the circumstances of the persons involved, that is to say, whether they are of more or less understanding'.[8] An Inquisitor had to be flexible in his approach. But if his best efforts should fail, if the prescribed medicines had no effect, then the guilty had to be removed from the community — by exile, imprisonment, or death — to prevent the disease spreading further, for it was commonly believed in Italy that God punished society for the sins of its members.

The importance of the Inquisition's work was therefore recognised by Catholic society; but the Inquisitor's task was not simply to impose mandatory punishments. He had to learn about the motives of those under suspicion before deciding how to deal with them. And in fact, most suspects were found on investigation to be confused rather than committed. When truly 'engaged' heretics were discovered, the tribunals tended to assume they were inspired by evil motives, not by conviction.[9] This sort of heretic was not open to rational argument; he was obstinate and wholly untrustworthy, since his overwhelming ambition was to deceive the community for his own benefit.

Now all these characteristics of the true heretic were at times attributed also to the Jews. In 1563, for example, Cardinal Giammichele Saraceni referred to 'Jewish obstinacy and treachery', and in 1580, the Inquisitor of Pavia condemned a converted Jew, Carlo Ventura Mezzabarba, for returning to Judaism to become 'a limb of the devil, as truly you were before'.[10] Jews were clearly believed to be unreliable and obdurate, and inspired by the devil. But were they therefore necessarily subject to the Inquisition?

They could certainly not be described as heretics, for, as Umberto Locato, the Commissary-General of the Roman Inquisition observed in 1570, 'heresy is a kind of infidelity belonging to those who profess the faith of Christ, but who corrupt his doctrine'.[11] Only the baptised could become heretics: 'the Church does not judge those who are without, as the Apostle says'.[12] Non-Christians — Muslims and pagans as well as Jews — had therefore to be distinguished from non-Catholics — Protestants and Greeks, for example. A Jew could not be brought before the Inquisition simply because he was a Jew.

There were also significant worldly reasons for tolerating non-Christians in a Catholic society. Many important economic centres in Italy attracted non-Christian populations. Traders and sailors passed through on business, staying only briefly in lodgings; diplomats were posted to foreign missions; merchants, students, artisans or missionaries might settle for life. Government officials recognised that these migrants could benefit the local economy, and so improve their own revenues from taxation. In 1572, for example, the Duke of Savoy issued a wide-ranging charter of privileges to encourage Turks, Moors and Persians, as well as Jews, who might wish to trade in his territories. The same reasoning could be applied, of course, to non-Catholic migrants, and in some areas, both groups were as a result protected from ecclesiastical molestation.[13]

But this willingness to tolerate non-Christians and non-Catholics rarely allayed the resilient suspicion that any non-Italian might be an enemy. Muslims captured in war were often murdered, 'in order to deprive the Turk of the power to have men at his command';

those arrested by the Venetian government tended to die myster-
iously in prison. In 1588, government officials in Corfu arrested
two Muslim soldiers who had escaped to the island to seek Catholic
baptism, for fear they might be spies,[14] and even Greeks who were
formally in communion with Rome were thought to be secretly
hostile. 'It will be very difficult to find any native Greeks who are
not untrue', wrote one Theatine in 1581.[15] Often, non-Christians
and non-Catholics were believed to be working in alliance. In 1573,
for example, a Turkish convert to Catholicism really did use the
willing aid of a Greek family living in Venice to escape from Italy
and revert to Islam; and it was suspected that Protestants, Greeks
and Turks were all deceitfully hoping to win Catholics to their own
religious doctrines.[16] It was assumed that regular social contact
with the enemies of the Church might turn the faithful against the
authority of Rome: in 1596, Pope Clement VIII therefore ordered
Italian merchants not to reside in any city or territory that prohibited the free exercise of the Catholic religion, and influential
clerics occasionally called for the expulsion of non-Christians as well
as non-Catholics from Italian cities. In the early seventeenth century, the Papacy was still toying with the idea of a Crusade against
the infidel.[17]

So non-Christians and non-Catholics could be viewed as either
welcome economic assets or as dangerous saboteurs. But they were
also all potential converts to Catholicism. This became particularly
important in the later years of the sixteenth century, when the
Papacy was encouraging missionary endeavours in many parts of
the world.

## II

The Jews formed just one of Italy's religious minorities. The largest
community was perhaps in Rome: by 1586, there were about 3,500
Jews in the city, some 3.5 per cent of the urban population. The
Jewish population of Venice fluctuated between perhaps 0.5 per
cent of the total in 1516, when the Ghetto was established, to nearly
2.25 per cent by 1642.[18] Governments recognised the economic
advantages brought by these communities: Sixtus V, for example,
ordered Jewish immigrants to pay on arrival a tax of 20 *giulii* for
each male aged between 15 and 60 in their family, and a further
12 *giulli* each year thereafter.[19] Like other non-Christians, the Jews
could be tolerated as economic assets.

But in Catholic eyes, Jews had to be distinguished from all other non-Christians. They had played a part in God's plan for man's salvation; their faith and ritual prefigured the truths taught by the Church, and had been preserved as a witness to faith in Christ and His Passion.[20] As a result, Catholic intellectuals often expressed interest in Jewish belief and behaviour. Christian Biblical scholars were assisted by Jews, and Pope Leo X was happy to accept the dedication of Daniele Bomberg's 1517 edition of the Bible with Rabbinic commentaries. There was, too, a recurrent fascination with Cabbalistic doctrines.[21]

Many Christians, however, had a less cerebral interest in the Jews. During the 1560s, a Jew in Venice called Daniele used to sleep regularly with a Christian prostitute known as 'La Rossa' in the home of his fellow Modenese, Giovanni; and in the early 1570s, a Roman Jew calling himself Salvatore Ricciolto used to leave home at night in disguise to sleep with a Christian woman named Magdalena.[22] Social and professional contacts between members of the two faiths were common. We know of many occasions when Jews and Christians would eat or gamble together,[23] and in Mantua, the Jewish community organised a regular theatre company, under the direction of the noted playwright Jehuda Sommo da Porta Ariè, to entertain the Gonzaga court; Duke Vincenzo I once attended a party himself in the home of the Jewish entertainer Isaac Massarani.[24] In some towns, Christian servants worked, or lived, in Jewish houses, and Christians were employed by Jews as nurses, musicians or teachers.[25] Jewish teachers of music were especially respected: in the 1580s, a Jewish dance tutor in Venice called Giuseppe travelled to Mantua with one of his best Christian pupils, at the parents' request, for an extended study visit at S. Andrea.[26] Traders and businessmen maintained more formal contacts. Sixtus V tried to re-establish the silk industry in Rome by granting privileges to the Jew Magino di Gabriele,[27] and Jews were prized in many parts of Italy as medical practitioners. One noted Jewish medical, philosophical and Biblical scholar, Davide de Pomis, worked valiantly in Venice during the plague of 1575-7, and later cared for Sixtus V.[28]

But Jews were perhaps most familiar to Christians as bankers and money-lenders. No economy could function effectively without credit. Christians could not borrow readily from each other, because usury was condemned by canon law and by secular governments; the solution was to permit lending by Jews.[29] The principle was clearly stated by Duke Ranuccio I Farnese of Parma in 1589:

the experience of past times has demonstrated and made known that, in order to avoid the greed and avarice of bad Christians, it is less evil to permit the Jews to live in our state — except in the cities of Parma and Piacenza — and to act as bankers for needy Christians, who can then be assisted with money, as opportunity and necessity dictate, without having to rely on the more damaging and wicked contracts entered without Christian piety, as usually happens at present.[30]

But many Catholics continued to express their hostility to Jewish lending. In 1548, two leading Venetian patricians, Tommaso Mocenigo and Girolamo Polani, received substantial support in the Senate when they argued that 'lending at interest is disapproved by all divine and human laws; it is the means by which the Jews, committing various robberies and extortions, consume and devour the people of this our city'.[31] There can be little doubt that such opinions were often inspired by economic rivalry; they were certainly used in some cities by members of wealthy Christian families to justify the establishment of *Monti di Pietà*, alternative sources of credit that remained under Christian control. Pius V, too, opposed Jewish lending — but did not hesitate to set up a new interest-yielding *Monte* in 1571, when he needed cash for his own government expenditure.[32]

Catholics could also put forward less obviously self-interested arguments for limiting or preventing contact with Jews. According to the bishop of Ischia in 1555, the very presence of Jews among Christians was 'damaging and dangerous'.[33] Concern was often expressed, for example, about sexual relations between Jews and Christians since it was unlikely that Jewish mothers would trouble to have their children baptised.[34] A similar concern for the Sacraments inspired those who feared that Jewish physicians would not remind their Christian patients to confess as they neared death.[35]

Some Catholics believed that Jewish hostility also affected the material security of the Christian community. According to Giulio Marcello, who taught at the University in Rome, the Jews expected the Messiah to appear immediately after the destruction of Rome by the Turks. No Jew could therefore be trusted, for they would pass strategic information to the Turks in order to hasten the Messiah.[36] These anxieties were apparently justified by information received during 1568 of a conspiracy in Cyprus, involving a Jewish friend of the Duke of Naxos who had imported gunpowder to Famagusta in preparation for the Turkish invasion.[37]

But even in times of peace, some Catholics believed that, just as God punished communities for tolerating heretics, so he would punish them for tolerating Jews. On the night of 17 April 1559, a flysheet was pinned to the door of the cathedral in Cremona, urging the immediate expulsion of the Jews:

> People of Cremona: do not fail to ensure that these Jewish dogs are expelled from this blessed city, for otherwise you will suffer ruin; if you knew the great blasphemies that these impious dogs are saying against our Saviour Jesus Christ, you would realise that just one of their blasphemies would be sufficient to ensure ruin for ten cities, or even for one thousand.

God would devastate the whole city because the Jews had insulted Christ.[38] The same nervous reaction greeted reports that Jews had mocked processions carrying the Sacrament, or had damaged Christian images, or had profaned the consecrated Host.[39]

The real threat from Judaism might actually have been more insidious. It was often assumed that Christians who maintained regular, friendly contacts with Jews would become accustomed to the notion of an alternative system of beliefs, and so begin to nurture doubts about Catholic doctrine. The Jews denied, for example, that Christ was the Messiah, and that he rose from the dead; if these opinions spread among Christians, belief in the Incarnation would be endangered.[40] In this way, the Jews cold be seen as the allies of Christian heretics and of other non-Christian groups in a combined assault on church teaching.[41]

A case was therefore made for prohibiting all contacts with the Jews. As Giorgio Sommariva remarked in 1480, they could never be trusted: they 'cheat everyone who takes their word on trust . . . it will be understood by everyone here that the entire Jewish people is the enemy of our Christian blood'.[42] But it is important to emphasise that this crudely hostile stereotype was only rarely adopted in Italy.[43] A man could hardly be blamed for being born a Jew, and his adherence to Judaism was often explained as the fruit of ignorance rather than of malice — an ignorance his religious leaders had an interest in preserving.[44]

The most effective way to reduce the danger posed by Jews was therefore to convert them. Once removed from the influence of their leaders, it was believed, they would surely come to recognise the obvious truth of Christianity. In 1577, and again in 1584, Gregory

XIII ordered adult Jews to attend sermons in Hebrew every Saturday; Clement VIII insisted that at least 200 men and 100 women should be present.[45] This ideological operation was assisted by material temptations. Privileges and concessions were granted to Jews to provide evidence to Christian goodwill; 'our wish is', wrote Leo X, 'that you may, by experiencing one act of liberality, have the ability to be enticed by the same liberality to approach to the true light of the orthodox faith'.[46] But if such inducements were at all necessary, conversion was perhaps less attractive than Catholics liked to admit and the commitment of converts less secure than they would have hoped. Certainly the disadvantages of conversion were considerable. A convert lost all contact with his Jewish relatives, and with the community and lifestyle in which he had previously lived;[47] Jews viewed converts with hostility, and avoided their company. Conversion therefore required a traumatic change of identity. The aggressive zeal of some converts may have been, as Professor Brian Pullan has suggested, a means of justifying to themselves 'an act of seeming treachery'.[48]

## III

Catholic attitudes to the Jews in early modern Italy therefore ranged from welcoming toleration to implacable hostility. It is not easy now to make any accurate assessment of how widespread any of these attitudes may have been within the population as a whole; but it is possible to show that they all influenced the policies of governments and the judgements of the Inquisition.

As Léon Poliakov has suggested, Italian governments generally adopted more generous policies about the Jews than rulers elsewhere in western Europe;[49] but legislative attitudes could change rapidly, and not all governments followed the same policies at the same time. The provisions of medieval canon laws were designed to mark Jews off from Christians, and to reduce contacts between them. Jews were therefore supposed to wear distinctive clothing, and to stay indoors on Good Friday; Christians were forbidden to take employment with them as servants; no new synagogues were to be built in Christian territories.[50] Some governments enforced these provisions. From 1446, for example, Jews in Venice had to wear a yellow circle on their clothing.[51] Some governments — especially those subject to Spanish influence — were uniformly hostile throughout the Early Modern period. But others were more generous. The Este were always tolerant: even in the later fifteenth century, freedom of religion was guaranteed in Ferrara, where a Jewish *scuola* was established in 1481, and Bernardino of Feltre's sermons were stopped in 1493.[52]

The early sixteenth century saw some improvements in the Jews' position. A new synagogue was founded in Mantua in 1513 for example, and — despite the establishment of the first ghetto in Venice in 1516 — the period from about 1518 to the mid-1530s was fairly peaceful. The first two synagogues in Venice were founded in 1529 and 1532; and in 1535, the Papacy even removed the requirement on Jews in Ancona to carry a distinguishing badge.[53] By contrast, the Jews were persistently harrassed in nearly all parts of the peninsula between about 1566 and 1583. In 1566, the Venetian government renewed legislation ordering Jews indoors on Good Friday, and prohibited their employment of Christian servants. The Medici eventually gave way to papal pressure to adopt more stringent policies: in 1567, they ordered Jews to wear a yellow hat when outdoors, and established ghettos in Florence and Siena in 1570 and 1571. In 1569, Pius V expelled all Jews from the Papal States, except those resident in Rome and Ancona: some 900 were obliged to leave Bologna. They were further prohibited from residing in Piacenza and Parma from the 1570s and the Gonzaga passed laws banning Christians from serving Jews in 1581.[54]

The significance of these changes can perhaps be most easily appreciated by comparing the regulations governing Jewish life issued by Sixtus V and Clement VIII. Both insisted on the canon law requiring Jews to carry a distinguishing mark; but where Sixtus seemed to encourage contacts between members of the two faiths, Clement seemed determined to prevent them. In 1586, Sixtus allowed Jews to work and live throughout the Papal States, and to associate freely with Christians; he permitted them to open new synagogues and to follow their own laws. He even licensed Jewish physicians to treat Christian patients, a practice prohibited by Paul IV more than 30 years earlier. But in 1592, Clement VIII prohibited a wide range of activities which brought Jews and Christians together: no Christian was now to enter a Jewish shop, house or synogogue; no Jew was to visit a Christian prostitute, talk to any Christian after midnight, or eat with a Christian at any time. Jews were not to teach, employ or serve Christians, or use their physicians, midwives or tutors. Christians were not to become indebted to Jews. Social converse was made almost impossible.[55]

Such differences in approach seem to have been the result of economic and political considerations, as well as of rival ideological commitments — though the balance is not always easy now to assess. It is clear that in times of war or international tension, Jews were often regarded with suspicion because of their supposed sympathy for the Turks — especially if they had not been born in their place of residence. In 1568, for example, just before the War of Cyprus, Jews not born in Cyprus were expelled from Famagusta.[56] In times of peace, however, the Jews' economic value was more appreciated: Sixtus V improved their legal status because he wanted to encourage their skills and capital in an area already suffering the economic difficulties of the later sixteenth century.[57] Clement VIII also recognised their value, and was prepared, as Cardinal Santori told the Florentine Ambassador in 1595, to tolerate them in Rome and Ancona 'in respect of trade'; but his own commitment to the ideal of Catholic purity was too strong to allow any other contacts.[58]

In theory, the Inquisition should have been motivated solely by ideology, and Inquisitors certainly expressed concern occasionally at what the tribunal in Reggio Emilia called in 1598 the 'very great familiarity between Jews and Christians'[59] — though it was recognised that some matters fell outside their jurisdiction.[60] Over one offence, however, the Inquisition had indisputed authority: any Christian who converted to Judaism was likely to be investigated and punished severely as a heretic.[61] Christians who had themselves circumcised, adopted Jewish names, and lived openly as Jews could be easily identified; but, aware of the Inquisitors' concern, many apostates chose to disguise their new convictions under an unchanged Catholic lifestyle. Books written to guide Inquisitors therefore often included hints on how to recognise secret Judaisers. In the seventeenth century, for example, Prosper Farinaci warned Inquisitors to beware of any Christian who rarely went to Church, or who associated frequently and on friendly terms with professing Jews — those who entered business agreements with Jews, attended their festivities, or simply ate and drank with them.[62] This sort of behaviour was often observed among the descendants of converts, for Judaism, it was sometimes argued, was imbibed with a mother's milk, and so passed from one generation to another, even within families who lived publicly as Christians.[63]

But what authority did the Inquisition have over Jews who were never baptised? In 1429, Pope Martin V accepted the principle that Inquisitors should not interfere in any way with the legitimate activities of the unbaptised;[64] but the effectiveness of this principle was often seriously limited in practice. Thomas Aquinas had already argued in the thirteenth century that infidels, including Jews, should be prevented from blaspheming, impeding or subverting the faith, by force if necessary. In the fourteenth century, Nicolau Eymeric wanted Jews who encouraged Christians to commit errors to be subject to the Inquisition as well, and his argument that the pope had authority over infidels and Christians was echoed in 1570 by Umberto Locato, who maintained that, since the pope was the Vicar of Christ, 'he has power not only over Christians, but also over all infidels, since Christ truly has power over everyone'.[65] By the 1560s, it was generally agreed that the Holy Office should investigate Jews accused of trying to convert Christians, and Marquardus de Susannis argued in 1568 that they should also investigate those accused of blasphemous practices, like crucifying lambs on Good Friday.[66]

The most comprehensive statement of Inquisition powers over unbaptised Jews was finally made by Gregory XIII. In the bull *Antigua iudaeorum improbitas* published on 1 July 1581, he listed ten cases in which Inquisitors might proceed against Jews and other infidels.[67] The most significant clauses were perhaps those in which Gregory allowed tribunals to act against infidels and Jews who invoked demons, and who denied beliefs held by their religion in common with Christianity. He here endorsed a principle that had for some two centuries been under intermittent discussion. Eymeric had argued in the fourteenth century that Jews who rejected beliefs, like monotheism, that they shared with Christians were to be treated as heretics; in 1570, Umberto Locato repeated the argument, adding that Jews who sacrificed to demons should also be punished.[68]

After 1581, the provisions of Gregory's Bull were reiterated by nearly every Inquisitors' manual, legal textbook and Holy Office decision dealing with the Jews.[69] Copies were forwarded to tribunals throughout Italy.[70] Unbaptised Jews were therefore less likely to evade Inquisition jurisdiction after 1581 than before; and since Inquisitors frequently corresponded with each other, some kind of common approach was likely to develop — especially when they took instruction from Rome.[71] In 1597, for example, the Inquisitor in Parma wrote to the Congregation for advice about a denunciation against some Jews in Colorno, who had employed a number of teenage girls as resident servants and, it was suspected, as bedfellows too. Certainly the girls no longer attended Christian services or received the Sacraments. On 17 January 1598, after a lengthy and by no means unanimous discussion, the Cardinal Inquisitors decided that in all such cases, tribunals should be informed that the Jews involved were indeed subject to their jurisdiction, because of the risk that the Christian employees might be tempted to convert to Judaism.[72]

The demands of ideology could, however, conflict with the political or economic requirements of secular governments. This was particularly awkward when the Inquisition wanted to investigate charges against the Marranos — a term used in Italy to describe Christians of Jewish descent, usually members of families which had migrated from Iberia. In 1492, 1497 and 1536, Jews in Spain and Portugal had been forced to choose between baptism or exile. Many who chose baptism later migrated to Italy, where they, or their descendants, reverted to Judaism, and so entered the Inquisitors' jurisdiction. Others continued to live as Christians in Italy, but found themselves dangerously exposed to the suspicion that they had returned to Judaism in secret. The Marranos were never entirely trusted. In 1556, the local government in Ancona referred to 'the great wickedness of the treacherous Marranos', and Paul IV's opinion has become notorious: 'we want to see the whole lot burned', he growled to the Venetian Ambassador's secretary in December 1558.[58] Government orders expelling them were issued by Venice in 1497 and 1550, by Naples in 1515, and by Urbino in 1558.[74]

But some governments were at times prepared to tolerate and even to encourage their presence despite church opposition. Marrano communities flourished in Savoy and Ferrara, for example, until 1580 and 1581; another was created deliberately at Livorno by Duke Ferdinand I in 1593.[75] The economic advantages of a stable Marrano community could be considerable: popes Alexander VI, Julius II, Paul III and Julius III were all prepared to tolerate in Ancona the descendants of 'New Christians' who had reverted to Judaism, because of their trading connections in the Levant, and the credit they made available to the local economy. Between 1551 and 1555, the Venetian government tried hard to persuade the Marrano Mendes sisters to keep their huge fortune invested locally. Marrano refugees were welcomed in Pesaro in 1557, partly at least because many were reported to 'have great wealth and do good business'.[76] In the later 1580s and early 1590s, governments encouraged Marrano immigrants to settle at Venice, Livorno and Ancona, again for economic reasons.[77] Girolamo Matteucci noted the Venetian government's fear in 1588 that Marranos who were expelled from Christian societies would take their skills and wealth to Turkish territories, and so finance the Ottoman war effort;[78] and in 1595, the Florentine ambassador in Rome warned Cardinal Santori 'how much damage would be done to business and trade if exemptions and privileges are not granted to these Jews'.[79] And no Catholic government could ignore requests from the Turkish authorities to favour their own Marrano subjects in times of peace, for fear of providing grounds for retaliation against Christian traders, or even for renewed military hostilities.[80] Leaving aside the requirements of ideology, then, we should expect to find governments willing to favour the Marranos, as well as the Jews, in times of economic difficulty; and to read of growing hostility in times of war or economic confidence.[81]

And when the Marranos were most valued, governments were prepared to challenge the Inquisition. After the loss of Cyprus, for example, which disrupted trading links with the East Mediterranean, the Venetian government promised immunity to Jewish merchants then resident in Christian territories if they immigrated in the following two years: they could not be punished for apostasy or any other religious offence committed in the past, 'not even if in other times they have lived as Christians, as long as for the period in which they reside in this city, they live continuously as Jews'.[82] Similar orders effectively limiting the rights of Inquisitors were issued in Venice in 1589 and again in the 1590s, in Milan in 1435, 1533 and 1580, in Mantua in 1522, by the Papacy in 1547, 1549, 1552, 1533 and 1594, in Florence in 1548, 1551 and 1593, and in Savoy in 1572.[83] Inquisitions were undoubtedly affected by such orders. The tribunal in Venice received information against at least 32 named individuals between 1548 and 1588 for openly reverting to Judaism in Italy; no action seems to have been taken against those denounced before the expiry of the legislation of 1573, and we know of no denunciations for this offence at all after the 1589 contract with the Sephardim.[84] The orders in fact encouraged immigrants to revert publicly to a Jewish way of life, and so left only secret Jews and local converts who changed their minds liable to prosecution in the Marrano communities.

Jews who converted to Christianity in Italy had perhaps some excuse for failing to sustain a strictly orthodox Catholicism. At an early stage in an otherwise highly successful ecclesiastical career, the convert Fra Sisto da Siena, for example, had to abjure his erroneous beliefs about predestination.[85] But a full and public reversion to

Judaism — a voluntary return to the ghetto and its restrictions — was, if proved, less easy to absolve. In December 1572, a Florentine named Giacomo, from Montevarchi in the Valdarno, denounced a personal acquaintance called Salomone Dardeso to the Commissary General of the Holy Office in Rome. Salomone had, he claimed, been baptised some ten years before, and had then lived publicly as a Christian; but in April 1572, Giacomo had seen him again in Florence, this time dressed as a Jew.[86] The penalty for this offence, when proved, was always severe. On 24 July 1611, after vespers in St Peter's in Rome, seven Jews suspected of this offence were exposed in an *auto-de-fe*; six made their abjurations, and were sentenced to a whipping; two of them were also sent to the galleys for ten years each. The seventh was more obstinate, and was delivered to the city governor 'to be burned alive, because he wished to die a Jew'.[87] But without a confession this kind of charge was difficult to corroborate, and the Inquisition in Venice was rarely able to bring such cases to a conclusion. Only five individuals were pronounced guilty there in the sixteenth century: all had confessed their guilt without torture, and only one, Giacomo Francoso, received a really severe punishment — 20 years in the galleys and a split ear for receiving baptism four times in one year.[88]

Judaism practised in secret was even harder to prove. The commitment of 'secret Judaisers' is not easy now to determine, but penitents who confessed were often treated with remarkable leniency. In 1617, for example, the Inquisition in Ferrara investigated Cesare d'Este della Mirandola, a convert who admitted under torture circumcising one of his sons. His sentence simply put him in the care of his parish priest, and ordered him to present himself once a month to the Inquisition.[89] Only two suspects were declared guilty in Venice in the sixteenth century: Gaspar Ribeiro, who died, apparently, impenitent, before the investigation was complete, and Filipe de Nis, who confessed in 1586 and was simply ordered not to leave Venice. Of the other two dozen or so denounced to the city's tribunal between 1555 and 1591, none received any punishment at all, and Filipe was released after two years.[90]

In all the Inquisition cases discussed so far, the tribunals were investigating the lives of men and women who had been, or might have been, baptised. But as we have seen, they were in some circumstances entitled to act against unbaptised Jews as well. In October 1566, for example, the Cardinal Inquisitors in Rome ordered a Jew who had blasphemed, apparently in Ancona, to be whipped; a hole was cut in his tongue, and he was threatened with execution if he committed the offence a second time.[91] This unusually severe sentence was in tune, perhaps, with the new mood in Rome symbolised by the election of Pius V. Unbaptised Jews who found it convenient to live as Christians could also be punished severely. In the summer of 1549, an assistant priest at S. Anzolo in Venice was called in the middle of the night to confess a foreigner who had been dangerously wounded in a brawl at a brothel in the Calle del Pestrin. The Inquisition subsequently discovered that the foreigner was in fact a Portuguese Jew called Francisco Olivier, who had recovered sufficiently from his wounds two days after the fight to be carried back to the ghetto. Witnesses suggested he had previously lived both as a Christian and as a Jew; he argued that he had always lived as a Christian, though circumcised as a child by his father, and occasionally dependent on Jewish relatives for charity. He was sent to the galleys for four years, and then exiled for life from all Venetian territories.[92] The tribunal was undoubtedly influenced by Francisco's admission that he had slept with Laura, one of the Christian prostitutes who worked from the Calle del Pestrin. The Congregation in Rome was, like many lay Catholics, disturbed by the thought of any sexual union between Christians and Jews, and in 1567 made ten years in the galleys the standard punishment for Jews who slept with Christian prostitutes.[93]

Denunciations were also received against Jews who had demonstrated an open hostility to Christianity by mocking or damaging Christian images and symbols, or by insulting Christians or converts — though not all were pursued with great determination. In 1588, for example, a Greek trader called Lashari reported a Levantine Jew called Caim Saruch to the Inquisition in Venice for calling him a dog; the tribunal questioned two witnesses, who confirmed the charge, but then took no further action.[94] Attempts by Jews to convert Christians, or dissuade converts, were treated more seriously: in 1595, two Portuguese were arrested in Rome, who, it was reported, 'have been going about persuading some other Portuguese Marranos to be circumcised here in the city'.[95] The penalty might be severe: in February 1583, Giuseppe Saralvo, a fruitful proselytiser among Marranos, was passed by the Ferrara tribunal to Rome for execution.[96]

All these offences had long been subject to Inquisition jurisdiction, but Gregory XIII's bull of July 1581 undoubtedly provoked in some areas a marked, though perhaps only temporary, increase in the number and range of cases against the unbaptised. In Venice, the tribunal made a number of orders in the 1580s to limit contacts between Christians and Jews,[97] and tribunals throughout the peninsula paid more attention to Jews who employed Christian servants. At the turn of the century, the Inquisitor in Modena wrote to the Congregation in Rome to ask whether he could act against a Jew of Nonantola called Vitale who had employed three Christian women during the last ten days of his wife's pregnancy; and in 1615, the tribunal in Ferrara did prosecute a number of local Jews with Christian servants.[98]

The ability of a tribunal to act on a denunciation was therefore influenced by changes in both the intellectual and the political climate. Church legislation might extend the range of its activities; government ambitions might reduce it. The Papacy was aware of these pressures, and occasionally used them to bargain over individual suspects. In January 1559, for example, Paul IV told Venice he was prepared to release three suspect Marranos who had been trading in the city under the terms of a treaty with the Turks, in return for a promise that the government would not in future permit Marranos to use Venetian ships.[99]

But even without any external pressures, the tribunals allowed themselves some discretion when passing sentence. Theorists argued, for example, that young converts who reverted to Judaism should be treated more leniently than adults;[100] and tribunals were careful to take account of the suspects' personal circumstances. In October 1555, the Venetian Inquisition agreed to sentence the convert Elena de' Freschi Olivi to house arrest only, despite the very serious charges of blasphemy brought against her, 'having been made aware, by much evidence, that she is mad, and of an unsound mind'.[101] Cases inspired by personal vendetta were normally dismissed. In January 1584, for example, the Venetian tribunal received a denunciation for secret Judaism against a convert from Naples called Pacifico. It named as witnesses Giacomo Pozuol, a broker at the Rialto, and Alessandro Scarpa and Giovanni Scampogiato, who lived in the same lodging house as Pacifico, and worked like him in the pearl trade. The tribunal's investigations gradually uncovered a complex web of hostility between these four men, who had already appeared as litigants before the lay courts of the *Giustizia Vecchia* and the *Piovego* about a debt of rather less than 20 lire which Pozuol owed Pacifico. In April 1584, the tribunal released Pacifico, and in due course sent Pozuol to the galleys. Scarpa and Scampogiato disappeared — perhaps they had left Venice altogether. The tribunal exiled them in their absence.[102]

This lengthy account of the Inquisition's dealings with the Italian Jews may suggest that Judaism was perceived as an ever present threat; but Inquisitors actually had more pressing problems to deal with most of the time. Cases against Jews and Judaisers formed in fact a very small part of a tribunal's regular activities, even in areas where Jews were relatively numerous. Reliable statistics are available for only a few cities as yet, but a pattern may already be emerging. Between 1549 and 1594, the Inquisition in Lisbon dealt with nearly 2,000 cases against Jews; in Naples, the Holy Office handled only 38 between 1564 and 1599, less than five per cent of the total. In Venice, just over 70 cases involved Jews in the second half of the sixteenth century — again, less than five per cent of the total — and in the seventeenth century, that proportion fell to just over two per cent. The Italians were certainly not obsessed with Judaism.[104]

But the tribunals were closely involved in one further aspect of Jewish life. We have already seen that the church authorities were disturbed by the thought that Jews might persuade Catholics to doubt fundamental beliefs like the divinity of Christ. The same concern was in part responsible for papal legislation which restricted Jewish publishing. Hebrew books were thought to contain 'abuse against the Trinity', and in 1563, a Modenese physician named Agostino was denounced to the Inquisition for owning a Paris edition of Maimonides' *Morè Nevochim* which, one convert said, spoke against Christ.[104] Papal and Inquisition documents criticised Jewish books, and the Talmud in particular, for their alleged blasphemies, and for preaching superstition, impiety, heresy and hatred of Christ and the Saints; at times they were even accused of distorting the meaning of the Mosaic Law and of encouraging acts against the laws of nature. Clement VIII and later authors accused them of obscenities too.[105]

According to some sources, this hostility was encouraged by converts, like Giovanni Battista Eliano, the grandson of Elias Levita; but little was done to control Jewish printing before the 1550s.[106] On 12 August 1553, the Congregation of the Holy Office in Rome published an edict ordering secular rulers, bishops and Inquisitors to collect and burn all copies of the Talmud found in Jewish homes and synagogues. The edict was published by a number of governments, including those of Venice, Ferrara and Florence, and it was reinforced the following year by a Bull issued by Julius III ordering the seizure of all Jewish books that mentioned Christ. In 1557, Jews were forbidden to own any Hebrew books except the Old Testament.[107]

But in a number of cities, the Jews mounted a surprisingly successful defence campaign. In Milan, for example, Don Ferrante revoked the order to observe the Holy Office edict after Jewish protests, and in the following years, copies of the Talmud were still printed and circulated in Spanish Lombardy.[108] The Index issued by the Papacy after the Council of Trent again permitted expurgated editions of the Talmud.[109] The Inquisition tribunals continued to supervise Jewish publications in the later sixteenth century, but responsibility for their content was now passed directly to the Jewish communities themselves, who had to pay Christian censors (usually converts) to approve the final texts: the Mantua community paid Allessandro Scipione Renato 20 *scudi* between June 1589 and June 1590 for expurgating their books.[110] Clement VIII renewed the total prohibition of the Talmud in 1593 and 1596;[111] but by then the Congregation of the Index was increasingly responsible for supervising publications, and the Inquisition's direct interest became more limited.[112]

The loss to the Jewish communities when their books were burnt was considerable. Over 1,000 copies of the Talmud were destroyed in Venice in 1553, and as many as 12,000 in Cremona in 1559. Even in the seventeenth century, Jews found in possession of prohibited titles had their copies burnt and their other property confiscated.[113] But Clement VIII had stated clearly in 1593 that Inquisitors should use their discretion when deciding which additional penalties to impose; and the inconsistent application of the laws against Jewish publication suggests that the Inquisitors may not all have been unthinkingly hostile. There certainly was a fear that Christians would be influenced by Hebrew books, but not everyone, even in Rome, believed the Talmud should be burnt.[114] Some Catholics encouraged the study of rabbinic works as an aid to conversion: if they were printed accurately, their testimony to the truth of Christianity would surely become too obvious to ignore.[115]

The control of Jewish books was therefore not a simple matter. If they were corrupting, they had to be kept from both Catholic and Jewish readers; if they reinforced the claims of Christianity, they should be approved. Nearly all Inquisitors would have accepted the Church's responsibility to 'preach the gospel to every creature'[116] and some became directly involved in missionary work. Fra Dionigi Costacciaro, for example, had taught converts in Ancona in the 1560s before his appointment as Inquisitor in Florence; there he continued to preach to the Jews in public, and was responsible in 1583 for the conversion of the learned rabbi Jochiel di Pesaro.[117]

It was because of their missionary interests that tribunals occasionally intervened to discipline uncommitted converts before their baptism, even though it was not clear that they could ever be charged with heresy or apostasy.[118] Conversion, rather than punishment, was the Inquisition's primary interest. In 1598, Giulio Paolo fled from the *Casa dei catecumeni* in Ferrara. The Holy Office arrested him, but then seem to have accepted his plea to put it all down to 'youthful restlessness'. He was required simply to promise to return to Christianity, and given no punishments at all.[119]

## IV

The Catholic response to the Jews in Early Modern Italy was less uniform than a casual glance at the sources might suggest. Some individuals certainly did believe that they posed a threat to church and society, and denunciations to the Inquisition contain their share of assertions which expose a repellent antisemitism. The denouncers were often, no doubt, inspired by prejudice, though some, motivated perhaps more by economic or personal rivalries, may have used the language of bigotry merely to increase the force of their accusations. But governments were not always prepared to side with racial and religious hatred, and Inquisition tribunals rarely reflected it in their proceeedings. Many investigations were never concluded, and those individuals who were found guilty were often treated with great leniency.

The records of the Inquisition cannot therefore be used as evidence for a single form of Catholic antisemitism. The tribunals spent only a small part of their time investigating Jews: the Holy Office in Naples, for instance, packed all but one of its 38 sixteenth-century trials against Jews into a relatively short period between 1569 and 1580.[120] The Inquisition was largely dependent on denunciations to stimulate its activities, so irregularities like these may well be the result of a short-lived and local growth or decline of popular hostility. But more denunciations never led automatically to more persecution: investigations might be dropped, or never initiated, for a wide range of legal, technical or political reasons, and the tribunals' preoccupations did not in any case always mirror those prevalent in Catholic society. Their interest in conversion, for example, is most evident in sentences passed after about 1580, in a period of economic difficulty that may have aggravated popular prejudice against the Jews even as it encouraged governments to favour them. This interest may have persuaded Inquisitors to follow up more denunciations than before — and then to treat suspects more leniently.

A desire to convert the Jews is, admittedly, just as 'antisemitic' as a desire to burn them: if successful, both policies eliminate the Jewish communities. At one level, therefore, the Inquisition must always be seen as a weapon for uniformity, even when it treated the Jews leniently. But the willingness to ignore denunciations, drop investigations, and take account of the suspects' personal circumstances, make it impossible to charge the Inquisitors with any systematic programme of persecution against the Italian Jews in the sixteenth and seventeenth centuries.

## Notes

1. The Biblical references are to John 5: 1, 4, 5. Recent studies of the cycle include F. Cortesi Bosco, *Gli affreschi dell'oratorio Suardi: Lorenzo Lotto nella crisi della Riforma* (Edizioni Bolis, Bergamo, 1980). I am most grateful to Mr Jeremy Warren for introducing me to the frescos.

2. Archivio di Stato di Venetia (hereafter ASVen), *Santo Uffizio* hereafter (*SU*), b.62, *processo* 'Corfiut fra Giovanni Francesco', denunciation of 5 December 1590.

3. *SU* b.24, *proc.* 'Enriches Agostino, Gomes Edoardo', denunciation received 9 March 1555.

4. Archivio Segreto Vaticano (hereafter ASVat), *Fondo Borghese*, serie I, 340-4, fol. 36r: the edict is undated.

5. ASVat, *SS. Venezia*, 26 fol. 268v.

6. ASVen, *SU* b.153, advice of Bartolemeo Salvadego, Erasmo Graziano and Cornelio Frangipani in a letter of the Doge to the rectors of Brescia, 12 August 1595.

7. Cf. the comments of the legate's auditor to Giovanni Laureto in October 1553 printed by M.E. Pommier, 'L'itinéraire religieux d'un moine vagabond italien au XVI<sup>e</sup> siècle', *Mélanges d'archéologie et d'histoire, LXVI* (1954), p. 322.

8. Biblioteca Apostolica Vaticana (hereafter BV), *Patetta*, 145, fol. 30r. I am grateful to Dr James Robertson of the University of Dundee for drawing my attention to this volume.

9. For a fuller discussion, see N. Davidson, 'Il Sant' Uffizio e la tutela del culto a Venezia nel '500, *Studi Veneziani*, n.s., 6 (1982).

10. BV, *Vat. Lat.* 6792, fol. 106r; Library of Trinity College, Dublin (TCD), 1225, fol. 160v.

11. *Opus quod iudiciale inquisitorum dicitur ex diversis theologis et I.U.D. per fratrum Unbertum Locatum . . . extractum* (Apud Haeredes Antonii Bladii, Romae 1570), pp. 119-21.

12. *Le Carte Strozziane del R. Archivio in Firenze: Inventario: Serie prima* (2 vols, Tipografia Galileiana, Florence, 1884-9), p. 491 (letter of Lelio

Torelli to the secretary of the Duke of Florence, 27 November 1557). The Biblical reference is to I Corinthians 5:12; it had already been used by Thomas Aquinas, in the Summa Theologica: *Sancti Thomas Aquinatis . . . Opera Omnia iussu impensaque Leonis XIII P.M. edita* (Ex Typographia Polyglotta, Rome, 1882), p. 89.

13. The Savoy charter is printed by M. Lattes, 'Documents et notices sur l'histoire politique et littéraire des Juifs en Italie', *Revuew des études juives,* V (1882), pp. 231-7.

14. See, e.g., ASVen, *Consiglio dei Dieci, Secrete,* reg. 10, fols. 10r, 31v; *Quarantia Criminal,* filza 94, *proc,* 33 and 34; *Consiglio dei Dieci, Criminali,* reg. 11, fols. 7r-v, 9r-v, 32r.

15. BV, *Vat. Lat.* 6782, fol. 36r (letter of Don Gregorio to his brother, the priest Luigi de Ponte, 21 July 1581).

16. See ASVen, *SU,* b.35, *proc.* Giorgio turco, Demetri Francesco', fols. 2r-8v, 11r, 15v-17r, and the undated letter of Andrea Barbaro; BV, *Vat. Lat.* 10945, fol. 62v (concern about the activities of English travellers in the early seventeenth century).

17. See BV, *Vat. Lat.* 10945, fol. 124r; ASVat, *SS. Venezia,* 9, fols. 155v-6r; V. Peri, ' "L'incredible risguardo" e "l'incredibile destrezza": la resistenza di Venezia alle iniziative postridentine della Santa Sede per i Greci deu syiu dinubu', in H.-G. Beck and M. Manoussacas (eds), *Venezia, centro di mediazione tra orienta e Occidente (secoli XV-XVI): aspetti e problemi* (2 vols, Leo S. Olschki, E.A. Pertusi, Florence, 1977), pp. 624-5.

18. M. Sanuto, *I Diarii* (57 vols, Visentini, Venice, 1888), vol. 22, col. 109; J. Delumeau, *Vie économique et sociale de Rome dans la seconde moitié du XVIᵉ siècle* (2 vols, E. De Boccard, Paris, 1957), vol. 1, p. 281; B. Pullan, *Rich and Poor in Renaissance Venice: The Social Institutions of a Catholic State, to 1620* (Basil Blackwell, Oxford, 1971), pp. 546-7; B. Pullan, *The Jews of Europe and the Inquisition of Venice, 1550-1670* (Basil Blackwell, Oxford, 1983), pp. 156-7.

19. Archivio di Stato, Rome (hereafter ASR), *Camerale II,* 40 (Ebrei), 2, brief of 6 October 1586.

20. Cf. ASR, *Camerale II,* 40 (Ebrei), 2, constitution of 13 February 1429; ASVat, *Misc. Arm.* IV, 10, fol. 110r; Locato, *Opus,* p. 189.

21. Cf. E. Natali, *Il Ghetto di Roma* (Tipografia Della Tribuna, Rome, 1887), p. 214; F. Secret, *Les Kabbalistes chrétiens de la Renaissance* (Dunod, Paris, 1964), pp. 126, 238, 328; F. Secret, 'Notes sur les Hébraisants chrétiens et les Juifs en France', *Revue des études juives,* CXXVI (1967), p. 433; P. Zambelli, 'Cornelio Agrippa, Sisto da Siena e gli inquisitori', *Memorie domenicane,* n.s., *III* (1972), pp. 163-4.

22. ASVen, *SU,* b.20, *proc.* 'Targher Giovanni modenese', denunciation of 6 November 1565 and deposition of 13 November 1565; ASR, *Camerale II,* 40 (Ebrei), 3, document of 20 November 1572.

23. Cf. ASVen, *SU,* b.31, *proc.* 'Stichiano fra Aurelio', deposition of prison warder's wife, 8 May 1572 (Venice); *SU* b.36, *proc.* 'Abraam detto Righetto', fols. 3r-v (Florence); *SU,* b.52, *proc.* 'Mandolino (ebreo)', interrogation of 18 May 1584 (Muggia).

24. F. Marotti, *Lo spettacolo dall'Umanesimo al Manierismo: Teoria e Tecnica* (Feltrinelli, Milan, 1974), p. 241. S. Simonsohn, *History of the Jews in the Duchy of Mantua* (Kiryath Sepher, Jerusalem, 1977), pp. 526-7.

25. See for example *SU* b.47, *proc.* 'Briani Paolina', protest of Osain 'turco', 31 December 1581; *SU* b.53, *proc.* 'Commedianti', depositions of 6 April 1584; *SU* b.57, *proc.* 'Ferro Alessandro', interrogation of 7 June 1586; ASVat, *Fondo Borghese*, Serie II, 64-5, fol. 57r.

26. ASVen, *SU*, b.55, *proc.* 'Giuseppe Ebreo, Mantova', interrogation of 19 March 1585.

27. Delumeau, *Vie*, I, p. 507.

28. ASVat, *SS. Venezia*, 26, fols. 477r, 494v; *SS. Venezia*, 28, fol. 282r.

29. See for example ASR, *Tribunale Criminale del Governatore, Processi, secolo XVI*, 96. fol. 1v; *Tribunale del Governatore, Processi, 1554*, 19, *proc.* 5; *Bandi*, 2, nos. 178-80; Pullan, *Rich and Poor*, pp. 432-6.

30. Printed in B. Colombi, *Soragna: Cristiani ed Ebrei, otto secoli di storia* (Luigi Batte, Parma, 1975), p. 268.

31. ASVen, *Senato, Secreta*, reg. 66, fol. 57r.

32. Cf. ASR, *Bandi*, 4, no. 100 (motu proprio of 7 march 1569) with *Bandi*, 5, no. 31 (bull of 17 December 1517); R. Segre, 'Bernardino da Feltre, i Monti di Pietú e i banchi ebrei', *Revista Storica Italiana, XC* (1978), pp. 825, 829-30.

33. ASVat, *Misc. Arm.*, V, 248, fol. 70v.

34. ASVen, *SU*, b. 162, letter of Giacomo Foscarini to the Capi, 29 November 1574; cf. *Compilazione delle Leggi*, b. 188, fols. 135r-v, Senate law of 11 April 1443.

35. Cf. P.C. Ioly Zorattini, 'Gli Ebrei a Venezia, Padova e Verona', in G. Arnaldi and M. Pastore Stocchi (eds), *Storia della cultura veneta dal primo Quattrocento al Concilio di Trento*, NER, III/1 (Pozza, Vicenza, 1980), p. 563.

36. BV, *Vat. Lat.* 3933, fols. 18r, 19r. Giulio may have been a convert; his statement was possibly written in the later 1560s.

37. Biblioteca Nazionale Marciana, Venice (hereafter BMV), *It. VII*, 213, fol. 279v; *It. VII*, 810 (7290), entry for 1 June 1568; *It. VII*, 364, fol. 48v.

38. Printed in R. Segre, *Gli ebrei lombardi nell'eta spagnola: storia di un espulsione* (Accademia Delle Scienze, Turin, 1973), p. 33.

39. See for example ASVen, *Consiglio dei Dieci, Lettere di Rettori, Udine*, b.170, letter of 29 August 1543; BV, *Vat.Lat.* 6792, fol. 79r; ASR, *Tribunale Criminale del Governatore di Roma, Sentenze originali*, b.2, 1556, no. 46.

40. See for example the argument against the Resurrection repeated by Fra Girolamo Garzoni da Verola after hearing it, he said, from a Jew in Bologna (ASVen, *SU*, b.52 *proc.* 'Garzoni Girolamo', fol. 16v); and the comments of the Theatine Giovanni Battista Castaldo in his *Vita del Santissimo Pontefice Paolo Quarto* (G. Cassiani, Modena, 1618), p. 130. Cf. U. Cassuto, *Gli ebrei a Firenze nell'eta del Rinascimento,* Tipografic Galletti E. Cocci, Florence, 1918), p. 91; K.R. Stow, 'The Burning of the Talmud in 1553, in the Light of Sixteenth Century Catholic Attitudes toward the Talmud', *Bibliothèque d'humanisme et renaissance, XXXIV* (1972), pp. 446-7.

41. Cf. the comments of Girolamo Muzio in a letter of September 1553 from Pesaro printed by P. Paschini, 'Episodi della Contro-Riforma in lettere inedite di Girolamo Muzio', *Atti e Memorie della Società Istriana di Archeologia e Storia Patria, XXXIX* (1927), p. 365; and the opinion of Giulio Marcello in BV, *Vat. Lat.* 3933, fol. 19r. These assumptions seemed

occasionally to be supported by evidence presented to the Inquisition: see for example *SU*, b.10, *proc.* 'Benedetti fra Benedetto, Venezia; Racer Giovanni Maria, Candia', abjuration and sentence of Giovanni Maria, 27 February 1552; *SU*, b.11, register of proceedings against Francesco Merlara and others dated 1553, undated abjuration of Angelica, wife of the sword-maker Giangiacomo.

42. Georgius Summarippa veronensis, *Martyrium Sebastiani Novelli trucidati a perfidis iudeis*, Diligentia Bernardini Celerii De Luerg (Tarvisii, 1480).

43. Cf. B.S. Pullan, 'The Inquisition and the Jews of Venice: the case of Gaspare Ribeiro, 1580-1581', *Bulletin of the John Rylands University Library of Manchester, LXII* (1979), pp. 215-16.

44. See for example M. Stern, *Urkundliche Beiträge über die Stellung der Päpste zu den Juden* (H.Fiencke, Kiel, 1893), p. 162.

45. See Natali, *Il Ghetto*, pp. 225-7, 229; C. Roth, *The History of the Jews of Italy* (The Jewish Publication Society of America, Philadelphia, 1946), pp. 315-16; A. Milano, *Il Ghetto di Roma: illustrazioni storiche* (Staderini Editore, Rome, 1964), pp. 269-75; *Encyclopaedia Judaica* (16 vols, Keter Publishing House, Jerusalem, 1971), vol. XIV, cols 1184-5.

46. ASVat, *Arm. XXIX*, 67, fol. 125v. The same reasoning appears in the Middle Ages: see for example Thomas Aquinas, *Opera Omnia*, vol. VIII, p. 89; Martin V's constitution of 13 February 1429 (ASR, *Camerale II*, 40 (Ebrei), 2); and Eugenius IV's bull of 6 February 1433, printed by A. Neubauer, 'Pope Eugenius IV on the Jews', *The Jewish Quarterly Review, II* (1890), p. 530.

47. Paul III prohibited converts from contact with non-Christians, and encouraged them to marry born Christians (*Bullarium Diplomatum et privilegiorum sanctorum romanorum pontificum* (24 vols, Sebastiani Franco et Henrico Dalmazzo, Augustae Taurinorum, 1857-72), VI, pp. 336-7); cf. BV, *Vat. Lat.* 6792, fol. 100r, proclamation of Cardinal Sirleto, July 1568.

48. Pullan, *The Jews*, p. 283.

49. L. Poliakov, *Historie de l'antisémitisme* (4 vols, Calmann-Lévy, Paris, 1955-77), vol. 2 (1961), p. 304.

50. *Corpus Juris Canonici*, ed. E. Friedberg (2 vols, ex officina Bernhardi Tauchnitz, Lipsiae, 1881), vol. II, cols 772-3, 776.

51. ASVen, *Compilazione delle Leggi*, b.188, law of 3 November 1446.

52. S. Bongi, *Inventario del R. Archivio di Stato in Lucca* (4 vols, Tipografia Giusti, Lucca, 1872-88), vol. 1 (1872), p. 211; L. Amabile, *Il Santo Affizio della Inquisizione in Napoli* (2 vols, Lap, Città di Castello, 1892), vol. 1, pp. 112-20; Roth, *The History*, pp. 187-8, 254, 268, 283; Pullan, *Rich and Poor*, p. 460; Segre, 'Bernardino', p. 53.

53. M. Radin, 'A Charter of Privileges of the Jews in Ancona of the Year 1535', *The Jewish Quarterly Review*, n.s. *IV* (1913-14), p. 233; Simonsohn, *History*, p. 568; D. Jacoby, 'Les Juifs à Venise du XIVᶜ au milieu du XVIᶜ siècle', in Beck and Manoussacas (eds), *Venezia, centro*, p. 210. The decree establishing the Venetian Ghetto is printed in Sanuto, *Diarii*, vol. 22, cols 85-7.

54. ASVen, *Senato, Secreta*, reg. 66, fol. 546r; V. Sandi *Principii di storia civile della Repubblica de Venezia dalla sua fondazione sino all'anno di N.S. 1700* (6 vols, Sebastian Coleti, Venice, 1755-6) vol. 3 (1756), pp. 444-5; *Le Carte Strozziane*, I, p. 491; A. Battistella, *Il S. Officio e la riforma religiosa in*

*Bologna* (2 vols, Anichelli, Bologna, 1905), vol. 2, pp. 148-9; Cassuto, *Gli ebrei*, pp. 101-2; P. Prodi, *Il Cardinale Gabriele Paleotti (1522-1597)* (2 vols, Edzioni Di Storia e Letteratura, Rome, 1959-67), vol. 2 (1967), pp. 201-2; L. Poliakov, *Jewish Bankers and the Holy See: From the Thirteenth to the Seventeenth Century* (Routledge & Kegan Paul, London, 1977), pp. 181-3; Simonsohn, *History*, p. 115.

55. The texts of the regulations, dated 6 October 1586 and 17 August 1592, are in ASR, *Camerale II*, 40 (Ebrei), 2 and 3 respectively. Paul IV's bull 'Cum nimis absurdum' of 14 July 1555, printed in *Bullarium*, VI, pp. 498-50, was put into effect in Rome by the Vicar-General in an order of 23 July (ASVat, *Misc. Arm.* V, 248, fol. 70v).

56. B. Arbel, 'The Jews in Cyprus: New Evidence from the Venetian Period', *Jewish Social Studies, XLI* (1979), pp. 29-30.

57. Pullan, *Rich and Poor*, pp. 545-6; and cf. Pullan, *The Jews* pp. 169-71, 180-1.

58. ASR, *Camerale II*, 40 (Ebrei), 2, bull of 2 July 1593; Archivio di Stato, Florence (ASF), *Medici*, 3310, fols. 297v-8r. Giulio Antonio Santoria often appears in the documents as 'Cardinal Santa Severina', identified by the name of the diocese in Calabria of which he was archbishop before his election to the College of Cardinals.

59. Cited by Poliakov, *Jewish Bankers*, p. 129; the report referred to Scandiano.

60. The Dominican Bernardo da Coma argued that Jewish usury should be subject to the Inquisition (see his *Lucerna inquisitorum hereticae pravitatis* (Apud M.A. Zalterium, Venetiis, 1596), p. 71) but this view was rejected by the Roman Congregation in 1612, Stern, *Urkundliche Beiträge*, p. 177.

61. See for example Locato, *Opus*, p. 22.

62. Prosper Farinaci, *Opera Turidica* (9 vols, Sumtibus Wolfgang, Mauritii Endteri, VIII, Noribergae, 1686), vol. 8, p. 26.

63. See for example ASVat, *Fondo Borghese*, Serie II, 64-5, fol. 55v: a statement of Sixtus V, in the presence of the Congregation of the Inquisition, that infants brought up by their Jewish parents 'superstitione, et perfidia corrumpantur, aut illam cum lacte imbibant'.

64. ASR, *Camerale II*, 40 (Ebrei), 2, constitution of 13 February 1429.

65. Thomas Aquinas, *Opera Omnia*, VIII, p. 89; *Directorium Inquisitorum R.P.F. Nicolae Eymerici* (Aedibus Populi Rorian, Romae, 1578), pp. 244-5; Locato, *Opus*, p. 184.

66. See, for example, *Tractatus Marquardi de Susanis iurisconsulti Utinensis. De Iudaeis et aliis infidelibus* (Cominum de Tridano Montisferrati, Venetiis, 1568), fol. 157v; Locato, *Opus*, pp. 22, 186, 190; *Repertorium inquisitorum pravitatis haereticae. Correctionibus et Annatationibus Praestantissimorum Iurisconsultorum Quintiliani Mandosii, ac Petri Vendrameni decoratum et auctum* (D. Zenarum, Venetiis, 1575), p. 490.

67. Printed in *Bullarium*, VIII, pp. 378-9.

68. Eymerici, *Directorium*, pp. 244-6; Locato, *Opus*, pp. 183-5.

69. See for example ASVat, *Fondo Borghese*, Serie II, 64-5, fols. 86r-8r; BV, *Vat. Lat.* 10945, fol. 92v; *Patetta*, 145, fols. 29v-32r; Stern, *Urkundliche Beiträge*, pp. 170, 172-6, 178; and, in addition to the manuals and textbooks already cited, B. Ugolino, *Tractatus de offico et potestate episcopi* (Apud Andream Phaeum, Romae, 1617), p. 196.

70. See for example a reference to a letter of Cardinal Sabelli containing the bull addressed to the Inquisitor of Verona in ASVen, *SU*, b.153, packet marked '1612: giuramento di secretezza'.

71. Cf. cases cited by Pullan, *The Jews*, pp. 45-50, 55-7.

72. ASVat, *Fondo Borghese*, Serie II, 64-5, fols. 86r-8r.

73. C. Feroso, 'Di alcuni Ebrei portoghesi in Ancona sotto Paolo IV', *L'Archivio Storico per le Marche e per l'umbria, I* (1884), p. 693; BMV, *It. VII*, 80 (7298), entry for 20 December 1558.

74. D. Kaufmann, 'Die Vertreibung der Marranen aus Venedig im Jahre 1550', *The Jewish Quarterly Review, XIII* (1901), pp. 525-9; Roth, *The History*, p. 302; Arbel, 'The Jews', p. 24.

75. S.W. Baron, *A Social and Religious History of the Jews* (18 vols, Columbia University Press, New York and London, 1969), vol. 14, pp. 135-6; G. Laras, 'I Marrani di Livorno e l'Inquisizione' in *Atti del convegno 'Livorno e il Mediterraneo nell'età Medicea'* (V. Bastogi Editore, Livorno, 1978), pp. 82, 90; P.C. Ioly Zorattini (ed.), *Processi del S. Uffizio di Venezia contro Ebrei e Giudaizzanti (1548-1560)* (Leo S. Olschki, Florence, 1980), pp. 32-5.

76. *Le Carte Strozziane*, I, pp. 491-2; Baron, *Social*, XIV, pp. 35-6; Poliakov, *Jewish Bankers*, pp. 176-7; Pullan, *The Jews*, p. 179.

77. Laras, 'I Marrani', pp. 82-9; Pullan, *The Jews*, pp. 187-9.

78. ASVat, *SS. Venezia*, 26, fol. 268r.

79. ASF, *Medici*, 3310, fol. 481r.

80. Cf. the letter of 9 March 1556 from the Sultan to the Pope (in ASVat, *AA, Arm. I-XVIII*, 6542, fols. 80r-v) with Navagero's report of 25 April 1556 that the Ancona authorities had been ordered not to execute more Marranos for fear of provoking an attack by the Turkish fleet (in BMV, *It. VII*, 1097 (9445), fol. 172v; see also fols. 194v-5r).

81. Cf. the remarks of Jacoby, 'Les Juifs', pp. 214-15; B. Pullan, 'A ship with two rudders: "Righetto Marrano" and "The Inquisition in Venice" ', *Historical Journal, XX* (1977), p. 40; Pullan, *The Jews*, pp. 174-5, 181-2, 186, 189-90.

82. ASVen, *Consiglio dei Dieci, Secrete*, reg. 10, fols. 159r-v.

83. Orders restricting Inquisition authority on the Terraferma were also issued by Venice in 1548 and 1566. For Venice, see ASVen, *Senato, Secrete*, reg. 66, fols. 56r-v; Sandi, *Principii*, III/1, p. 445; L.A. Schiavi, 'Gli Ebrei in Venezia e nelle sue colonie', *Nuova Antologia di scienze, lettere ed arti*, 3rd series, *XLVII* (1893), p. 512; Pullan, *The Jews*, pp. 52-4, 78-9, 86-8. For Milan, see Baron, *Social*, vol. 14, p.127; S. Simonsohn, 'Un privilegio di Francesco II Sforza agli Ebrei del ducato di Milano', in *Scritti in memoria di Sally Mayer (1875-1953)* (Jerusalem Post and Goldberg Press, Jerusalem, 1956), p. 317; Segre, *Gli Ebrei*, p. 82. For Mantua, see Simonsohn, *History*, p. 112. For the Papacy, see Stern, *Urkundliche Beiträge*, pp. 108-12; A. Milano, *Storia degli ebrei in Italia* (Giulio Ein Audi, Turin, 1963), p. 250; Baron, *Social*, vol. 14, pp. 36-7; A. Toaff, 'Nuova Luce sui Marrani di Ancona', in E. Toaff (ed.), *Studi sull'ebraismo italiano in memoria di Cecil Roth* (Barulli, Rome, 1974), pp. 261-2; Poliakov, *Jewish Bankers*, p. 177; Pullan, *The Jews*, pp. 188-9. For Florence, see C. Roth, *A History of the Marranos* (The Jewish Publication Society of America, New York and Philadelphia, 1932), pp. 214-15; Laras, 'I Marrani', pp. 84-5, 90-2; Baron, *Social*, XIV, p. 126. For Savoy, see Lattes, 'Documents', p. 233; Pullan, *The Jews*,

pp. 182-3.

84. Cf. the Florentine government's strenuous efforts to secure the release of the Marrano merchant Giacomo Ispariel, arrested on the orders of the Roman Inquisition in the spring of 1602, until his escape to Venice two years later (ASF, *Medici*, 3318, letters of 30 May, 7 and 14 June, 16 November 1602; *Medici*, 3320, letters of 16 and 24 April, 1 and 26 May 1604).

85. For Sisto da Siena's own account, see *Bibliotheca Sancta, a F. Sixto Senensi . . . collecta* (Apud Franciscium Senensem, Venetiis, 1566), p. 844.

86. ASVen, *SU*, b.33, *proc.* '1572, 1573: Denuncie. Codega Marc' Antonio (and others)', denunciation of 18 December 1572.

87. Rome, Archivio Capitulare di S. Pietro, *Diarii*, 28, entry for 24 July 1611 (I am most grateful to Dr Noel O'Regan of the University of Lancaster for providing a transcript of this document). Two further suspects were absolved.

88. ASVen, *SU*, b.7, *proc.* '*Contra Francoso Jacobum*' (now printed by Ioly Zorattini (ed.), *Processi (1548-1560)*, pp. 67-78). The other four are Marc'Antonio de Electis, in *SU*, b.159, fols 30r-1v, 70v, 79v; *SU*, b.36, *proc.* 'Abraam detto Righetto' (who changed his story later); *SU*, b.32, *proc.* 'Giovanni Battista'; and Antonio Rodrighes, discussed by P.C. Ioly Zorattini, 'Note sul S. Uffizio e gli ebrei a Venezia nel Cinquecento', *Rivista di Storia della Chiesa in Italia, XXXIII* (1979), p. 504.

89. A. Balletti, *Gli Ebrei e gli Estensi* (Anonima Poligrafica Emiliana, Reggio Emilia, 1930), p. 218.

90. ASVen, *SU*, b.45, *proc*, '1584: Contra Gasparem Ribiera'; *SU*; b.54, *proc.* 'De Filippi Salomone (and others)'. In 1555, Trisatão da Costa confessed his guilt, and was expelled by the government; but the Inquisition took no action against him (see Ioly Zorattini (ed.), *Processi (1548-1560)*, p. 263). On the reality of 'secret Judaism', see comments of Pullan, 'The Inquisition', pp. 214-20, 230.

91. BV, *Vat. Lat*, 10945 fols 32v, 92v.

92. ASVen, *SU*, b.8, *proc.* '1549: Contra Franciscum Olivierum' (now printed by Ioly Zorattini (ed.), *Processi (1548-1560)*, pp. 79-91).

93. BV, *Vat. Lat.* 10945, fols 53r, 92v.

94. ASVen, *SU*, 62, *proc.* 'Saruch Caim'; cf. the charges in *SU*, b.8, *proc.* 'Ebrei' (now printed by Ioly Zorattini (ed.), *Processi (1548-1560)*, pp. 93-4), which the tribunal did not apparently take too seriously.

95. ASF, *Medici*, 3310, fols 481r-v.

96. Roth, *The History*, p. 314.

97. See for example ASVen, *SU*, b.64, *proc.* 'Moretto Giorgio', orders of 15 May and 10 June 1589.

98. ASVat, *Fondo Borghese*, Serie II, 64-5, fols 99r, 265r-70r; Balletti, *Gli Ebrei*, p. 154.

99. BMV, *It. VII*, 810 (7298), entries for 25 October 1558 to 14 January 1559; *It. VII*, 213 (8836), fols 176r-v.

100. See, for example, *Repertorium*, pp. 354-5.

101. Ioly Zoratti (ed.), *Processi (1548-1560)*, pp. 190, 222-3.

102. ASVen, *SU*, b.54, *proc.* 'Pozuolo Giacomo (and others)'. Occasionally, inquisitors allowed themselves to be bribed to pass less severe sentences — see for example Feroso, 'Di alcuni Ebrei', pp. 698-9; Toaff,

'Nuovo luce', pp. 262, 273-4 — but such cases do genuinely seem to have been rare.

103. Figures from *L'Archivio Storico Diocesano di Napoli*, ed. G. Galasso and C. Russo (2 vols, Guida Editori, Naples, 1978), pp. 724-91; and Pullan, *The Jews*, pp. 9-10, 13, 91-2, 201. Cf. the remarks of Baron, *Social*, vol. 14, p. 137; P.C. Ioly Zorattini, 'Processi contro Ebrei e giudaizzanti nell'archivio del S. Uffizio di Aquileia e Concordia', *Memorie storiche forogiuliesi*, *LVIII* (1978), p. 144.

104. F. Secret, 'Notes sur Giullaume Postel', in *Bibliothèque d'Humanisme et Renaissance*, *XXII* (1960), p. 384; ASVen, *SU*, b.17, 'Agostino da Modena medico', deposition of 16 October 1563.

105. In addition to the documents cited in notes 127 and 131, see ASVat, *Concilium Tridentinum*, 74, fols 169r-76r; BV, *Patetta*, 145, fol. 33r; Sisto da Siena, *Bibliotheca*, pp. 193, 199-202; Locato, *Opus*, p. 224.

106. Natali, *Il Ghetto*, p. 83; W. Popper, *The Censorship of Hebrew Books* (KTAV Publishing House, New York, 1969), pp. 25-6, 31.

107. Stern prints the Congregation's edict (*Urkundliche Beiträge*, pp. 99-102), but dates it 12 September; the original in ASVat, *AA. Arm. I-XVIII*, 1592, is dated 12 August. Julius III's orders are in ASVat, *Arm. XLI*, 72, fol. 321r; *Arm. XLII*, 1, fols 61r-2v; and *Directorium*, separate pagination of *Literae Apostolicae*, pp. 94-5. See also Stern, *Urkundliche Beiträge*, pp. 104-8; D. Kaufmann, 'Die Verbrennung der Talmudischen Litteratur in der Republik Venedig', *The Jewish Quarterly Review*, *XIII* (1901), pp. 536-8; Cassuto, *Gli Ebrei*, pp. 385-6; Balletti, *Gli Ebrei*, p. 90; Roth, *The History*, pp. 292-3; Stow, 'The Burning', pp. 441-2.

108. Cf the failure of the Rome community to dissuade the Congregation in 1553 (BV, *Vat. Lat.* 6177, part II, fols 359r-v) with the success reported by Stern, *Urkundliche Beiträge*, pp. 117-26; Simonsohn, *History*, pp. 417-18, 691; Segre, *Gli ebrei*, pp. 31-6.

109. Balletti, *Gli Ebrei*, p. 89; Roth, *The History*, p. 305. The Jewish appeal to the Council appears in ASVat, *Concilium Tridentinum*, 74, fol. 168r.

110. Cf BV. *Vat. Lat.* 10945, fol. 92v; Stern, *Urkundliche Beiträge*, p. 170; Popper, *Censorship*, pp. 72-3, 75, 77-8, 100; Simonsohn, *History*, pp. 687-92.

111. *Bullarium*, X, pp. 25-8; Simonsohn, *History*, pp. 689, 691.

112. Cf. Stern, *Urkundliche Beiträge*, pp. 158, 166.

113. Cf. Stern, *Urkundliche Beiträge*, p. 176; J.W. Montgomery, 'Sixtus of Siena and Roman Catholic Biblical Scholarship in the Reformation Period', *Archiv für Reformationsgeschichte*, *LIV* (1963), p. 224; Popper, *Censorship*, p. 100; *Encyclopaedia Judaica*, vol. XV, pp. 770-1. For an account of the structure and significance of the Talmud, see J. Bowker, *The Targums and Rabbinic Literature* (Cambridge University Press, Cambridge, 1969), pp. 53-69.

114. Cf. Stern, *Urkundliche Beiträge*, pp. 161-2; Baron, *Social*, vol. 14, p. 354; Stow, 'The Burning', pp. 458-9.

115. A new edition of the Talmud with Catholic marginal interpretations was published in Basle by Froben between 1579 and 1581 with the approval of Cardinal Sirleto; its title page notes that the text 'iuxta mentem Sacri concilii Tridentini expurgatum et approbatum, ut non modo citra impietatem verum etiam cum fructu a nostris legi possit.' Cf. the comments

of Sisto da Siena, *Bibliotheca*, pp. 110-11; Stow, 'The Burning', pp. 436-7, 443-6, 455-7; F. Parente, 'Il confronto ideologico tra l'Ebraismo et la Chiesa in Italia', in *Italia judaica; Atti del I convegno internazionale* (Ministero per i beni culturali e ambientali, Rome, 1983), p. 309.

116. Mark 16:15.

117. BV, *Vat. Lat.* 6184, part I, vol. 172r; *Vat. Lat.* 6195, part I, fols 100r-1r; P.S. Medici, *Catalogo de' neofiti illustri usciti per misericordia di Dio dall'ebraismo* (V. Vangelisti, Florence, 1701), pp. 59-60.

118. Cf. Farinaci, *Opera*, VIII, p. 25; Pullan, *The Jews*, pp. 68, 272-7.

119. Balletti, *Gli Ebrei*, p. 220.

120. Galasso and Russo (eds), *L'Archivio Storico*, pp. 724-91.

# 3

# The Impact of Protestantism in Spain
# 1520-1600

*Jaime Contreras*

## Introduction

On 10 December 1520, when Martin Luther publicly burned the papal bull *Exsurge Domine* at Wittenburg, in Spain, in the extreme southwestern part of Europe, the frenzied clash of arms could be heard everywhere. Castile and Aragon were suffering the effects of a cruel civil war: the Comunero movement in Castile and the Germanía of Valencia. Outwardly, these conflicts indicated limited acceptance of the sovereignty of their new king Charles I, who had already been elected Emperor Charles V of Germany; but, in reality, Comuneros and Agermanados represented the violent expression of serious social tensions which had originated many years earlier, well before the death of Queen Isabella in 1504.

Now, in 1520, in the turmoil of war, it seemed that the entire social order as well as the political structure that the Catholic Sovereigns had erected were about to collapse like a pack of cards. Among the pillars of that structure, the Inquisition occupied a prominent place. Nevertheless, from the time of the Queen's death powerful winds had battered the Tribunal of the Holy Office, threatening it with collapse and destruction.

Between 1504 and 1520, a succession of furious attacks emanating from important social strata along with a number of serious mishaps contributed to the semi-paralysis of that tribunal of the faith which the Catholic Sovereigns had created with such enthusiasm and maintained with such careful attention. Let us describe, briefly, its misfortunes.

The judicial activity of the Inquisition, which had formerly been as frenzied as it had been cruel, was now reduced to a minimum. The *converso*-Judaiser, the main and preferred victim of inquisitorial activity, had virtually disappeared. With rare exceptions, the curve of condemnations fell vertically and the Tribunal found that, all at once, its preferred 'clientele' no longer existed![1] Obviously, this is not to say that conversos as an ethnic group had been destroyed by the tragic repression of previous years but simply to indicate that the Holy Office was encountering difficulty in detecting its particular 'heresy'. Whatever happened, the result of this paralysis was a forced reduction in inquisitorial staff and the disappearance of many tribunals. Of the seventeen that existed in the time of Inquisitor General Torquemada, only seven remained by 1506.[2]

Instead of trying to accommodate itself to this new conjuncture, however, the Holy Office continued to be obsessed with the converted Jew. There were still many of these, but the majority, far from continuing to commit heresy, had assimilated the new religion as the indispensable condition for rising to privileged positions in the church or in the public life of many cities.[3]

This giddy ascent caused an almost excessive concern to the Inquisition and the groups that it represented, so they attempted to curtail it even when, in order to do so, they had to carry out a programme marked by strong racist overtones. Without doubt this proved to be a difficult task not only because it was becoming more and more difficult to detect conversos practising heresy but because their abandonment of Judaic practices permitted them to marry into Old Christian families of impeccable rank and lineage.

The Inquisition's policy of 'firing to annihilate' the conversos was an arbitrary and indiscriminate action that, logically enough, provoked a violent reaction that was led by important social strata whose lineage was above suspicion.[4] For the first time, the Holy Office was becoming troublesome for many in Castile.

Protests were not long in coming, and with greater or lesser intensity they spread throughout the land. As we already know, it was in Córdoba where they attained their greatest expression. There, the insane proceedings of Inquisitor Lucero provoked such agitation that the Crown was forced to initiate an investigation in order to repair the damage that the Inquisition had caused. For the first time, the Inquisition was forced to sit on the bench of the accused. The tribunal was the famous ecclesiastical congregation of 1508.[5] The prudent attitude of Cisneros and strong royal support saved the tribunal from explicit condemnation but its prestige was deteriorating and its necessity had become a matter of public debate. Several years later, the anti-inquisitorial tone adopted by the Comuneros is evidence that the embers of this debate had not been entirely extinguished. In the middle of the war there was still distrust of the Inquisition in many parts of Castile.[6]

As a result, when the events of 1520 took place in Wittenburg, very few in Spain suspected that they would not only serve to rehabilitate the Holy Office but convert it into one of the leading political institutions of the Catholic monarchy. In fact, the Reformation arrived at a very opportune moment as much for the Imperial forces locked in their struggle with the Comuneros as for the Tribunal of the Faith which quickly discovered a new heresy whose repression would serve to solidly re-affirm the precarious and uncertain basis of its own existence.

## 1520-1540: The Inquisition and the spectre of Luther

The Inquisition made use of Luther; this appears to be an obvious conclusion. The first news about the events in Germany had hardly arrived in the Iberian Peninsula when already the mark of heretic had been attached for ever to the figure of the Reformer. Doubtless he remained a far-off, almost mythical personage, but very quickly a strategy was designed that would make him into a kind of bogyman. We know that it was at the Diet of Worms that the first Spaniards encountered Luther: a Luther already firmly established in the maturity of his doctrines, extremely obstinate and unwilling to compromise. Alfonso de Valdés, the humanist and Latin secretary to the Emperor, saw in this recalcitrant attitude 'the evil seed of heresy'.[7]

But the news could not be hidden and very quickly a whirlwind of rumours ran through the peninsula. Some were filled with eagerness and curiosity while, in others, fear presaged evil auguries.

Expectation and curiosity were the first reaction of a small group of courtiers, humanists and Erasmians. For them, the Reformer was a figure sufficiently attractive to hope that his doctrine would provide the great shock that would finally start the long-hoped-for 'reform of morals'.[8] There we have, as a unique example, the exceptional figure of Juan de Vergara,[9] also present at Worms and representing the belief of many Spaniards in the essential goodness of the reform idea, a project welcomed unselfishly and ingenuously by certain Illuminists,[10] by groups of Comuneros[11] and by a few cells scattered in the district of Valladolid and Seville.[12] Such were the Spanish 'partisans' of Luther who mythicised Luther's endeavour. Taken together, they formed a barely recognisable but highly cultivated group. For the rest of the population, Luther was no more than a deformed image which was soon to become the target of the coarsest epithets of official propaganda.

Between 1520 and 1521, political authority and its most important institutions attempted to create the image that, for the future, would be published abroad until the entire social fabric was satiated with it. Underlying this image was a fearful defensive attitude that manifested itself in two significant ways: for the authorities, Luther was both 'a dangerous heretic' and a chief agent of political subversion. Both images constituted the gravest accusations because they presupposed the rebellious denial of the universal political formula that the Emperor had devised for the entire Christian world and would tend to undermine the foundations of the established political and social order. As a consequence, a strategy was formulated and, on 7 April 1521, the Inquisition took the first step by prohibiting the works of the Heresiarch. Since Lutheranism brought with it an enormous revolutionary potential that was especially dangerous for Spain because it coincided with a difficult political situation when the king was absent in Germany and the country was enflamed by revolution, Luther's ideas therefore had to be stopped at the frontiers. If this could not be accomplished it would 'cause a great tumult and further enflame passions at a time when certain towns in these kingdoms have risen in rebellion'.[13]

What was to be done? Principally, it had become necessary to re-create the most uncompromising ideological mechanisms and re-affirm the repression of intellectual and religious dissent. In order to accomplish this, nothing could be more effective than once again to re-establish the prestige of the Holy Office and abandon the 'rash and cowardly' proposals to reform or even abolish it.

Shortly after the end of the Comunero Revolution, strong statements about the Lutheran peril were made in Castile and serious measures were adopted to contain it. Everyone knew, or ought to have known at least, that Luther was an enemy heretic. But some suspected that there were partisans and sympathisers of the great Heresiarch even within the Iberian peninsula itself. It was, therefore, necessary to exercise extreme caution because among the many apparently orthodox intellectual concepts and religious ideas then circulating in Castile there were some that might contain the seeds of heresy.

At court, in the shelter of Imperial forces, Erasmian spirituality was all the rage. Important persons in the inner circle of the Emperor's advisors were professed Erasmians. Gattinara, the Grand Chancellor, was one of these and Alonso de Manrique, the Inquisitor-General himself, was another. All of these men represented a connection with the Erasmian phenomenon in Europe as a whole. Nevertheless, in spite of its important influence in Spain, the Erasmians represented a tendency that many stigmatised as springing from an excessive fondness for foreign customs and, as a result, it could not hope to awaken strong popular support. Along with this, and protected by the wide amnesty that followed the end of the Comunero movement, there was yet another current that attempted to combine Caroline Europeanism with the more popular spirit of the Crusade. This was a spirit that had remained alive despite obvious vicissitudes since the time of the Catholic Sovereigns so that when Charles presented his proposed Crusade against the Turks he was appealing to a strongly rooted emotion. From the Messianic perspective of the Crusade, therefore, it was not difficult to respond powerfully to the Lutheran threat.[14] There were, therefore, two different ideas: one peaceful, the other bellicose — two ideas which divided the highest political circles and ended with the victory of the hawks.

In this struggle the forces controlling the inquisitorial machine stood more for the second approach than the first. Representing the Supreme Council rather than the Inquisitor-General himself, these forces eagerly deployed the most repressive ideas and imposed a hard line. The Lutherans themselves were not the first victims of this campaign; instead it was the phantoms of Lutheranism who were rooted out and eradicated. For the Suprema, these phantoms were composed of certain groups of university intellectuals, persons inclined towards an interiorised and affective spirituality and, above all, the Illuminists of Toledo because it was not difficult to find an obvious parallelism between their views and the Lutheran concept of Grace.[15]

Soon, the first cases were begun. Some, very few to be sure, were of popular origin. These were men who had heard of Luther and immediately saw in him the almost mythical figure justifying their own critical and discordant ideas. Others, those of greater significance, came from higher social levels. Perhaps the most significant of all was the case of Juan de Vergara. Vergara was caught by the iron net of the tribunal of Toledo, and those who shared his views, including the Inquisitor-General himself, could do nothing for him. Vergara abjured 'de vehementi' as an Erasmian and 'defender' of Luther.[16] This case was clear proof that the Inquisition had become interested in removing certain spiritual ideas from Spanish intellectual and religious life. These were ideas that, however imprecise their outlines, were already marked as tributaries of the same river: Illuminists, Erasmians, Dexados, Irenists were all roots joined to the same trunk, that embodied by Martin Luther.

Little by little, between 1520 and 1540, the model of repression was created. Of course, this was a struggle against ghosts but it had a spectacular result: Luther became converted into a bogyman.[17] This repressive model, which had not yet openly formulated the mechanics of punishment, had two principal objectives: (a) to prevent the dissemination of reformist literature, and (b) to keep a close watch upon, and if necessary prosecute, any demonstration of support for the Reformation however remote and ambiguous it may have been.

As a result of this, Spain began to close in around itself. Trent was just around the corner, and the idea of systematic aggression by the enemies of the faith, repeated incessantly, had settled in the minds of both great and small. The attitude that emerged was one of defence at all costs of 'nationalistic' values. We are entering the 1540s which would bring with them long years of religious intransigence, an intransigence which corresponded closely with the moral strictness of a triumphant Calvinism which had burst forth, marginalising Lutheranism and initiating the 'reform of the Reformation'

## 1540-1560: The victory of the Holy Office

Regardless of the vantage point from which they are regarded, the middle years of the sixteenth century mark a profound turning point. By this time, Castile was fully committed to meeting the demands of the imperial idea even though this required efforts and caused strains that earlier generations had not experienced. The Emperor's struggle against the Protestant princes of Germany not only caused profound intellectual uneasiness, but also required a constant infusion of resources whose negative economic effect was already being felt in various parts of the kingdom.

Charles I attempted to spread the burden among all social groups but the nobility and the clergy took pains to remind him of their right to fiscal immunity. In the same way, the representatives of the urban elites, fortified behind the walls of the Cortes, did not hesitate to deflect the Crown's demands towards the popular classes.

At the same time, from the heights of their corporate privileges, the ruling groups sought to impose a kind of social occlusion in order to cut off at the roots the desire for social advancement of those who, enriched by an expanding economy, sought to crown their gains with the lustre of honour and privilege. The Kingdom was becoming more feudalised than ever before. As a result, the predictable social tensions that were being generated had to be channelled towards external objects. In this way, Luther and the Reformation became the main enemies of the state. Of course, this was not only for socio-economic reasons; there were also powerful political and ideological arguments but it also seems obvious that the aggressive xenophobia that characterised the anti-Protestant crusade did not obscure its indirect interest in alleviating possible social tensions. Howsoever we characterise this 'swerve into dogmatism', it had an important impact on everyday life. It was said that the times of joy and optimism had given way to an atmosphere of fear and foreboding. These were the 'sombre men' spoken of by Braudel.[18] These were the men of the Tridentine generation, the men of the age of Philip II, dangerous and 'arduous' times, as Teresa de Jesus called them.[19]

The events that were to mark out this period became evident very quickly: the opening of the Council of Trent in 1545, while in Castile in 1547 Cardinal Siliceo, principal supporter of the most closed and inflexible position, imposed the famous Statute of Purity of Blood in the diocese of Toledo.[20] Between those two years, in 1546, another important event took place: the nomination of Fernando de Valdés as Inquisitor-General.[21]

This appointment was made for a very specific reason: 'to confront an unstable religious situation under constant attack by European Protestantism'.[22] Such were the Emperor's orders and the Inquisitor responded fully to the desires of his master. In the future, the Inquisition would become converted into the ideal instrument to brake the Protestant offensive in the Hispanic Kingdoms. In fact, the entire reorganisation of inquisitorial structures that Valdés put into place, the broad range of cases that were assigned to the Holy Office and all the campaigns of conversion and repression that began at that time, had, as background, the obsession with Protestantism.

As we have already said, this obsession took two forms: one, the heresy that was printed; the other, heresy openly avowed. In both cases, the Inquisition tried to eradicate the 'pollution' when it had been discovered and immobilised.

The book, which was the carrier of heresy in print, became the object of careful attention. These were the years when the edicts and catalogues of prohibited books began to proliferate. This was not simply an effort to prohibit the works of Protestant authors but to outline and delimit a 'universe of heterodoxy' in the words of

Virgilio Pinto.[23] It was not merely a matter of identifying and intercepting printed heterodoxy but also of indicating exactly what the Christian should read and also had to believe.

The printed word and the opinion emanating from the university or the pulpit also became the object of meticulous attention. During this period, the archives of the Holy Office are full of visits of inspection to bookshops and libraries. Universities, cathedral chapters, monasteries and private individuals had to endure the minutely cautious inspection of the agents of the Tribunal. Every one of them, as the letters to and from the Supreme Council attest, sought the same goal: to expurgate heresy. But what heresy? The heresy that can be found in the edict of 1551, that which was hidden among the holy books that were included in the general censorship of bibles of 1554, and above all, that which was carefully gathered together in the enormous Index of 1559.[24] It is here that we meet, for the first time, that 'universe of heterodoxy' referred to by Virgilio Pinto. Here we have the open heresy of the Protestant author but here we have, too, carefully gathered together, all the forms of heterodoxy — an enormous range of 'superstitious errors' which, according to the new censors, was rooted in literary production, in works of a scientific nature and even in religious works of Christian doctrine. Everything was carefully reviewed, and almost everything was mutilated. A reign of fear had been imposed and orthodoxy rode on the croup of a politico-ecclesiastical ideal that sought to apply the most absolute severity. As a logical consequence the book, that 'silent heretic', was, from then on, at the mercy of the Inquisition.

And, along with the book, which was the chief populariser of heresy, the Holy Office also prepared itself to sift through the entire social fabric in search of those who believed in Lutheranism. A great deal has been written about the closeness of many intellectuals of the period to the doctrine of the Reform, and although this did not encompass the Inquisition's entire plan of action it was of grave concern to the inquisitors in the middle years of the century. Small but well-educated social groups made up of intellectuals and well-known ecclesiastics comprised the main objective of the tribunal.

The years 1558 and 1559, as is well known, produced the great anti-Lutheran outburst. During the years immediately before that, everything appeared calm, yet, to keen ears, a dull subterranean rumbling presaged some spectacular shock. For some time the rejuvenated Tribunal under the dedicated leadership of Fernando de Valdés had been working frantically and in the deepest secrecy.

Rumours, information and witnesses were collected and with them an explosive dossier was created that was revealed in 1558 and had its most spectacular success in the following year.

Were these dates purely accidental? It is difficult to reply with any degree of assurance. Nevertheless, from a purely speculative standpoint, it is important to indicate certain coincidences. This is a time of transition between two distinct epochs. Charles cedes his power to Philip II; an Emperor, with a European and universal perspective, gives the highest responsibilities to a Hispanicised Philip. In Yuste, Charles ponders his failure: Germany divided; Flanders aroused and turbulent; the unity of the 'Universitas Christiana' now seemingly impossible and, finally, his own inheritance fragmented, irreversibly, as a result of sordid rivalries among his own family. The peace of Cateau-Cambrésis with the French is the only solid achievement that remains of the Caroline period. Philip II inherited this situation and accepted it as inevitable, but he did attempt to repair the edifice. Heresy had been the cause of all of these evils, and, as a consequence, heresy had to be punished. In this context, someone in his inner circle spoke to him about the information being accumulated by the Holy Office and . . . his response was not long in coming. The flames illuminated the land of Castile. Was this the end of an epoch or the beginning of another? Perhaps both at the same time, but it is certain that spectacular effects flowed from these events. The first and most important of these was the full confirmation of one option: the Counter Reformation was transformed into the political philosophy of the kingdom.

Let us quickly survey these events. Several *autos-de-fe* that were held in Valladolid and Seville succeeded in eradicating the nucleus of 'Protestants' discovered in the interior of Castile.[25] Were they really Lutherans?[26] This is an issue very difficult to clarify. Actually, all or almost all of those tried knew the works of the Reformers. They had even discussed these works passionately among themselves but . . . it does not appear that any of them had made an open profession of Lutheran faith. Almost all of them maintained, essentially intact, the Erasmian principles of their youth. And even some of their judges, disposed as they were to discover ample fields on which they could affirm the presence of the evil seed, had to place them close to the Illuminists.[27]

Howsoever it may be, it is certain that those *autos-de-fe* were a final chapter which saw the death of informal heterodoxies and religious ambiguity alike, all of them tainted with the colour of

Protestantism. This was the most important thing. We are dealing with a story in which minute 'enemies' were discovered in the early chapters and all of which, as time passed, ended by flowing into the river of a feared and powerful enemy: 'the sect of Luther'. The lesson that the People of God were meant to learn from this was simple and straightforward: every dissident whim, however insignificant, led inevitably to the deep ocean of Protestant heresy.

In the future, this People of God, which had to be guided like a meek a d submissive herd, would have to pay careful attention to the true identity of its shepherds. The *autos-de-fe* of Valladolid and Seville had revealed the existence of false prophets who guarded the herd disguised as good shepherds. Doctors Egidio and Constantino, who were both famous preachers, had directed the conventicle in Seville. Dr Cazalla, the most conspicuous leader of the group in Valladolid, had frequently mounted the imperial pulpit. What the Inquisition said, therefore, was certain: the evil seed had been spread among the favourite sons of the church. It was an enormous scandal and, as a consequence, the scalpel did not hesitate to cut the healthy as well as the sick with imprisonment, torture, confiscation and bonfires.

The effects were spectacular. 'The pedagogy of fear', as Bennassar described it, produced important results.[28] But, in spite of everything, the Inquisition was still not satisfied. With meticulous care, it prepared a final blow. On 21 August 1559, Bartolomé de Carranza, the Archbishop of Toledo, the Primate of the Spanish church, the foremost preacher of Flanders and a loyal and intimate servant of the Monarchy, was made prisoner by the Holy Office in Torrelaguna, a village of its own diocese near Madrid. It would be of little value to recount all the steps or describe the turbulent world of passions that led to this unfortunate event.[29] Perversity, cruelty and envy were responsible for burying Carranza in the cellars of the Inquisition. The most infamous accusations were levied at him and the worst of all was that he was intellectually close to certain points of Protestant theology. None of this appears to have been the case but these were difficult times for the faith. A terrible excuse permitted vengeance to disguise itself with the habit of truth and the sword of justice. Apart from this, there was the *raison d'état* that demanded that the victim become an important pawn in the tense diplomatic negotiations between king and pope.

But this was not all. The name of Carranza was used as an instrument to attain other goals as well. A rumour was allowed to circulate to the effect that Carranza was a prisoner because, on numerous occasions, he had not hidden his sympathies for some of the men condemned at Valladolid. This seemed to be demonstrated by some obscure passages in his book *Comentarios sobre el Catecismo Cristiano*. The accusation was already launched; after that came the lesson. As the Holy Office expounded it, the lesson was that the enemies of God and of 'these kingdoms' were acting with infinite cunning and that only the Inquisition, which kept watch over the peace and security of everyone, had been able to unmask and detain them. Neither the arms of the regiments nor the inspired words of the most illustrious preachers, nor the piety of the bishops and the brilliance of theologians, could have braked the offensive of the reformers. These were powerful arguments not only for supporting the Inquisition without reservation, but also for copying its methods. In this climate of religious exaltation, millions of individuals, mixing the aggressiveness of the judge with the fear of the victim, lent their eyes and ears to the task of collaborating with the Holy Office. For its part, the Inquisition did not fail to make effective use of this situation. These were the golden years of the Holy Office, the yeas when the Crown came to consider it the cornerstone of its 'constitutional' order.

## 1560-1600: The goals of a campaign of social control

The events described above brought about a significant change in the situation as the Inquisition became consecrated as the most effective instrument for social control and the prevention of heresy. Two methods were adopted by the Holy Office in taking up the challenge of the confrontation between the two irreconcilable religions that now divided Europe. The first was unleashed in the interior of the kingdom and had as its principal object the removal of 'impurities' from the mentality of the popular classes. This was an indirect method of combating heresy. The second tactic was employed on the borders at ports and customs posts. Both of these activities attempted to prevent rather than to 'cure', although the first was a task of providing security not against heresy but against a proximate heterodoxy. Nevertheless, what is most interesting is that this preventive strategy had certain ultimate goals: to assure social conformity and internal stability by magnifying the presence of the enemy, an enemy mythologised and, in reality, scarcely capable of operating effectively.

This radical propaganda had a very particular objective: the popular classes. Just as if it were dealing with some form of plague, the Holy Office felt that it was important to keep a close watch upon certain collective attitudes which were anchored in traditional religiosity and did not correspond to the Counter Reformation model. Of course these attitudes contained nothing of Lutheranism, but controlling them was a way of preventing any kind of approach to the ethics of the Reform. In this way, the Inquisitors became, in a certain sense, the disseminators of Protestant beliefs and practices that were unknown to the public. But this was a knowledge that, because of the propagandistic means employed (edicts of faith, *auto-de-fe*, censorship, etc.), presented a stereotyped image of the Lutheran as a brutal heretic, a foreign criminal and a political enemy.

Operating with these presuppositions, the Holy Office succeeded in characterising as 'suspected of being close to the doctrine of Luther' many persons whose only crime was to entertain a somewhat critical moral attitude. In reality, it was only from a position of the most extreme inflexibility that one could extract vague and far-off echoes of Protestant ideas.

Obviously, such people were neither Protestants nor anything like them. Nevertheless, there was an important group among the cases begun during this period that deserved special attention from the inquisitors. These were the cases of foreigners, travellers, immigrants, etc. who were watched because they were suspect by their very nature.[30]

It was feared that these foreigners would at least reveal, if not explicitly propagandise for, the ideas of the Reformer. Certainly there were few actual preachers among them but what worried the Holy Office was their contact with the public. Although this happened very infrequently, when it did occur the result was a crude and distorted image of Protestantism. Real proselytism was very rare and with little chance of success. Several factors contributed to this: vigorous prosecution of cases, very intense physical surveillance that was carried out by inquisitorial agents, the so-called *familiares* and commissioners, the effective support of the clergy and finally the support of the civil authorities. The result was the creation of an atmosphere of hostile xenophobia that penetrated, successfully, wide sectors of the population. If, in reality, there were popularisers of the Reform, they did not enjoy any great degree of success among Spain's Catholic population.

This seems to have been the reality; but it did not prevent inquisitors from thundering over the landscape and shouting about the snares and dangers of heresy. They contended that the Holy Office had clear evidence about this danger and that its prisons were full of 'Lutherans'.

What did they mean to suggest with this clamour? What did this fearful 'Lutheranism' consist of them for them? By 'Lutheranism', the inquisitors understood a confused and deformed body of dogmas, doctrine, beliefs and moral practices that had been fashioned out of a variety of readings or from the confessions of accused persons. There are glaring differences between the theology and morality of the Reformation and what was tried as such by the Inquisition. Instead of 'dogmatic Lutheranism' what we encounter in the case files of the Holy Office is something much more confused that might be called 'sociological Lutheranism'. This distinction is important in order to define more precisely the attitude of the Holy Office with respect to Protestantism. This tendency for the 'sociological' places squarely before us the coordinates that mark out the Inquisition's objectives. Everything that was in the least suspicious with regard to the religious framework, or the political and social order, was qualified as heresy.

Jean Pierre DeDieu has worked out the different variables by which the Inquisition recognised its version of a 'Lutheran'.[31] In the first place, a 'Lutheran' was anyone who praised the Reformer or any of his basic ideas. In the second place, a 'Lutheran' was anyone who expressed opinions or carried out any actions against the clergy and denied the spiritual faculties and social privileges inherent in its sacerdotal function. Apart from these two essential matters, DeDieu has demonstrated that dubious opinions respecting indulgences, the cult of saints, the validity of the sacraments, justification by faith or the free and personal interpretation of scripture — in other words the essential nucleus of the reformed doctrine — were of secondary importance for the Tribunal.

These were elements, then, that defined a Lutheran for the Holy Office. This is what the Tribunal stated when it drew up its edicts and this is what can be gleaned from the great majority of the cases that were initiated for this motive. Thus a new kind of heretic could be recognised. This was a modern form of heresy but so dangerous that, because of its attacks on religion and state, it deserved to be placed in the same position of infamy and marginalisation as the two other social enemies who 'believed in the sect of Moses and Mohammed'. None of these could be considered Christian, because Christianity is synonymous with believing in and affirming 'what is believed and affirmed by our Holy Mother the Church of Rome'.

Here is the key. But it is also important to emphasise the fact that the anti-Lutheran strategy was not only a negation of the Reformation but, principally, a strategy for imposing the Counter Reformation. In other words, we are in the presence of an 'educational' programme that attempted to propagate the post-Tridentine model of Christianity because it was this prototype that best corresponded to the ideal model of social conformity.

In marked contrast to the heretic, who was a social enemy, the person who affirmed the sacerdotal power of the clergy, accepted the validity of the sacraments and kept up a devotion to the saints was both a good Christian and, as such, a faithful subject. In the last analysis, a Christian was someone who accepted in an inclusive or general way 'the Scripture as believed and taught by the Holy Mother Church'. This was the evangelical programme of the Counter Reformation; a programme defined in opposition to the spectre of Lutheranism.

Luther, Protestantism, the Reformation, heresy, etc. are all spectres that form the negative model: the disfunctional, the subversive, the dangerous. In contrast to this model, there was formulated what was socially positive and contributed to social and political harmony.

Of all these contrasting forms of behaviour, it is vital to distinguish the 'mode of being Christian' as the one that was most outstanding. By means of the social attitude of 'being Christian', the individual was linked to his local community, his 'sacralised' political authority and the universal church. It is in this way that the individual comes fully to possess his rights as a social actor. As a result, it was necessary to repress all public demonstrations of divergent views. Such repression must be carried out openly and publicly because dissent itself was an open and public phenomenon.

The Inquisition, even though it acted in secret, had a tremendous amount of influence with suspicion and fear as its main arguments. On account of all this, the Tribunal sought to punish, not so much the expression of elaborate conceptual arguments, but rather those attitudes or public activities that inspired a certain suspicion even though they were common enough in everyday life.

Matters as diverse as an ironic reference to the ecclesiastical estate or an irreverent comment on the Eucharist or, simply, some sarcastic reservation about oral confession, were motives for suspicion. All of this was enough to make the Tribunal pick up its ears, fearful of finding, not the bright shining seed of Luther, but some vague and far-off echo. Pinning this down was no easy task. Each and every one of the relevant circumstances had to be investigated: the accused's place of origin, witnesses, locations, attitudes, occasions. After that, came the hard questions: who, where, when, with whom, etc. These were all questions with only one goal: to locate and isolate the odd, singular and foreign.

Doubtless, this was a policy with xenophobic overtones but it was also crowned with spectacular results. Many found themselves before the bar of the Holy Office more because they were foreign than because they were Lutheran. The foreigner was always a potential enemy because it was alleged that his very nature inclined him towards heresy.

In order to counteract any influence from abroad, Catholic nationalism deployed an enormous propaganda machine while watching the frontiers and setting up strict mechanisms of control.[32] But all of this, even though sufficient, was not enough. In reality, what was most important was the pressure on the individual. The 'educational' programmes that were set up were designed so that each Christian Spaniard became an impregnable fortress within himself. Discovering heresy meant following a path that began with a rigorous analysis of one's own conscience and terminated in the conscience of one's neighbour. Therefore, it was desirable to acquire a subtle inquisitorial sensibility for oneself in order to penetrate other people's minds. Following such programmes, the desired model individual, as reflected in the Old Christian, could be attained and along with it religious purity and social stability.

Of course, it is difficult to determine the exact influence that a programme, pursued with all the force of a systematic and long-lasting propaganda campaign, had on each individual. It is also difficult to tell what effects this propaganda had when it was disseminated from the institutions of the state itself. From what we know now, it seems that inquisitorial activity, above all in the second half of the sixteenth century, had different results in each region; but here again, we cannot determine what these differences were. The number of cases that were tried for suspicion of Lutheranism were considerable in some tribunals, above all in those on the frontiers.[33] In these regions, there is obvious evidence of a severity capable of dissuading groups of foreign Protestants. In spite of this, the formidable apparatus that was deployed had other functions that should be mentioned.

The inquisitors themselves believed that this apparatus was more than was strictly necessary to control the entry of Protestant heretics. In spite of that, it was maintained and even reinforced on numerous occasions. This was because it was not designed exclusively for the foreign heretic but also for the Christian of the interior. Exaggerating the importance of Protestant heresy was a way of achieving the interior 'peace' that the monarchy needed in order successfully to confront the exigencies of its foreign policy while at the same time guaranteeing the imposition of social and ideological control in the interior. Therefore, Luther and Protestantism in general became a permanent spectre in sixteenth-century Spain which was made to 'collaborate' in the task of stabilising a feudal, aristocratic and authoritarian social order. Never was an enemy made use of so profitably.

## Notes

1. Jean-Pierre DeDieu, 'Los cuatro tiempos de la Inquisición', in B. Bennassar (ed.), *Inquisición Española: poder político y control social* (Crítica, Grijalbo, Barcelona, 1981), pp. 15-39. Ricardo García Cárcel, *Orígenes de la Inquisición Española* (Ediciones Península, Barcelona, 1976), pp. 167-75.

2. J. Contreras and J.P. DeDieu, 'Geografía de la Inquisición Española: La formación de los distritos 1470-1520', *Hispania, 144* (1980), pp. 37-93.

3. S. Haliczer, 'Construcción del Estado, decadencia política y revolución en la Corona de Castilla 1475-1520', in *Homenaje a García de Orbaneja* (Moneda y Credito, Madrid, 1976), pp. 301-23.

4. Tarsicio Azcona, *'La Inquisición Española procesada por la Congregación General de 1508'*, in *J. Pérez Villanueva (ed.), La Inquisición Española, nueva visión, nuevos horizontes* (Siglo XXI, Madrid, 1980), pp. 89-163.

5. Tarsicio Azcona, in Pérez Villanueva (ed.), *La Inquisición Española*, p. 89.

6. J. Pérez, *La revolución de las Comunidades de Castilla 1520-1521* (Siglo XXI, Madrid, 1977), pp. 543-5; S. Haliczer, *The Comuneros of Castile. The Forging of a Revolution 1475-1521* (University of Wisconsin Press, Madison, Wisc., 1981), p. 152.

7. M. Andres, 'La Imágen de Lutero en España hasta 1559', in J. Belloch Zimmermann and A. Rodriguez Sánchez (eds), *Lutero y la Reforma* (Universidad de Extremadura, Cáceres, 1984), p. 65.

8. A. Redondo, 'Luther et L'Espagne', *Mélanges de la Casa de Velázquez, I* (1965), pp. 109-65; J.E. Loughurst, 'Luther in Spain (1520-1540)', *Proceedings of the American Philosophical Society, 12* (1959), pp. 65-93.

9. J.E. Loughurst, 'Alumbrados, erasmistas y luteranos en el proceso de Juan de Vergara', *Cuadernos de Historia de España, 38* (1958), pp. 107ff.

10. M. Costa, *Proceso inquisitorial contra María de Cazalla* (Fundación Universitaria Española, Madrid 1978).

11. M. Andres, 'Lutero y la Guerra de las Comunidades', *Norba, 4* (1983), pp. 307-23.

12. J.I. Tellechea, 'La reacción española ante el luteranismo 1520-1559',

*Diálogo Ecumenico, 6* (1971), pp. 325-41.

13. J.I. Gutierrez Nieto, 'Los conversos y el movimiento comunero', *Hispania, 24* (1964), pp. 337-61.

14. M. Aviles Fernandez, 'El Santo Oficio en la primera Etapa Carolina', in J. Pérez Villanueva and B. Escandell (eds), *Historia de la Inquisición en España y América* (3 vols, Biblioteca de Autores Cristianos, Madrid, 1984), vol. I, p. 467.

15. A. Márquez, *Los alumbrados* (Taurus, Madrid, 1972), p. 159.

16. Loughurst, 'Alumbrados, p. 107.

17. J.P. DeDieu, 'El modelo religioso: rechazo de la Reforma y control de Pensamiento' in Bennassar (ed.), *Inquisición Española*, pp. 231-69.

18. F. Braudel, *Las civilizaciones actuales* (Tecnos, Madrid, 1966). Cited by B. Escandell 'El viraje dogmático de los años cuarenta', in Pérez Villanueva and Escandell (eds), *Historia de la Inquisición*, vol. I, p. 440.

19. J.I. Tellechea, *Tiempos Recios: Inquisición y heterodoxias* (Ediciones Sígueme, Salamanca, 1977), p. 14.

20. A.A. Sicroff, *Los estatutos de Limpieza de Sangre. Controversias entre los siglos XV y XVI.* (Trad. Esp. Taurus, Madrid, 1985), pp. 125-69.

21. J.L. Gonzalez Novalin, *El Inquisidor General Fernando de Valdés 1483-1568* (Universidad de Oviedo, Oviedo, 1968), pp. 163-96.

22. J.L. Gonzalez Novalin, 'La época Valdesiana' in Pérez Villanueva and Escandell (eds), *Historia de la Inquisición*, vol. I, p. 541.

23. V. Pinto, *Inquisición y control ideológico en la España del siglo XVI* (Taurus, Madrid, 1983), pp. 149-97.

24. J.M. De Bujanda, *Index de L'Inquisition Espagnole, 1551, 1554, 1559* (Centre d'études de la Renaissance, Université de Sherbrooke, Quebec, 1984), pp. 163-205.

25. Archivo Histórico Nacional, Sección de Inquisición, leg. 2075 and 3189.

26. M. Bataillon, *Erasmo y España* (Fondo de Cultura Económica, Mexico, 1950), pp. 699-737.

27. Gonzalez Novalin, 'La época Valdesiana', p. 554, n. 67.

28. Bennassar, *Inquisición Española*, pp. 94-125.

29. See J.I. Tellechea, *Fray Bartolomé de Carranza y su tiempo* (2 vols Guadarrama, Madrid, 1968).

30. M. Jimenez Monteserín, 'Los luteranos ante el Tribunal de la Inquisición de Cuenca, 1525-1600', in Pérez Villanueva (ed.), *La Inquisición Española*, pp. 690-736.

31. J.P. DeDieu, 'El modelo religioso', pp. 247-52.

32. J. Contreras, *El Santo Oficio de la Inquisición de Galicia. Poder, sociedad y cultura* (Akal, Madrid, 1982), pp. 527-70 and 609-27.

33. See the collection of letters and summaries of cases sent by the regional tribunals to the Suprema, Archivo Histórico Nacional, Sección de Inquisición.

# Part II
# The Inquisition and Popular Culture

# 4

# Popular Religion in Cuenca on the Eve of the Catholic Reformation

*Sara Nalle*

It all began with the vision. Bartolomé Sánchez, aged 50, was walking home from harvesting at dusk around St John's Day (24 June — Midsummer's Eve), 1550,[1] when next to St Sebastian's Chapel he saw in the air a shining vision of a woman standing between two men. Above the woman floated a bird, whose extended wing tips touched the mouths of the two men.[2] Bartolomé dropped to his knees and prayed five Our Fathers together with five Hail Mary's and then three of each, all the while begging the Lord to tell him if what he saw was a good or bad sign. The vision disappeared and Sánchez, whose farming was not going well, felt much consoled in his heart. He never said a word to anyone, but ever after that evening, 'I went about wondering to myself what that [vision] could have been.' At Lent the next year, he went to confess with his village priest, Martin Almazán. To prepare himself, he bought a book of hours in Spanish from Hernan Zomeño, a neighbour.[3] He opened the book at the hours for the Conception of Our Lady and discovered a coloured illustration representing himself returning from harvesting. When he went to confess with Almazán, he took the book with him and showed the priest the prayers and the figure of himself. Almazán could not fathom it. He granted Bartolomé absolution but he refused to judge the vision. 'Don't tell anyone about this,' he warned Bartolomé, but Bartolomé wanted to understand. He took the book around to friars and learned persons, and confessing his story to them at their feet, he would ask them what it meant. Meanwhile, Almazán died, and the next year, during Lent, 1552, Sánchez went to confess the vision with the new village priest, Bachiller Barca. He could not have chosen a worse moment to do so. Just the day before, Bartolomé had been excommunicated for not paying his tithes. This common abuse of the sentence of excommunication angered Sánchez. He told Barca, 'the one who excommunicates people and the one who reads the sentences [in church] ought to be stoned'. When Barca pointed out to Sánchez that he was one of those who had been excommunicated, Sánchez became indignant and went off without getting his confession. Finally, a Dominican friar from a nearby monastery at Carboneras came to preach on St Thomas' Day (7 March 1552). Bartolomé went to confess with his friar and showed him the book. 'It's the devil,' pronounced the friar in good Dominican fashion and refused to grant Bartolomé absolution. He ordered Sánchez to come to the monastery and not to say anything to anyone if he valued his life.

It was now close to Easter, 1552. The friar's words profoundly upset Bartolomé, who became more determined than ever to get absolution. He decided that he would go to the monastery as a penitent even though the friar had not demanded this. Sánchez made a hempen rope and wrapped it around his torso five or six times. Then he took some saddlebags and filled them with five stones weighing altogether 25 pounds. The night before Bartolomé was to go to the monastery, he hid his things under a threshing shed so his wife would not see them and ordered his boy, Bartolomico, to read his favorite prayers to him from the books of hours. Sánchez was too excited and upset to read himself. Bartolomico began to pray the Passion of Our Lord. It was then that Bartolomé suffered the first seizure. He fell from his chair shouting, 'Get thee away, cursed Lucifer; I did not grant thee leave to enter in here!' and begged for assistance from God and His saints.[4] Bartolomé's wife and neighbours came running, but as he could not explain to them what had happened, they all went home except for García Pérez, a weaver, who wanted to sit up with Bartolomé. Pérez advised Bartolomé not to go to Carboneras, and in the morning, when Pérez left for work, he shut Bartolomé inside the house to prevent him from leaving. Sánchez, however, escaped with the help of a passing child, slung his saddlebags over his shoulders, and set off towards the monastery. García came after him. Relieving him of the bags, García persuaded Bartolomé to go home and wait there until García brought the priest, Barca, to his house. When the priest came, he said to Sánchez, 'Let's go to mass; later we'll talk.' Apparently, Bartolomé recovered his bags and rope and put them on again to go to mass.

The day Bartolomé Sánchez showed up in church with his saddle bags and ropes went down in the oral history of Cardenete. Pablo Herrero remembered:

Sánchez was walking around with one shoe on and the other off carting some saddle bags, and he carried inside them five stones. He said that he carried them in honour of the five wounds [of Christ]. He came this way from his house to the parish church and inside the church, I heard him shout and say, 'St Francis faith and St. Peter rock'. . . and the parish priest [Barca] took him outside the church.[5]

Juan Cabellero:

I saw Sánchez walking with a cap on his head,[6]one shoe on and the other off, and a staff. I asked him why he was walking around with one shoe on and the other off, and he relied, 'Because the world is going topsy-turvy'. Then I saw him in the church this way on his knees and he was saying 'Come here, Peter,' and, 'Anyone here want to debate with me?' and other things that seemed nonsense to me.[7]

Sánchez continued in his troubled state, without, however, causing any more public scenes. His friend, Bartolomé de Mora, began to watch out for him.[8] One day close to Christmas, Sánchez appeared bewildered, so Mora and two others tied him up with a rope. Sánchez reacted by accusing them, 'You've tied me to the column like the Jews did Christ! Who is the one to give me the first lash?' whereupon Mora and his friends untied Sánchez and took him to the church (although Bartolomé claimed that they stripped him down to his shirt and left him, and he had to bite his way free).[9] Mora decided to take Bartolomé to a priest in the nearby village of Monteagudo, who would be able to tell them if Sánchez was possessed by a devil and cure him. The priest, though, could not find any trace of possession and gave them some medicines instead.[10]

Up to this point, Christmas, 1552, as far as most of Sánchez's neighbours were concerned, he had not done much to make them doubt his overall sanity. He certainly had done nothing worthy of the attention of religious authorities outside of his native Cardenete, a large village (population 1,400 in 1591)[11] in the Castilian diocese of Cuenca, whose seat was located 180 kilometres to the east of Madrid. Pilgrimages to shrines, visions, and harsh penances were a normal part of sixteenth-century Spaniards' religious life.[12] In the bishopric of Cuenca alone, according to an official count in 1583, there were more than 800 rural chapels, at about an average of two shrines per community.[13] More intractable problems they took further afield, as Bartolomé did, to powerful regional shrines, such as Our Lady of

Texeda or Our Lady of la Zarza, two Marian shrines located in the eastern half of the bishopric, where miraculous cures were commonly effected.[14] Although less common, visions occurred regularly in the diocese and elsewhere, particularly in the vicinity of shrines. For example, in 1557 several villagers in Buendía, on the opposite side of the bishopric, testified how they had seen a bright red cross in the sky.[15] Finally, nothing could be more natural than a self-imposed physical penance, particularly at Eastertide. Whole brotherhoods in Cuenca were dedicated to flagellation at Easter. Or, in imitation of Christ, individuals wandered off to caves and hermitages where they subjected themselves to terrifying disciplines and prolonged fasts.[16]

Although Bartolomé's behaviour may seem bizarre to a modern observer, when taken in context his actions made a certain amount of sense. Prior to having his vision, Sánchez, father of four young children, had fallen on hard times and had come down in the world. Once an independent farmer, Sánchez now during the harvest season migrated south in search of temporary work in the fields. During the winter months, he worked for others in the village at the lowly trade of wool combing. In the midst of his difficulties, he experienced a vision which comforted him. For nearly two years, Sánchez had been unable to resolve the meaning of the vision and the book of hours. By his own admission, the vision began to obsess him, so much so that he began to have thoughts 'beyond what the Holy Mother Church orders' — thoughts which made him feel as if 'he was going to burst'.[17] In addition, during all that time, he did not receive absolution. He would not confess with his parish priest because he was feuding with him, and the Dominican would not absolve him unless he came to the monastery, 22 kilometres distant. What better way to go than as a pilgrim to the monastery, which housed an important relic, a piece of miraculous liturgical cloth from Daroca?[18] Bartolomé's friend Pérez had tried to prevent him from going to the monastery because he believed that Bartolomé should go to his parish priest first. But when Bartolomé walked into the church carrying his saddlebags and rope, his fellow parishioners did not recognise his penance for what it was because he had chosen relatively unusual disciplines. Most physical disciplines in Spain recalled some obvious aspect of Christ's passion. Penitents walked barefoot and shirtless, flogged themselves, or carried a wooden cross over their shoulder.[19] Sánchez used heavy stones that symbolised Christ's wounds and wore the traditional rope of a condemned prisoner wrapped around his body. In short, Sánchez seemed more desperate than insane, or as one witness commented, more of a rascal than a crazy man.[20]

No, what began to bother the villagers of Cardenete about Sánchez was neither his behaviour in church nor his occasional fits, but his ideas about religion. As Bartolomé explained first to his neighbours and then later to the authorities, the vision he had experienced set him thinking and asking questions. He buttonholed 'Catholic persons, ecclesiastics, friars, abbots, and preachers' for any information he could get. Over the course of several years, he formed his own ideas about doctrine which he later proudly maintained 'sprang from his imagination'.[21]Around January 1553, Sánchez suddenly began to talk freely and earnestly about religion to anyone in Cardenete who would listen to him. The villagers had tolerated Sánchez's visions, shouting, and eccentric behaviour. They drew the line, however, at heresy. Within weeks, in March 1553, Bartolomé was sitting in chains in the town jail while Barca, the parish priest, collected testimony for the *señores inquisidores* in the mountain city of Cuenca.

Barca called nine witnesses, all men, who had known Bartolomé from two years to upwards of forty.[22] As was normal with such commissioned investigations, Barca had a list of questions prepared for him by the inquisitors (based on a denunciation that has been lost) that the priest was to put to each witness in succession. The questions went straight to the point. The inquisitors wanted to know if Sánchez presented any signs of illness or insanity (to which everyone replied no); if he had done anything that could be taken for a sign of insanity (to which most responded by referring to the incident in the parish church); and if Sánchez had said anything that touched on the affairs of the Holy Office. In short, was Sánchez a heretic?

The witnesses unanimously stated that Sánchez had begun espousing his heretical views during the previous three months, that is just prior to and during Lent, 1553. In effect, Sánchez had mounted his own Lenten campaign that competed with and contradicted the church's programme of sermons that prepared the faithful for the annual rounds of obligatory Eastertide confession, communion, and celebration. Sánchez was very clear to everyone about four points. He was not going to confess with priests because they were cursed and excommunicated. Instead, he would only confess his sins to God, who knew what they were. Third, the eucharist was no more than some flour and water mixed together and Christ never formed part of it, and lastly, the cross was just a post and he was not going to worship an idol.[23]

In addition to the beliefs above, Sánchez occasionally was heard to mention others. He held that the Christian faith was the worst of the three religions of the 'book' — Christianity, Judaism, and Islam. He refused to baptise his children. The pope was a villain and papal indulgences did nothing to get souls out of Purgatory. The famous sudarium in Jaén, known as the Veronica de Jaén, that miraculously preserved an image of Christ's face was a fraud. Bartolomé had seen it and it was just a sheet of paper. Finally, the incorrupt body of Cuenca's own San Julian was not in the cathedral where they had put it — it had ascended to heaven!

In short, Sánchez was a veritable fountain of heretical and blasphemous ideas. He was most consistent in his anticlericalism.[24] All nine witnesses remembered hearing Sánchez attack priests. He offered no reasons for his hatred of the clergy, but one might suppose that his excommunication for non-payment of his tithes when he was desperately poor was a factor. Once having rejected the priesthood, key elements of the Catholic faith came tumbling down around Sánchez's feet. Wicked priests controlled confession. Priests stained with sin could make Christ appear miraculously in the host and then deny His saving grace to those not worthy of receiving it. Cursed priests brandished crosses and crucifixes when God had forbidden worship of idols. Clearly, Sánchez was not going to jeopardise his soul by putting his faith in a priest!

The villagers of Cardenete reacted to Sánchez's declarations with shock, amazement and concern but admonitions and warnings from friends like Juan Cabellero did nothing to sway Sánchez from his ideas.

Some of the witnesses recalled that after reproving Bartolomé, they attempted to discover the origin of his bad religion. Francisco Ruiz first tried to correct Sánchez after listening to him attack the priesthood, the papacy, images, the Trinity. . . . Since Sánchez would not hear him, Ruiz gave up for the moment and went home. A few days later, Ruiz sought out the wool-comber to ask him where he had got his ideas from — did he have some book?

> Sánchez replied, no, he did not have any kind of book; it was a divine grace that he had. I asked him where did the divine grace come from and he answered that one day when he was coming from harvesting in the valley at Yémeda next to Cardenete by St Sebastian's Chapel, a very luminous and comely figure came to him and he had been much consoled by it.[25]

So, Bartolomé Sánchez claimed he was a visionary. He believed that he had received a divine grace that enabled him to understand deeper truths. He was intractable, filled with the insolence of one who is convinced that God is on his side. Sánchez's neighbours, however, did not believe him for a moment. Sánchez may have had a vision, people do, after all, but no one was going to elevate the wool-comber to the status of a God-favoured seer on that account. Particularly when he spouted such radical ideas.

Sánchez's neighbours and associates echoed perfectly the growing religious conservatism of the 1550s. Prior to this time, for over half a century, ecclesiastical and secular elements of the Spanish church had experimented with different aspects of religious reform.[26] However, the growing hostility between the Catholic and Protestant camps after the collapse of the Regensburg reunion conference of 1541 and the discovery of Protestant cells in Valladolid and Seville in 1557-8 marked a decisive change in the history of Catholicism in Spain.[27] The conservatives had been right all along — the only way to deal with Protestantism was to eliminate the causes of its appeal and erase all trace of Protestant thought in Spain.

Sitting in his damp cell of Cardenete, Bartolomé Sánchez could not know of the changing currents abroad in Spain and Europe, nor that in an infinitely small and yet integral way, he had been caught up by them. He sat and waited the inquisitors' pleasure, and thought more about his blasphemous religion.

At that moment, spring 1553, the Tribunal of Cuenca's two inquisitors, Pedro Cortes and Enrique de la Cueva, were occupied elsewhere in their district. In August 1553, Inquisitor de la Cueva departed on a tour of Siguenza that would last for over a year.[28]As was normal, while one inquisitor left on inspection, the other stayed behind in Cuenca to handle any cases that came to the tribunal's attention via denunciations or that had been resolved in the field while on the previous tour. Inquisitor Cortes presumably had completed his tour in the spring and summer of 1553, and began to work on his backlog of cases during the fall. In October, Cortes sent for Bartolomé Sánchez. Sánchez arrived at the headquarters of the Cuenca tribunal on 19 October 1553. The warden, Diego de Tapia, received him, removed his fetters, and put him in the 'courtroom' jail. Bartolomé's hearing before Inquisitor Pedro Cortes would begin the following morning.

After having Bartolomé Sánchez brought before him, Inquisitor Cortes ordered him to lower his hood, kneel to the altar and to the crucifix and the images of Our Lady and the other saints there, and pray that the Lord help him to clear his conscience if Sánchez had done anything to offend Him. Sánchez refused. Instead, he began to give the inquisitor a lesson in his personal theology. He would not humble himself before the idols and he worshipped only the Trinity of God the Father, the Son, and the Mother, who were in Heaven.

At this very first hearing, Sánchez set the tone for his first trial for heresy, which would run from 11 November 1553 to 7 June 1554. Sánchez was disobedient, articulate, commanding and crafty. Eight months in jail in Cardenete and one night in the secret prison of the Holy Office did not frighten him, nor did Inquisitor Cortes's presence cow him into submission. Clearly, Sánchez was not like other peasants who crossed the Inquisition's path. Many at their first meeting with the Señor Inquisitor, when ordered to kneel and pray, burst into tears or forgot their prayers. Not Sánchez. Likewise, at this first encounter, Cortes also showed something of his style. Cortes was patient with Sánchez. He took great pains to teach Sánchez the correct doctrine and to understand his prisoner. Cortes' mission, after all, was not to burn heretics but to save souls. Although the inquisitor was a judge, he was also a priest, and Christian charity demanded that Cortes try to cure Sánchez's troubled soul. Had Sánchez been a *converso* or *morisco*, Cortes might have adopted a more callous attitude towards his prisoner. On the whole, Spain's converted minorities elicited little sympathy from the Inquisition, which viewed the minorities' transgressions as further evidence of their bad faith and danger to society.[29]Sánchez, however, was an 'old Christian', a peasant, and a member of the majority Catholic population of Castile. Cortes would, therefore, make every effort to rehabilitate Sánchez. At Sánchez's second trial for heresy several years later, a less sympathetic inquisitor would remind Sánchez that Cortes and others had always treated him with love.

With love, then, Cortes reassured Sánchez that the church did not order Christians to worship idols made of stone, wood, or paint. The images merely served to symbolise God and his saints and to remind Christians of their power in this world. Sánchez ignored Cortes's explanation of the use of images in the church and continued to elaborate on his interpretation of the mystery of the Holy Trinity. Logically enough, he pointed out to Cortes that a trinity of the Father, the Son, and the Holy Ghost made only two persons, not three. Only when the person of the Mother is added, is there a trinity. Patiently, Cortes explained to Sánchez the doctrine of the Trinity. 'The Virgin Mary is not God, but a creature created by God and to believe anything else is heresy, a grave error, and those who do not give up their ideas go to Hell.'

Sánchez noticed that Cortes was writing copiously and became suspicious. He suggested that they stop for now. Tomorrow or another day he would answer Cortes's questions but he did not have to say more than what served God. At this point, Cortes also had had enough of debate. He ordered that Sánchez be forced to sit in his chair so that he would kneel to the altar. Sánchez knelt, but turned towards the wall. When Cortes reprimanded him, Sánchez replied that he knelt to Heaven and he had no other altar than God the Father, the Son, the Mother and the Holy Ghost, and he had nothing more to say. Then, as requested, he got up and swore to tell the truth according to law by the cross of Cortes's table.[30] Returning to his kneeling position, he reiterated that God was his altar and he would not humble himself before idols because he did not believe in them. With that, Sánchez declared that he had a headache and the hearing was adjourned.

The next morning, 21 October, the hearings resumed. When Sánchez entered the courtroom, Cortes motioned to him to kneel in front of the altar. Sánchez countered that he still believed what he held the day before and turned towards the wall to pray. For the next two and a half weeks, after repeating this ritual each morning, the inquisitor and the wool-comber debated theology. In addition to disputing the nature of the Trinity and images, Sánchez explained his beliefs concerning sin and confession, the doctrine of the cross, the meaning of the Gospel, the eucharist, the Temple, the clergy, and baptism. With each day's passing, Sánchez grew more angry and intractable.

Sánchez began to express his considerable hatred for the church in Messianic terms. As in other Christian societies, there existed in Spain a strong undercurrent of popular, revolutionary millenarianism that surfaced whenever the social order weakened.[31] The most recent outbreak had occurred during the revolt of the Comuneros (1520-1) when Sánchez had been a young man. Sánchez's own village had participated in the revolt by joining in a popular uprising against the local lord, the Marquis of Moya.[32] Perhaps from one of the numerous visionary preachers who still criss-crossed Castile, Sánchez had incorporated this Messianic tradition into his own religious ideas.[33] Early on in the hearings, Sánchez explained how Christ had been crucified against His will and God would send a judge to seek justice against Christ's murderers. Through the story of the Temple priests of Jerusalem, Sánchez associated Christ's murderers with the priests of the church hierarchy. The promised judge, Bartolomé claimed, was Elijah, who would come to conquer the Devil and the Antichrist with true faith.[34] When Cortes explained to Sánchez that the prophets had foretold Christ's voluntary sacrifice on the cross, Sánchez asked for an adjournment. By the time the court reconvened two days later, Sánchez's anger for the church had turned directly against the Inquisition, which he attacked in prophetic, near-incoherent terms. He began by saying that God would send a messenger (himself) to proclaim the truth. Once the messenger had spoken, it was only fair to allow him to return home to feed his wife and children. But when God sent Christ to speak the truth, He had been killed. The fate of those who murder someone who speaks truthfully is eternal death. Sánchez switched to the present and became specific.

> The Inquisition and its officials have killed and sentenced and burned many people without cause. It has held as heretics those who say that the Messiah is not yet come . . . . It is now one thousand five hundred and some years since the Messiah that the Inquisition believes in has come. I believe that that one is the son of God incarnate and the Virgin Mary [but] this other Messiah who is coming, Elijah, is the justice that God sends for those whom the Inquisition has killed without cause. This Elijah . . . was born fifty-two years ago or so, and he is here on earth, born and raised in Cardenete.[35]

Sánchez realised that he had gone too far. When Cortes asked him what were the reasons for believing that he was who he claimed to be, Sánchez declared sullenly that he was the son of man and woman, no one had believed Christ either, and refused to say any more about it.

Although Sánchez would not claim again in his first trial that he was Elijah, his belief that he held God's special favour manifested itself in other ways, particularly when he spoke to God in his prayers. Because prayer was the most direct means of communication with God, the church strictly controlled it. If a Christian did not know his prayers, he was powerless to call on God for His protection and grace. On the other hand, if one prayed incorrectly, the meaning of religion could be altered drastically. In the 1560s, as fear of Protestantism spread in Cuenca and the church's indoctrination efforts gained momentum, the inquisitors asked an ever-wider circle of defendants to recite their prayers to the tribunal. At first the inquisitors discovered that many Conquense peasants were grossly ignorant of their prayers. As the Catholic Reformation progressed, their catechisms improved, so that by 1600 nearly all peasants could recite their prayers in the Inquisition.[36] No peasant, however, dared to speak to God as directly or in such a disturbing manner as did Bartolomé Sánchez.

Like many devout persons, Sánchez spoke of God both through the traditional prayers of the catechism and in his own personal language. On 3 November, Cortes questioned Sánchez about his background and Christian education. While following closely the original wording of each prayer of the catechism, Sánchez had changed the sense of each so that they reflected his prophetic and potentially revolutionary relationship with God and the Virgin Mary. In the 'Hail Mary' he called on the Mother of God to pray not for 'we sinners' but for Sánchez and the people of Israel. Bartolomé used the phrase 'people of Israel' in the sense of the long-suffering chosen of God, who some day would be redeemed from their misery.[37] Sánchez's interpretation of 'Our Father' was more radical. He prayed to God to work His will through Sánchez. God would provide for Sánchez, the people of Israel, and whomsoever else He saw fit to help. In the final prayer, the Creed, Bartolomé changed the wording so that he only believed in God and His church, not in Scripture or in the Holy Mother Church.

The wool-comber had also fashioned his own prayers which he recited spontaneously at the beginning of the hearings of 6 and 11 November. Not limited by established forms, Sánchez's personal prayers were openly defiant of the system. Clearly preoccupied by his imprisonment and the danger he faced, on 6 November, Sánchez called on God thus:

Lord God, thou art the bread.
Lord Son, thou art the wine.
Holy Virgin Mary, thou art the flesh.
Lord, by the most holy Trinity do not let me fall
and if I should fall, thou shalt raise me up.
Lord, teach me thy wisdom, reveal thy goodness.
Let all see in me the wonders of thy most holy enlightenment
so that in thy name I might overcome and conquer
this weight that thou hast given me with the Antichrist and the Devil.[38]

(Ibaneta's note: by this weight he means his trial.)

Five days later, on 11 November, the day Sánchez would be formally charged with heresy, his thoughts turned to revolution.

> My Lord, thou has said that Him Whom thou gave us
> thou wouldst make a fortress in His power.
> So Lord, please maketh a fortress in my might
> and please scatter the proud with the will of His heart
>> and usurp the powerful
>> and exalt the humble
>> and fill the hungry with goods
>> and leave empty the rich
>> so that we may receive the people of Israel[39]

When challenged, Sánchez made it clear that he believed that he spoke for God, who would save him from all danger, including inquisitors and their stakes.

While the hearings went forward, Cortes made preparations for Sánchez's trial. Cortes hoped for the cleanest solution: Bartolomé's confession followed by reconciliation with the church, all without the need for a long trial. Thus, the judge encouraged Sánchez to explain all of his beliefs in order to establish what they were and how to separate him from them. This approach patently failed; Sánchez willingly explained his religion but refused to listen to the inquisitor, leaving Cortes no other choice but to proceed with preparations for the trial which began on the morning of 11 November.

That morning, Diego de Tapia read the accusation. The prosecution's indictment is the heart and soul of any Inquisitorial trial, the barometer of the institution's mood. As the court's religious watchdog, the prosecution's role was to take the most extreme position possible regarding the transgressions in question. Prosecuting attorney de Tapia submitted a four-page indictment that listed seven detailed charges summarising Sánchez's alleged beliefs concerning the nature of the cross, Christ's death, confession, mass, baptism, indulgences, and the Trinity.[40] Tapia accused Sánchez of heresy but, significantly, as yet the prosecution did not identify a single one of the wool-comber's beliefs with Lutheranism or any other formal heresy. All the same, the prosecutor did take seriously the danger represented by Sánchez's beliefs. He called for the maximum sentence: confiscation of property, excommunication, and relaxation to the secular arm, in other words, death.

Meanwhile, as the presiding judge, Pedro Cortes had two

responsibilities to carry out, to investigate the case thoroughly and to ensure that Sánchez was defended according to law. Cortes renewed his efforts to uncover the source of Sánchez's ideas. Cortes could not accept that Sánchez had arrived at his beliefs on his own; like Bartolomé's neighbours Ruiz and Caballero, the inquisitor was convinced that Sánchez had got his ideas from someone or perhaps out of a book. Cortes regularly urged Sánchez to reveal the names of the persons who had taught the wool-comber what he knew. Each time, however, Sánchez maintained that he had no teacher other than God.

Cortes also arranged for Sánchez's defence. On the day of Sánchez's indictment, Cortes gave Bartolomé a transcript of the accusation and asked him to pick a lawyer from the canons named to his case. Sánchez, however, refused, declaring that the only lawyer he wanted was God.[41] At his next hearing, he announced that he had burned the indictment and he refused to defend himself against any of the testimony read in court. Stubbornly, Sánchez manoeuvred his trial into a cul-de-sac; his refusal to co-operate forced the tribunal towards sentencing. On 28 November, Cortes gave Sánchez 24 hours to reconsider and sent Dr Vergara once again to talk to the heretic. The next day Cortes had his answer. After a long conversation with Vergara, Sánchez told the court, 'I have thought all last night and this morning and I don't plan on going back on what I've said.'[42]

At this critical juncture, Sánchez's trial took an unexpected turn. Several years later, the notary, Juan de Ibaneta, explained what happened.

At the beginning of this trial, at the very first hearing that was held with Bartolomé Sánchez, he entered the audience room like an enraged or possessed man, gesturing and saying many foolish things . . . I remember that one of the things he said was that he had seen a celestial vision in a pasture and that he had been very frightened by it and he even lost consciousness. . . . Taking in account his foolishness and the things he said, since the capacity and judgement necessary for such a grave matter were lacking in the defendant, I asked the inquisitor to postpone his prosecution until it could be determined if he was possessed or had lost his senses.[43]

Cortes stopped the trial. Throughout the winter months and into the spring, Dr Vergara worked on Bartolomé's conversion while

Cortes conducted interviews with Sánchez's warden, jailor, cellmate, and the court doctor to evaluate the prisoner's state of mind. All four maintained that Sánchez was sane and quite reasonable, except, perhaps, when he spoke of his trial.[44]

The weeks passed. The month of April, early spring, had come to Cuenca. For the inquisitors, Pedro Cortes and Enrique de la Cueva, who had returned from Sigüenza for Easter, the arrival of spring meant that Easter was at hand; the time had come to clear their docket in preparation for the annual *auto-de-fe* in the city's main square. After several unsuccessful hearings with Sánchez during the month, on 26 April the tribunal met and voted on Sánchez's case. Ibaneta recalled

> They decided that maybe [Sánchez] would return to God if they threatened him with death, and they had voted the decision they did to frighten him, not because they wanted to burn him. I heard Dr Vergara [say] . . . that if he had not been convinced that when [Sánchez] arrived at the [execution] ground, he would return to God and come to his senses, under no circumstances would he have agreed to vote because he was convinced that [Sánchez] was possessed or insane.[45]

The sentence was carried out three days later. Stripped to the waist and mounted backwards on an ass, Sánchez was led down the narrow, steep streets of Cuenca to the field outside the city walls known as the Campo de San Francisco where heretics and criminals were executed. When Sánchez caught sight of the stake, he begged for mercy, showed signs of repentance, and clamoured to confess his sins. City officials hurried him inside the nearby Franciscan monastery where, in a chapel dedicated to the Name of Christ, Sánchez declared that everything he had said was 'public error' and begged again for God's mercy and the Inquisition's penancing. They brought him a cross 'and he adored it and kissed it with his mouth and eyes, saying "adoramuste Christi et benedicimus tibi". '[46] The inquisitors had won . . . or so they thought.

Bartolomé Sánchez was not burned as a heretic on the Campo de San Francisco. In the weeks that followed, he appeared a changed man. He recited his prayers correctly, shedding tears profusely and beating his breast in contrition. He no longer postured as God's angry prophet. Instead, he came to his hearings dabbing his eyes with a handkerchief. He began to attribute his actions to the influence of the devil or his own insanity. Point by point, he retracted each one of his heresies. God had not inspired him; no, he thought up everything on his own; it had all come out of his 'imagination'.[47]

Pedro Cortes accepted Sánchez's conversion and on 7 June 1554 Sánchez was reconciled with the church and sentenced to perpetual imprisonment in Cuenca.[48] Sánchez could count himself a lucky man. The mood of the tribunal was changing as the inquisitors began to worry more about the spread of heretical ideas. So, when Bartolomé Sánchez escaped to Cardenete in April 1556, began spouting his heresies and publicly burned his penitential tunic in the town square, the new inquisitors, Riego and Moral, had reason to be concerned.[49]

After Sánchez was sent back to Cuenca, the court wanted to know why he had returned to Cardenete and relapsed into his old heresies. Had he faked his conversion? 'Yes,' Sánchez replied, 'you had me in prison and you were going to burn me. I still believe what I did before.' Back in his cell, Sánchez had time to reflect. Perhaps his cellmate, Alonso Sánchez (no relation), a legal secretary, alerted Sánchez to the grim reality of his situation. Relapsed heretics customarily were not given a second chance by the Holy Office. Alonso persuaded Sánchez to say that the devil had deceived him.[50] At his next hearing, on 30 April, Sánchez entered the audience room crying and claimed that he had been possessed by the devil for four years. 'I take back everything I've said before and now. I beg for mercy, pardon, and penitence.' The new prosecutor, Alonso Serrano, was not convinced. On 19 June, he warned the inquisitors not to believe Sánchez. 'Furthermore,' he added, 'many of his opinions are the same as what the Lutherans teach. He isn't crazy; he's a heretic with evil intentions!'[51]

Like their predecessors, Riego and Moral could not bring themselves in good conscience to proceed against Sánchez. Then, as now, the insane legally were not held responsible for their actions. But where did the line between religious inspiration and insanity begin? In its decisions regarding Sánchez in 1554 and 1556, the tribunal wrote that it could not try Sánchez for heresy without some scruple of conscience. On the other hand, almost everyone who had ever known Sánchez, priests, peasants and doctors, thought he was completely sane.

Riego and Moral decided to punish Sánchez for burning his *sanbenito* and hold him in prison under observation. After one year passed Sánchez petitioned the court to allow him to return to Cardenete for the harvest. Over the vigorous objections of the prosecutor, Serrano, the inquisitors released Sánchez to the custody of his village priest.[52] He remained in Cardenete until spring 1558, when, after scandalising his neighbours, he disappeared for a month (he said he went on a pilgrimage to Guadalupe). He was re-arrested on his return and sent back to Cuenca in June.[53] At that moment, news of the discovery of Protestants in Valladolid had just reached Cuenca.[54] Despite the atmosphere of paranoia that gripped the Inquisition from Inquisitor-General Valdés down, Riego and Moral resisted the temptation to include Sánchez in the Protestant terror. Instead, in August, they decided to send him to an insane asylum in Zaragoza where they hoped he would be cured.[55] Sánchez promptly escaped and reappeared in Cardenete early in 1559. Several villagers sent a letter to the tribunal requesting Sánchez's detention, arguing that 'a man so heretical ought not to be with people, but where he deserves'. No action was taken, however, until the diocesan inspector visited the village in 1560 and wrote back that Sánchez sounded like a Lutheran to him, whereupon Bartolomé was arrested and sent to the capital. He arrived there on 28 March. After reviewing his case, his new inquisitor, Licenciado Padilla, ordered Bartolomé to stay in the city and report to the prison until the Suprema decided what to do with him. With Ibaneta's hopeful note that the Suprema's answer was expected shortly, the case record of Bartolomé Sánchez versus the Inquisition of Cuenca comes to an end.[56]

The trial of Bartolomé Sánchez, peasant visionary and heretic, drew to a close just as the Tribunal of Cuenca entered the most intense period of activity in its 350-year history. Although heresy could be imported from abroad, church officials knew full well that the seeds of religious rebellion — widespread anticlericalism, doctrinal ignorance and religious disobedience — lay scattered all over Spain. While it is unusual to find all of such attitudes present in one man, and in such extreme forms, Bartolomé Sánchez's case reveals the wide range of heterodox ideas that circulated among ordinary people in sixteenth-century Castile. During the Counter Reformation, part of the Inquisition's mission became to discover and control the unrest. Accordingly, the Tribunal of Cuenca increased its caseload dramatically between 1540 and 1569. In the decade 1540-9, the tribunal processed approximately 370 cases. Between 1550 and 1559, the total rose to 605, and between 1560 and 1569, the worst years of the Protestant scare, the court handled an astounding 960 cases.[57] After Bartolomé Sánchez, many more Conquenses of humble origins would be arrested for criticising the clergy, the sale of indulgences and the superstitious use of images. In all, between 1554 and 1600, the Tribunal of Cuenca tried 82 persons on specific charges of Lutheranism; hundreds more came before the court to account for their sacrilegious behaviour, heretical oaths or suspicious-sounding words.[58]

Religious discontent occasionally mixed with social unrest was indeed widespread among the people of Cuenca, yet Conquenses' inchoate expressions of dissatisfaction never tipped the balance of popular opinion against the church. As the inquisitors worked extensively with the common folk of Cuenca throughout the 1560s and the early 1570s, they began to realise that there were no native-born heretics in Cuenca, only disaffected and ignorant peasants. Since the reign of the Catholic Sovereigns, leading members of the Spanish church had been arguing that the solution to religious ignorance and the 'physic' against heresy was mass education. The inquisitors in Cuenca wrote back with satisfaction to the Suprema how their edicts of faith were teaching the people what was sin and what was not sin.[59] When Gaspar de Quiroga, bishop of Cuenca, became Inquisitor-General of Spain in 1573, he changed the focus of the Holy Office to the pedagogical goal of teaching Spaniards the elements of Tridentine morality and faith. In their edicts, inquisitors continued to define the essentials of the Islamic, Jewish and Protestant faiths, but they added to these, special exhortations against fornication, blasphemy, witchcraft and fortune-telling.[60] At the same time, through other channels, the Christian education of the people began in earnest. It was a long and arduous process, one that would involve the reform of the parish clergy and a total restructuring of local religious life within the guidelines set down by the Council of Trent. But it would be done. Ironically, in the end, Bartolomé Sánchez had been a prophet of sorts, although, not as he had thought, of the coming of an egalitarian, priestless age. Instead, in his defeat, Sánchez heralded the triumph of the Catholic reformation under a revitalised and authoritarian church.

## Notes

1. As in all of Europe, Midsummer's Eve in Spain was a night charged with magical significance. This was the night, according to Ana Gonzalez, a married woman of 30 from the city of Cuenca, that one was supposed to pick vervain and place it under the altar cloth so that it would be blessed the next morning at mass. Then the plant could be used to ask Our Lady

83

for riches (Archivo Diocesano de Cuenca (hereafter ADC), *Inquisition*, leg. 387, exp. 5498 (1615).

2. ADC, *Inquisition*, leg. 196, exp. 2216, fols. 120r-122v (hereafter '*Proceso*'). This account of the vision and Sánchez's attempts to understand its significance are taken from his confession made in 1556.

3. Literacy and book-ownership among Castile's peasant *labradores* during the sixteenth century were not as rare as one might think. Fifty per cent of male *labradores* questioned by the Inquisition of Cuenca knew how to read; one out of seven persons admitted to owning a book. S. Nalle, unpublished MS, 'Literacy and Culture: A Second Look at the Revolution in Education in Early Modern Castile'.

4. *Proceso*, fol. 121v. Sánchez may have meant his house, but clearly, his fear was that the devil was entering inside *him*.

5. Testimony given 22 March 1553, *Proceso*, fol. 3r.

6. Other witnesses also said that Sánchez was wearing a pilgrim's bonnet, which matches with his intentions.

7. *Proceso*, fol. 7r.

8. What follows is Mora's testimony, given Cardenete in March, 1553. *Proceso*, fols. 14r-15r.

9. Ibid., fol. 122v.

10. *Processo*, fol. 14v.

11. Archivo General de Simancas, Dir. Gen. del Tesoro, leg. 1301. Cardenete was part of the Marquesado de Moya and was known for its woollen cloths. F. Pinel y Monroy, *Retrato del buen vasallo . . . D. Andrés Cabrera, primer marqués de Moya* (Imprenta Imperial, Madrid, 1677), p. 207.

12. On shrines and visions, see William A. Christian, Jr, *Local Religion in Sixteenth-Century Castile* (Princeton University Press, Princeton, NJ, 1980) and *Apparitions in Late Medieval and Renaissance Spain* (Princeton University Press, Princeton, NJ, 1981).

13. S. Nalle, 'Religion and Reform in a Spanish Diocese: Cuenca, 1545-1650' (unpublished PhD thesis, Johns Hopkins University, Baltimore, Md, 1983), p. 270.

14. Fr. Pedro Ponce de Leon, *Milagros y loores confirmados con muchos exemplos de la soberana emperatriz de los cielos, Santa Maria de Texeda, con discursos morales y espirituales para las personas devotas* (Seville, (1663?)).

15. ADC, *Inquisition*, leg. 202, exp. 2292.

16. Nalle, 'Religion and Reform', p. 260.

17. *Proceso*, fol. 121r.

18. This was the *hijuela de los corporales de Daroca*, a bit of cloth used to cover the chalice before the offering. The *corporales*, which had become stained with Christ's blood during mass, were used in the reconquest of Daroca.

19. Jean Muret, the French ambassador to Madrid in 1666, wrote that penitents who were content to carry a wooden cross and wear a crown of thorns 'are so common that hundreds of them are seen'. He also described encountering penitents who wrapped themselves tightly in a rope 'doublet' as had Sánchez. J.M. Diez Borque, *La sociedad española y los viajeros del siglo XVII* (SGEL, Madrid, 1975), p. 158.

20. *Proceso*, fol. 12v.

21. *Proceso*, fol. 89v.

22. The inquest is on fols. 2v-17v of the *proceso*.

23. Although Sánchez shared some beliefs in common with the Alumbrados, a mystic sect that appeared in the 1520s, he clearly was not part of the movement. He shares with them only their anticlericalism and iconoclasm; in his millennarianism, asceticism, hostility to free love, and desire for a social levelling, he demonstrates aspects of late medieval popular and Franciscan spirituality. A. Márquez, *Los alumbrados. Orígenes y filosofía* (Taurus Ediciones, Madrid, 1972), pp. 245-51.

24. Anticlericalism was common in sixteenth-century Spain, even in clerical circles. The 1531 *Synodal Constitutions* of Cuenca paint a lurid picture of the dismal state of the diocesan clergy. M. Bataillon, *Erasmo y España. Estudios sobre la historia espiritual del siglo XVI* (2nd edn, Fondo de Cultura Economico, Mexico, 1966); Nalle, 'Religion and Reform', pp. 27-30.

25. *Proceso*, fol. 6r. Barca burned the book of hours.

26. The Spanish Prereform and the influence of Christian humanism are two areas of Spanish church history that have received a great deal of attention. For a summary of this scholarship, see the *Historia de la Iglesia en España*, vol. III-1, *La Iglesia en la España de los siglos XV y XVI* (BAC, Madrid, 1980).

27. The best brief introduction in English to this period is in H. Kamen, *Inquisition and Society in Spain in the Sixteenth and Seventeenth Centuries* (Indiana University Press, Bloomington, Ind., 1985), Ch. 5.

28. A record of the visitation survives in the *Libro de testificaciones*, ADC, *Inquisición*, L-317.

29. This was particularly true of the *moriscos*, who had a history of rebellion and eventually were expelled from Spain in 1609. In the Inquisition of Cuenca, *moriscos* received much harsher treatement than Old Christians, even for the same offences. Kamen, *Inquisition and Society*, Ch. 6, and M. García Arenal, *Inquisición y moriscos, los procesos del Tribunal de Cuenca* (Siglo Veintiuno, Madrid, 1978).

30. *Proceso*, fol. 21v.

31. On millenarianism in general, see N. Cohn, *In Pursuit of the Millennium. Revolutionary Millenarians and Mystical Anarchists in the Middle Ages* (Oxford University Press, New York, 1970). For Spain, see J. Caro Baroja, *Las formas complejas de la vida religiosa (Religion, sociedad, y caràcter en España de los siglos XVI y XVII)* (Akal, Madrid, 1978), pp. 247-66.

32. The anti-seigneurial content of the Comuneros' Revolt in Cuenca was pronounced. The dangerous popular uprising against the Marquis of Moya was brutally suppressed. J.I. Gutierrez Nieto, *Las comunidades como movimiento antiseñorial* (Editorial Planeta, Barcelona, 1973), pp. 198-204. For the millennarian aspects of the *comunero* revolt, see R. Alba, *Acerca de algunas particularidades de las comunidades de Castilla tal vez relacionadas con el supuesto acaecer terreno del Milenio Igualitario* (Editoria Nacional, Madrid, 1975) which prints some of the prophecies related to the uprising.

33. Some of these preachers and their prophecies are collected in the popular work by A. Martinez Arancon, *La profecia* (Editoria Nacional, Madrid, 1975). See also Joseph Pérez, 'Moines frondeurs et sermons subversifs en Castile pendant le premier séjour de Charles Quint en Espagne', *Bulletin Hispanique, 67* (1965).

34. *Proceso*, fol. 24v.

35. Ibid., fol. 26v. The reader need not believe that Sánchez literally meant that he was *the* prophet Elijah. As angry as he was, the association with Elijah would have been natural for someone immersed in the metaphorical and anagogical language of the preachers whose learning Sánchez had sought out. Elijah came to save Israel from the idolatrous Baalite priests imposed by King Ahab. Sánchez himself was almost adamant in his anticlericalism and iconoclasm. An interesting comparison may be made with the Anabaptist leader Melchior Hofmann, a furrier, who announced from prison in 1534 that he was Elijah sent to herald the judgement of Christ and the glory of Strassburg. C. Krahn, *Dutch Anabaptism. Origin, Spread, Life and Thought (1450-1600)* (Martinus Nijhoff, The Hague, 1968), p. 110.

36. Nalle, 'Religion and Reform', p. 232. During the period 1564-80, 60 per cent of *labradores* and 30 per cent of fieldworkers could recite their prayers perfectly in the Inquisition. In the period 1581-1600, 88 per cent of *labradores* and 60 per cent of fieldworkers could recite their catechism. Before 1564, figures are less reliable because of the lesser numbers involved, but the percentage was below 30 per cent for both groups.

37. *Proceso*, fol. 51v.

38. Ibid., fol. 52v.

39. Ibid., fol. 55v.

40. Ibid., fol. 49v;

40. *Proceso*, fols. 57r-58v.

41. *Proceso*, fol. 59v.

42. Ibid., fol. 72v.

43. Ibid., fol. 144r. The notary's interventions in the case were completely out of order. When the tribunal underwent an extensive review by the Suprema in 1559, Inquisitor Riego was reprimanded for seeking Ibaneta's opinions (Archivo Histórico Nacional, *Inquisición*, leg. 1933, exp. 1).

44. *Processo*, fol. 76r.

45. Ibid., fol. 144v.

46. Ibid., fols. 88r-v.

47. Ibid., fols. 87v and 89r.

48. Ibid., fol. 92v. The complete sentence required him to attend mass on all holidays, confess thrice yearly, and pray at the shrine of Our Lady of the Bridge in Cuenca every Saturday. Perpetual prison was not that rigorous; Sánchez was allowed to leave the prison to work at his trade.

49. *Proceso*, fol. 103v. Sánchez had decided to look for work at nearby Villar del Saz, but was overcome by an urge to go home instead. When he got there, though, his wife and brother were not happy to see him, which upset him. (fol. 109r.)

50. Ibid., fol. 152v, confession of 22 June 1558. Alonso's trial is ADC, Inq. leg. 203, exp. 2296.

51. *Proceso*, fol. 118r.

52. Judging by the letters sent by the assistant priest of Cardenete, Sánchez's mental condition deteriorated between March and May, 1558 (*Proceso*, fols. 147r and 148r).

53. Ibid., fols. 149r-150v.

54. M. Jimenez Monteserín, 'Los luteranos ante el tribunal de la

Inquisición de Cuenca, 1525-1660,' in J. Pérez Villanueva (ed.), *La Inquisición española: nueva visión, nuevos horizontes* (Siglo Veintiuno, Madrid, 1980), pp. 722-3.

55. The asylum in Zaragoza was reputed to be the best in Spain. The hospital led the way in introducing occupational therapy for the mentally ill. The inquisitors in Zaragoza replied to Cuenca that the asylum did not have as much success as one had heard, but that they would do their best for Sánchez (*Proceso*, fol. 160r).

56. *Proceso*, fols 163r-v. Here the trial record comes to an abrupt end.

57. D. Pérez Ramirez, *Catalogo del Archivo de la Inquisición de Cuenca* (Fundacion Universitaria Española, Madrid, 1982). The catalogue may be used only as a general indicator of the tribunal's activity.

58. Jimenez, 'Los luteranos', p. 695.

59. Nalle, 'Religion and Reform', pp. 126-7.

60. See the chapters by J.-P. Dedieu in B. Bennassar (ed.), *L'Inquisition espagnole*.

# 5

# Magical Healing, Love Magic and the Inquisition in Late Sixteenth-century Modena

*Mary O'Neil*

Recent historical studies of sixteenth-century Europe have documented a 'reform of popular culture' in both Catholic and Protestant areas. Peter Burke has described this reform movement as the religiously motivated 'efforts of the educated to change the belief and behaviour of the rest of the population'.[1]

The errors of belief characteristic of the uneducated were summed up in the recurrent phrase 'ignorance and superstition'. Although the definition of each of these terms varied along confessional lines, 'ignorance' usually referred to a lack of basic doctrinal information, and 'superstition' always included the magical beliefs and practices common throughout Europe. Religious complaints about behaviour focused on blasphemy and prohibited sexual behaviour. A lamentable state of ignorance, superstition and immorality was thus seen as characteristic of the people of Europe, especially (but not only) those in rural areas.

To combat these problems, sixteenth-century church authorities undertook broadly conceived programmes of catechetical instruction for the laity, seminary training for clergy and prosecution of religious as well as moral offences in church courts. This campaign was conducted under varied institutional forms, from Lutheran parish visitations to the Calvinist consistories of Geneva and Scotland, but its goals remained strikingly similar across Europe.[2] Everywhere, educated religious elites felt the time had come to eradicate popular errors, whether of belief or behaviour. In Counter Reformation Italy, it was the local offices of the Roman Inquisition which undertook a systematic campaign to suppress those popular errors of belief categorised by theologians as superstitious.

'Superstition' was a common term of abuse in the religious polemics of the sixteenth century, but Catholic and Protestant reformers used it in very different ways. Calvin defined as superstitious the whole theory and practice of Roman religion, from transubstantiation to saints cults.[3] Although Catholics had finer, more traditional lines to draw in deciding what was and was not superstitious, the post-Tridentine church undertook a related effort to eliminate those activities that went beyond the appropriate boundaries of religious observance. Catholic reform documents from Giberti's *Constitutions* to the decrees of the Council of Trent point to the need to discourage excessive or unseemly behaviour in religious contexts. To some extent these provisions reflected concern for exaggerations of otherwise orthodox devotions, like the desire for 'fixed numbers of Masses and candles' denounced at Trent.[4] The definition by Martino of Arles, current in sixteenth-century Italy, of superstition as 'superfluous and vain religion, pursued in a defective manner and in wrong circumstances', could apply to obsessive religiosity, but also to magical practices current among both peasants and urban people.[5]

Despite the arguments of Renaissance intellectuals for a 're-formed and learned natural magic', mainstream theologians since the Church Fathers had maintained that magical effects were achieved only with the aid of the devil, and were necessarily implicitly diabolical. It was because of this orthodox assumption that magical powers derive only from a pact with the devil (whether implicit or explicit), which in turn implied apostasy from the true faith, that the Inquisition had acquired jurisdiction over cases categorised as superstitious.[6]

In the climate of the post-Tridentine reform, the local offices of the Roman Inquisition prosecuted such cases with increased frequency. After an intensive period of heresy trials against Protestants from the 1540s to the 1570s, magical and superstitious offences came to constitute the major focus of late sixteenth- and early seventeenth-century Inquisitorial activity.[7] This essay draws on the Inquisition archives of Modena to consider the nature and character of these magical beliefs and of the campaign against them in late sixteenth-century Italy.

The verbatim trial records reveal a world in which magical remedies were used to deal with the routine hazards of life, especially illness and disease. The major categories of superstitious error prosecuted by the Inquisition were magical healing, love magic and divination, with the largest number of cases directed against healers. Divination techniques were used in a variety of situations, most frequently to find lost and stolen objects, including buried treasure, and to identify thieves. While none of these was specifically 'religious' in aim, all used religious forms of intercession, especially appeals to the saints, in ways considered inappropriate by the church. A common form of theft detection involved balancing a sieve on a pair of scissors and saying, 'by Saint Peter and Saint Paul, tell me who has taken my money'; the sieve was expected to rotate at the mention of the thief's name.[8] The people who performed this *incanto del sedaccio* believed that it worked through the aid of the saints, but in the eyes of the Inquisition any procedure lacking ecclesiastical approval could only function through the aid of the devil.

The following discussion focuses on trials for magical healing and love magic, in an effort to identify the particular character of the Roman Inquisition's campaign against popular magical beliefs and practices. It will be argued that the distinctive feature of that campaign, in contrast to northern Europe where such campaigns frequently escalated into full-scale witch hunts, was the moderation of its approach to magical crimes. This moderation derived from procedural restraints common to both Spanish and Roman Inquisitions[9] but also from the categories used by the court to describe such crimes. For despite the assumption that all such procedures implied a resort to diabolical assistance, in practice the court distinguished clearly between implicit and explicit invocation of demons, reserving its harshest penalties for the latter, less frequent type of offence. The application of this distinction to the category of 'superstition' permitted the Inquisition to deal with popular magical practices as a serious but manageable problem for which a restrained and comparatively lenient approach was most appropriate.

In taking action against magical remedies, the church intended to reassert its clerical monopoly on legitimate access to the supernatural. Protestant reformers had rejected all efforts to influence or manipulate supernatural forces for human benefit (except for prayer), and stressed the need to accept given conditions as providential.[10] But Catholicism continued to offer a religion that was remedial in very concrete ways. Spanish towns related to saints and shrines on a contractual basis, offering vowed days of religious attention in exchange for specific actions, from controlling insects and weather to ending the plague.[11] This collective level of devotional life was supplemented in the Italian setting by a strong emphasis on remedies to individual misfortunes, especially sickness and possession. Since much illness was considered to be of maleficial origin (that is, the result of witchcraft or diabolical malice) and even natural illness could be alleviated by spiritual intervention, religious remedies were important tools for healing the sick. Refer-red to as 'ecclesiastical medicines' by the Franciscan Girolamo Menghi, the orthodox remedies of holy water, clerical blessings, pilgrimages and exorcisms were to be employed against problems of both natural and supernatural origin.[12] The remedial functions of orthodox Catholicism were not limited to shrines and saints, but personified in clerics whose powers to bless and heal, with the aid of God and the approval of the church, form a central theme of Italian exorcist writing in this period. Remedies were thus indis-putably orthodox and belonged squarely within the functions of religion.

In the eyes of the church, magical remedies not only competed with clerical ones, but competed unfairly, for their format was invariably syncretic, putting familiar Christian devices to purposes not approved by the church.[13] In a process that must be attributed to the independent creativity of popular tradition, remedial formulae and procedures were extrapolated from standard prayers and liturgical observances, retaining the orthodox framework but replac-ing the contents with requests and techniques judged inappropriate and hence superstitious by theologians.[14] Referred to by their users as *orationi* (prayers), *ricetti (recipes) and segreti* (secrets), but called in-cantations (*incanti*) by the court, the multiple sources of these for-mulae in traditional oral culture are inaccessible to historians.[15] But the pious aspects of many *segreti*, their explicit invocation of the saints, the use of masses, baptism, orthodox prayers and bless-ed candles as ancillary techniques indicate that many magical remedies developed as extensions of the remedial functions of orthodox religion rather than from some wholly separate non-Christian source.[16]

Defendants tried for superstitious offences by the Inquisition repeatedly asserted that they thought a given *oratione* was 'a good thing', or a 'matter of religion'. Much of the campaign against popular magic thus consisted of educating people about what was and was not within the bounds of appropriate religious interces-sion. To this end, Inquisitorial edicts were read by parish priests at Sunday mass, listing the possible forms of superstitious error in fairly specific detail and requiring the listeners to denounce offenders. An edict from Bologna reminded the faithful of their

obligation, under pain of reserved excommunication, to make known to the Holy Office, all those persons whom they know, have known or will gain knowledge of, who perform or have performed on their behalf incantations, acts of witchcraft (*stregarie, malificii*) or sorcery (*sortilegio*) and magical or necromantic experiments . . . especially with explicit or implicit invocation of the demon.[17]

Moreover, from the 1590s on, parish priests were required to question people in confession about their knowledge of 'matters pertaining to the Holy Office', such as heresy, superstition and blasphemy. Absolution for sins was routinely withheld pending denunciation to the Inquisition of one's own or one's neighbours' offences. Second- and third-hand testimony was accepted, but was followed up by subsequent questioning of the persons who had been heard to repeat first-hand information about such events. This coercive mechanism of linking absolution for ordinary sins to informant testimony generated hundreds of denunciations technically classified as *sponte comparantes missus a confessione*, the majority of which were always for blasphemy, and which clustered in Advent and Lent as people prepared to receive communion at Easter or Christmas.

Both the reading of edicts and the participation of confessors in producing these somewhat less than 'spontaneous' appearances led to a striking increase in trials for magical and superstitious offences. In Modena they rose from a high of eleven or twelve per decade in the period between 1550 and 1589 to a total of 73 in the 1590s alone. Taken by itself, this rise in prosecutions indicates that the ecclesiastical bureaucracy's new methods of searching out such cases were effective, and that an issue that had previously been dealt with only sporadically was now receiving sustained attention.[18]

## Magical healing

There is further evidence that this campaign succeeded not only in the identification and trial of offenders, but in the prevention of recourse to magical remedies as well. Testimony in many cases reveals that healers known for curing a given condition began turning away potential clients with the explanation that their confessors no longer wanted to absolve them when they did such things.[19] These refusals of service left the relatives of sick people desperate; many offered to 'take the sin upon themselves' in order to induce a reluctant healer to perform the traditional remedies for fevers and childhood diseases. The Inquisition was aware of the pressures on healers, and trials were conducted against those who procured such services as well as against those who performed them. In one Modenese case of 1599, a sick priest named Fra Girolamo Azzolini promised absolution to a reluctant healer called by his family to 'sign' his fever.[20] Several healers alleged to the court that they had received special permission (*licenza di segnare*) from their parish priests to perform their cures; though not all of them could substantiate these claims, a few of them did. The fact that 20 per cent of Modenese trials for superstition between 1580 and 1600 were directed against clerics is indicative of the Inquisitors' determination to eliminate this source of confusion for the laity.[21]

There were educational functions performed by this campaign against popular magic. Many of the people whose consciences were pricked by an edict or a confessor's reprimand seem to have been genuinely unaware that the procedures in which they had participated were considered illicit. In 1595 Donna Violante arrived in court 'asking forgiveness not once but a hundred times for having erred' by taking her child to a 60-year-old man, Antonio Coreggi, who was known to heal hernias. Coreggi's testimony in the case betrays no suspicion on his part that his cure, learned 50 years before, was an objectionable one: 'I did not think such things were bad, nor that they were sins. If I had thought they were bad, I would have confessed them and stopped doing them.'[22] Antonio's healing ritual was to be performed at sunrise, either on the feast of St John the Baptist or on Good Friday. It required splitting open a nut tree, making a breach large enough for the child to be passed through three times while a young boy read aloud from the Gospel of St John.[23] The various edicts against superstition had thus succeeded only partially in Antonio's case. He knew that superstition was bad, but it remained simply a synonym for a generic concept of sin as doing harm to others.[24] He did not categorise his admitted actions in the court's terms, nor did the Inquisitor stop to instruct him on the meaning of this theological term. It was the coercive setting of the trial itself which alerted him to the fact that his sunrise healing, effective though it might have been, was 'bad' and should be discontinued.

When asked 'whether he believed that these things were done with the aid of the demon', Antonio responded: 'I never thought that such things were done through the devil's power but rather through the power of God and I never invoked the name of the demon.' Although he was perceived by the court as a 'good man and well disposed towards telling the truth', Antonio was nonetheless found to be

> lightly suspect of apostasy from God to the devil for having held and believed that holy words, the most holy Gospel and holy days . . . can be used for ends other than those instituted by the Church.[25]

The traditional formula of 'apostasy from God to the devil' is retained but there is no indication that the Inquisitors saw Antonio as allied with the devil in any real sense; 'lightly suspect' was the most mild of guilty verdicts. The central theme of this sentence is not the technical theological one of the implicit diabolical pact, but a jurisdictional concept of superstition as misappropriation of ecclesiastical rites and symbols (similar to the definition by Martino of Arles quoted above).

This tendency to treat popular remedies as superstitious in an almost bureaucratic sense as the misuse by uneducated people of functions properly reserved to the church characterises the Roman Inquisition campaign against magical practices and causes it to differ markedly from related campaigns elsewhere in Europe which placed greater stress on the diabolical nature of popular magic.[26] Antonio's penance, for example, consisted of confession and communion four times a year (including Easter and the feast of St John the Baptist, 'the days on which you performed these superstitions') and recitation of the Rosary every Friday for a year; a simple set of orthodox observances was considered sufficient atonement for a superstitious healing career.

This was a light penalty; most sentences for superstitious healing included the public humiliation of standing in front of church during Sunday mass with a lighted candle and a sign describing one's offence. Antonio's case was somewhat different (but not drastically so) from the norm, in part because of his gender. The overwhelming majority of people tried for magical healing in Modena were women who knew how to 'sign' specific illnesses, especially fevers and childhood diseases. Common procedures included making the sign of the Cross (hence the term 'signing') over a sick person, sometimes accompanied by other prayers or formulae and by natural remedies (such as baths and herbal treatments); in return the patient's family would offer food or small sums of money. Healers were often poor, older women, whose cures take on the aspect of disguised begging in many cases; some of them pleaded economic necessity as a mitigating circumstance at their trials.

Although others stressed the contrary, that they had cured people for 'the love of God' and 'had never taken anything for it', small gifts especially of food were the normal acknowledgement of this service.[27]

Depositions by witnesses indicate that relationships between healers and their clients could be tense, marked by fear and apprehension. Indeed, Antonio Coreggi was among the few whose accuser had no complaints about his services but was motivated solely by her belated perception of the unorthodoxy of his methods. Many healers were denounced to the Inquisition by their former clients, especially after an unsuccessful cure like that performed by Diamente de Bisa on a sick two-year-old girl in 1599. The child's widowed mother, Ludovica Venterino, was clearly traumatised by watching this 'big, old and ugly woman' bathe her child first in water and then in ashes.

> I gave her seven *bolognini* because she asked me for them, and I also gave her a lunch of bread and onions . . . but she ate alone. For myself I would not have eaten in her company, because I was frightened just looking at her.[28]

Although Diamente assured the mother that she had performed the healing procedure many times before, she acted in a secretive and even menacing manner. One witness, Alfonso Cappini, testified that she had warned Ludovica

> to take care that she said nothing to anyone outside in the street, for she [Diamente] would know everything that was said, even that which threatened from a distance. And after she had left, that child died in a brief span of time two hours later. . . . It still frightens me because she was hideous to look at, really a witch's face, a diabolical woman.

Diamente was thus denounced to the Inquisition for 'having destroyed [*guasta*] and killed a child' through witchcraft. Failed cures often resulted in such charges even against healers with solid reputations and loyal clients; in Modena, accusations of *maleficium* were invariably against healers and bear a certain resemblance to malpractice suits.

But the response of the court to these charges is an instructive one, for the Dominican Inquisitor, Giovanni di Montefalcono, resisted the perception of Diamente as a *strega* which was put forward by the bereaved family. He conducted the trial in a manner that turned up other opinions about her and shed concrete light on her suspiciously secretive behaviour. It emerged during Diamente's own interrogation that her confessor had urged her to stop performing her 'superstitious medications'. Her fear that he would learn she was still doing them when requested accounted for her attempts to keep the participants quiet with mingled threats and hints about supranormal perceptual abilities. Furthermore, the Inquisitor considered the possibility that the cure had been a natural one and did not accept the automatic correlation between Diamente's procedure and the child's subsequent death. Finally, he commissioned the local priest to inform himself about Diamente and her reputation in the village.[29] Don Santus di Zanctis himself had a good opinion of Diamente, but was swayed by the rumours that now reached him.

> In the past I never heard anything bad about this Diamente, but once Your Reverence charged me fifteen days ago with gathering information . . . I learned that the said Diamente is called by the nickname *la strega* . . . and that she undertakes to heal children who have been bewitched.

But Diamente had defenders as well. The person who had known her longest, her *comadre* (co-godmother) Julia, testified favourably to her abilities as a midwife and a healer. Diamente herself told the court:

> My career is that of spinning, weaving and sewing, wearing myself out to make a living. I am a poor woman and possess nothing in this world . . . I have made a profession of signing certain sicknesses such as *rosapilla* [measles?] worms and the illnesses of little children. Nor do I know how to perform incantations, superstitions or any sort of witchcraft.

She recounted numerous successful cures so that the sum of her testimony made the case of Ludovica's child seem exceptional.

The court resisted her accusers' charge of witchcraft, but Diamente's testimony about her healing methods placed her firmly in the category of 'superstitious healer'. She was asked to 'explain the methods she uses to sign these sicknesses, the words she speaks and the objects she uses'. Her lengthy replies describe cures which used ointments and herbs along with the sign of the cross; the court was most interested in her cure for worms.

For the sickness of worms, I say these words without using any objects: 'On Holy Monday, Holy Tuesday, Holy Wednesday, Holy Thursday, Holy Friday, Holy Saturday, Easter Sunday, the worm dies and decays.' Then I make the sign of the cross over them.

The 'vain observance of times and days' implicit in these methods fit standard concepts of superstition; it was on these methods, freely admitted by the defendant, that the interrogation focused, not on the circumstantial evidence linking her to a child's death. She was guilty in the eyes of the court, but of performing 'superstitious medications,' not of *maleficium*. The vocabulary of witchcraft (*striga, malefica, guastare*) is introduced in this trial only by witnesses and is passed over by the court, which uses instead the vocabulary of 'superstition'. Diamente received a standard penance of standing in front of the parish church during Sunday mass, fasting on bread and water on vigils of the Virgin's feastdays and reciting weekly rosaries for a year.[30] It is a harsher sentence than Antonio's but for an accusation of murder by witchcraft in 1599 it is striking in its moderation.

Moreover this moderation was maintained in the face of pressures for stricter treatment of witches from the population at large. Many denunciations for *maleficium* were never pursued by the Modenese court despite the intensity of feeling conveyed by those who saw themselves as victims of such acts. In 1579 a woman named Pasqua denounced the healer who had failed to prevent the deaths of her two infants in insistent, decided language: 'I hope Your Reverences will see to this matter for this Maria is held to be a witch [*stria*] by the entire Villa di Fre.'[31] Although there is a clear malpractice aspect to this denunciation, much of the evidence cited against Maria Mariani by a parade of witnesses focused on her well-known and varied healing abilities, of which she herself had frequently boasted. A former client justified the admissability of such evidence by citing a local proverb: 'it is commonly said that those who know how to heal also know how to harm'.[32]

This perception that the power to heal, especially the power to heal the bewitched (*maleficati, affaturati* or *guasti*), implied the opposite power to harm was a standard facet of learned and popular witch beliefs alike. The theological category of *maleficia ad sanandum* (healing by means of witchcraft) succinctly expresses the same ambivalence, which was, moreover, theoretically required by the implicitly diabolical nature of any magical cure. All this makes the restraint exhibited by the Inquisition even more striking. The cases of Maria Mariani and others like her never even came to trial, despite popular demand, while people like Diamente and Antonio were punished less severely than habitual blasphemers.[33]

## *Incanti ad amorem:* Love magic

The most extreme penalties handed out by the Modenese Inquisition are to be found not in trials against healers accused of *maleficium*, but in the functionally distinct sphere of love magic. Notwithstanding the difference between causing harm and inducing affection, historians have tended to include these cases in studies of witch trials.[34] This practice has been questioned by one recent scholar; calling for closer attention to the specific acts attributed to and the social roles occupied by persons accused of witchcraft, Richard Horsely has argued that since love magic had a 'good end' it should not be dealt with as equivalent to harm done by *maleficium*.[35]

Yet the theologians did exactly that. No distinction between 'good' and 'bad' magic existed in the eyes of the church, for its concerns focused on the means employed, not on the moral status of the end pursued in any magical act. Officially classified as *maleficia ad amorem*, techniques designed to induce passion in another person were particularly objectionable to theological opinion. For in addition to their implicitly (when not explicitly) diabolical source, the express goal of love charms were coercion to sin through the subversion of free will. Interrogations in these trials centred on the question of whether the defendant believed that the devil could force man's will into sin. Counter Reformation theology was particularly sensitive to attacks on free will associated with predestinarian Protestantism, and was determined to maintain the sinner's responsibility for his own sins.

Paradoxically, this confessional polemic undermined assumptions of the diabolical efficacy of love magic. The abjuration written for Moranda da Fanano, denounced for incantations and *furfanterie* in 1600, illustrates this point:

> I swear that I believe with my heart and confess with my mouth that the demon cannot force the will and free choice [*volonta e libero arbitrio*] of man to do evil, and consequently I abjure and detest that heresy which says and holds the opposite, of which I have been judged lightly suspect for the superstitions and

diabolical experiments performed and taught by me to give passion to others.[36]

In effect, Moranda's trial for the superstitious use of love charms
turned into a trial for the heretical denial of free will implicit in
her actions. Inquisitors in the field, starved for the hard theological
issues in which they had been schooled, thus exercised their abilities
by detecting the finer heretical implications of what were essentially
predoctrinal popular errors.[37]The persons tried on charges of love
magic were guilty of various things, from heretical opinions on the
freedom of the will to 'apostasy from Christ to the devil' for believing
that their implicitly diabolical spells would work, but they were not,
in the theologians' eyes, able to do what they attempted and wanted
to do. By asserting the impossibility that such incantations could
cause a person to sin against his will, even with the aid of the devil,
the church effectively assumed a sceptical attitude about the reality
and efficacy of love magic.[38]

Popular belief did not reach this sophisticated theological level.
While sceptics do turn up in the trial records, they were often dis-
appointed users of love charms whose disillusion with the results
of their experiments followed an initial credulity.[39] Many of the
'spontaneous denunciations sent from confession' were made by
people who had requested that some love charm be performed on
their behalf; they were required to denounce themselves as well as
the person who had assisted them. Providers of these services often
claimed economic motivation and denied that they in fact believed
in what they were doing, but since the Inquisition was concerned
above all with the issue of belief, their testimony was clearly self-
serving and may not reflect their real attitudes.[40]

Depositions by and about victims of love magic represent the
clearest evidence of a general assumption that such procedures were
efficacious. The socially inappropriate love affairs in which these
people were involved were routinely perceived as the consequence
of *maleficia ad amorem*. From the point of view of the relatives and
friends of the socially superior individual, for whom such a
misalliance defied fundamental principles of social hierarchy, this
hypothesis served a crucial explanatory function. For those of lower
status, love charms conversely held out hopes of a sudden (indeed
magical) transformation of their circumstances. Most of the people
accused of using such charms in sixteenth-century Modena were
women; upper-crust names figure prominently in the lists of men
magically pursued by their amorously ambitious inferiors.[41]

Camilla Baclara was denounced in 1553 for 'having wanted to give a certain drink as a love potion to one of the Grillenzoni, but her mother scolded her and she didn't do it'. She was more successful with the son of another powerful local family, Giovanni Battista de Capelli, to whom she gave a drink containing magically prepared nutmeg (*noce moscato*), considered a powerful aphrodisiac. Her accuser testified about its effects:

> Giovanni Battista can find no rest without this woman, so that coming at night from the villa, he did crazy things out of his ardent desire for her. Returning to the villa he became sick, with a rash on his hands and face, and a fever too. But as soon as he was with her again he got better.[42]

Giovanni's symptoms were interpreted for him by a woman of his own social level, the 'gentlewoman Donna Francesca, wife of Dominus Hieronimus de Rubigis,' who reported Camilla to the Inquisition as a *malefica*. The blinded victim was not held responsible for his condition by public opinion, nor could he be expected to understand its cause as well as his relatives and friends.

Theologians might deny the possibility of coercion to passion, but ordinary clerics were not immune to the general belief in the efficacy of love magic. The Guardian of the Observant Franciscan convent of Santa Margarita, Fra Francesco Calais, appeared before the Modenese Inquisitor in 1599 to demand prosecution of a woman whom he blamed for the seduction of a friar.

> Finding myself in a great turmoil because of a priest of my order, Fra Costanzo di Sacriguano, I was told by Fra Gasparo da Carpo . . . how Fra Costanzo had apostasised against his will and was forced to throw off his habit. The wretched creature is staying in this neighbourhood, for he was bewitched by a prostitute called la Buratinazza . . . who makes him come to her by force.[43]

Like the accusation against Camilla, this case never came to trial, despite the Franciscan spiritual director's urgent plea. Bewitchment provided a face-saving interpretation of the inconstant Fra Costanzo's scandalous behaviour but it was precisely the inference that he had done all this against his will that was theologically unacceptable to the Inquisitors. The accusations of love magic most likely to result in a full-scale trial were not those which inferred magical scheming from symptoms like those experienced by these men, but rather those in which testimony about actual use of spells and charms was produced. And when such trials were undertaken, the cast of characters in Fra Francesco's deposition, a prostitute and a priest, figured prominently.

For the specialists in the field of love magic were prostitutes who used a wide array of procedures to attract and hold clients or lovers. They were usually younger, lower-class urban women, clearly distinct as a social group from the village healers whose rural poverty and age fit the traditional witch image more closely. Drawing on Fernando de Rojas's famous literary depiction of the magically adept urban prostitute, the Spanish historian Caro Baroja refers to such women as 'Celestina type witches'.[44] While they were technically considered *maleficae* because they performed *maleficia ad amorem*, depositions tended to describe these women as 'knowing how to perform incantations' and other *furfanterie* (roguery or rascally actions) rather than in the popular vocabulary of witchcraft (*striga*, *guastare*, etc.) used to denounce healers. While the two types of magical practitioners represent different social groups, the distinction between them should not be overdrawn; a prostitute's *incanti ad amorem* could be referred to as *strigarie* and some of these women knew a broad range of magical remedies, including techniques for healing and divination.[45]

Trials for love magic had occurred sporadically throughout the late sixteenth century, but their number increased significantly in the 1590s and dramatically after 1598. In that year, the Este Duke was forced by papal military pressure to withdraw from Ferrara to Modena, traditionally the second city of his duchy. As the court and army established themselves in Modena, the new capital attracted *donne di mala vita* from Bologna, Venice and Milan as well as from Ferrara. The Inquisition did not concern itself with the professional status or moral failings of such women, but only with their knowledge of magical spells and charms. Since many of them lived in the same neighbourhood and knew one another, they frequently shared secret formulae among themselves or with others, sometimes for money. Thus a denunciation against one woman could quickly implicate several others, leading to a group trial like that against Margarita Chiappona and seven other women in 1593 and 1594.[46]

The eight prostitutes tried in 1593-4 knew scores of devices to induce passion in another person. Many of their love charms called on the saints, including San Daniello and Santa Elena, but also on the Holy Spirit, and required the use of blessed candles or other religious apparatus in order to work. The *oratione di Santa Marta*,

confiscated from Margarita Chiappona, was 'to be said kneeling
and fasting for nine mornings with nine Pater Nosters, nine Ave
Marias, to the praise and reverence of Santa Marta that she might
fulfil what is asked of her'. This prayer makes its requests in highly
vivid and physical language.

> O Blessed Martha, for love of me go to that wood where Our
> Lord Jesus Christ baptised with his twelve Apostles. . . . Cut
> three branches of fire and flame and for love of me send them
> to the heart of N.N. Send them through the veins of the heart,
> of the head, of the lungs, through the marrow of the bones, the
> flesh of the legs, with such love that it beats and scourges, so
> that for my love he should suffer incessantly. . . . For love of
> me, take away from him drink, food, sleep, power that he might
> not go or stay, nor ride nor drive nor walk, nor have relations
> with any woman, until he should come to me to satisfy all my
> desire and do all that which I will ask of him.[47]

Such a 'prayer' was clearly superstitious in theological terms, since
it employed an orthodox, novena-like format to invoke the aid of
a saint for the inappropriate goal of leading someone into a sinful
relationship against his own free will. Moranda da Fanano's
abjuration states the orthodox position: 'the saints should not be
invoked for the purpose of helping and giving strength to commit
sins'.[48]

Assistance was also sought closer to home from priests, whose
ritual expertise was central to a variety of love charms. Some of
these operated without the priests' knowledge, as people hid objects
or pieces of paper containing magical formulae (*brevi*) under the
altar cloth so that masses would be recited over them. Another common procedure required taking a shoelace (*stringa*) belonging to the
desired person to mass; when the priest turned towards the congregation to say 'Dominus vobiscum', a knot was to be tied in the
shoelace while saying: 'I am not tying you, stringa, but the heart
of you, N.N., so that you can go to no one but me.'[49] This and
similar covert activities attempted to draw on the liturgical power
of the mass by reciting formulae that substituted for the priest's
own words, diverting their efficacy to magical ends.

Even more alarming to the church hierarchy was the active in-
volvement of priests in the application of orthodox ceremonies to
superstitious purposes. Inquisition trials document the fact that,
unlike the *capellano* of San Pietro who turned in Antonia Vignola's

handwritten prayer to the Inquisition, some priests agreed to perform masses over magical objects, while others participated in baptisms with similar goals. Camilla Baclara's accusers alleged in 1533 that with the aid of a more co-operative priest, she had managed to have 15 masses said over the *noce moscato* used in preparing the potion she gave to Giovanni Batista de Capelli.[50] The baptisms were usually reserved for magnets, since it was popularly believed that a magnet (*calamita biancha*) baptised with a given person's name would have the power to draw that person irresistibly to the possessor of the magnet. Antonia Vignola possessed a ring containing such a *calamita*; unsure whether to consider the magnet's alleged attractive properties as natural or magical, the court summoned an expert witness, the goldsmith Magister Pompeo Travis, to testify on the matter,

I: Whether he knows if the stone vernacularly called *calamita* can be put to use to perform acts of *maleficium*.

R: It is commonly held [*per publica fama*] that *calamita biancha* can be used for amatory incantations by touching a person's skin with the magnet. However, calamita does not have this power unless it is baptised or enchanted [*incantata*] by holy things.[51]

As a result of this belief, priests were sought after to perform clearly unorthodox baptismal ceremonies for these objects, complete with godparents, holy oils and ritual vestments. In several cases, priests undertook this procedure on their own initiative, with the intent to use the magnets for their private amorous pursuits. Indeed, the case of Fra Costanzo is something of an exception; more priests turn up in the trial records as users of love magic than as its victims.[52]

Although clerical defendants knew their magical activities were illicit, lay defendants commonly asserted, like Antonia Vignola in 1564, that their spells and charms, having love as their goal, were 'good things'. But this defence was undermined by the very nature of the enterprise. Love magic aimed at power and control over another person's feelings and actions; to that end it threatened symbolic and physical distress. The *oratione di Santa Marta*, for example, asked that its victim should 'suffer incessantly' and be deprived of 'drink, food, sleep, power' until he complied with the desires of the *incantatrice*. It is not surprising that persons who suspected themselves to be objects of attempted spells should experience extreme physical symptoms like those reported in the case of

Archimidoro Massetti and Giovanni Battista de Capelli.

The negative perception of love magic did not, therefore, derive simply from the imposition of clerical categories, but had independent structural roots. The idea that one can distinguish between 'good' and 'bad' types of magic, like the proposal to classify love charms as 'good magic' of an essentially different order from harmful *maleficia*, is not supported by sixteenth-century perceptions, whether popular or learned.[53] The difficulty in making such a distinction lies in the fundamental moral ambiguity of all magical operations; if power to heal could as easily be used to harm, the power to induce love (itself ambiguous from the perspective of its target) could also be used to induce hatred.

Indeed there was a large sub-category of love magic classified by the court as *superstitiones ad amore impedendo* which had as an express object the prevention or destruction of amorous feelings. Francesco Villano, in love with a local prostitute, submitted to his wife's recommendation that he got magical help to overcome his infatuation.

> Goaded by my wife because of my relations with Barbara Grafagnina, and I myself being desirous of detaching myself from her because of the great passion I felt for her, I did the things you have described at my wife's persuasion.[54]

It was to Barbara's colleague, Margarita Chiappona, that Francesco and his wife turned for assistance; she obligingly provided them with one of her many remedies. The line between *incanti ad amorem* and those *ad amore impedendo* was in any case a thin one, for most love charms, like the *oratione di Santa Marta*, included the prevention of sexual activity with others in their demands. The traditional explanation for male impotence was ligature caused by witchcraft, and impeding sexual relations was a major category of *maleficia* in both learned and popular belief.[55] Many of the Modenese spells live up to this reputation. An intensified variant of *la stringa* described by Caterina Scorana in 1593 declared, 'I do not tie you *stringa*, but the member of you, N.N., so that you can go to no one but me', thus explicitly asserting the intent to cause a ligature.[56]

The people who used love magic were determined to achieve their goals by any means available.[57] If many drew on the power of orthodox ceremonies or called on the assistance of the saints, some went further. Moranda da Fanano was required to 'abjure, detest and curse' her heretical use of an *oratione ad una stella*, and to confirm that 'it is not licit for faithful Christians to offer prayers to the stars in the manner of pagans'.[58] Since the church held that all such efforts were implicitly diabolical anyway, it could perhaps be expected that magically intent practitioners would bypass intermediate channels, calling directly on the *Gran Diavolo* to achieve the same ends. Of the 24 persons tried for love magic in Modena between 1550 and 1600, 14 used formulae that included some invocation of demonic assistance. These ranged from brief charms, like that used by Magdalena di Ferrara in 1552 to procure the return of absent husbands 'in the name of Lucifer and Beelzebub', to elaborate ceremonies drawing on learned sorcerers' techniques for conjuring demons. The only non-clerical male tried for *incanti ad amorem*, Basilio Brasigella, had learned his procedure from a 'book owned by a Franciscan friar' which included a solemn Latin surrender of body and soul to the devil.[59] The explicitly diabolical aspect of such charms, which confirmed learned theories about the implicit diabolism of other incantations, caused the Inquisition to react strongly in these cases.

Eugenia Claveria, a Modenese prostitute, was tried in 1599 for her 'diabolical secrets, amorous superstitions and incantations wherein the express invocation of the devil occurs various times'. The source of her denunciation was Camilla de Orlani, who had been refused absolution and referred to the Inquisition by her confessor for her participation in Eugenia's *incanto dei macaroni* during which she repeatedly invoked the *Gran Diavolo*.[60] Although Eugenia maintained that she 'had not believed that these things were sinful and displeasing to God, since they were things of love', she was sentenced to public whipping and exile from Modena, the most severe penalty imposed by the Modenese Inquisition for any offence short of unrepentant formal heresy. In the Modenese trials, this punishment of public whipping and banishment was reserved for habitual, unrepentant blasphemers and for practitioners of explicitly diabolical magic, especially prostitutes. It is probably not accidental that the most rigorous treatment should be given to prostitutes, whose cases were prosecuted more vigorously than those of other women.[61] Even though the Inquisition did not have jurisdiction over morals offences, the public humiliation and exile of prostitutes served the double function of punishing their superstitious activity and moralising the city at the same time.

## Conclusion

The comparatively mild character of witch trials in Italy has been commented upon by observers from the sixteenth century to the present. In his sceptical treatment of witch beliefs, *De praestigiis daemonum* (1566), Johann Weyer noted the Bolognese practice of whipping and exiling witches rather than executing them as an example of a more enlightened approach than that prevailing in northern Europe. Contemporaries were also aware that this relative leniency was associated with the Inquisition. Paolo Sarpi recorded the Venetian Grand Council's order that maleficial witchcraft 'be punished by the magistrates, because the ecclesiastical penalties are insufficient chastisement for such great wickedness'.[62] Henry Charles Lea and others have since singled out the *Instructio pro formandis processibus in causis strigum, sortilegiorum et maleficiorum (Instructions for trying cases against witches, sorcerers and those who perform maleficia)*, drawn up by the Holy Office in Rome and circulated in manuscript form from the 1620s on, as a crucial document in the seventeenth-century effort to curb the murderous excesses of witch trials by procedural reform.[63]

However, John Tedeschi has recently argued that this view incorrectly presents the *Instructio* as a radical innovation. Rather, he states, the '*Instructio*, by and large, was not enunciating new legal doctrines . . . but restating longstanding Roman theory and practice'.[64] The evidence presented here from Modenese trial records of the late sixteenth century clearly supports Tedeschi's argument that the moderating procedural recommendations associated with the *Instructio* were standard practice in the local offices of the Roman Inquisition well before 1620.

A passage in the *Instructio* frequently pointed out as a crucial innovation warns judges that

> when a woman is convicted of or confesses to having performed incantations or maleficia in order to heal or for any other purpose, it does not however necessarily follow that she is a formal witch, since the sorcery [*sortilegio*] can be performed without formal apostasy to the Demon.[65]

Modenese trials in the 1590s against persons using magical remedies clearly conform to this model, for they do not treat the accused as formally allied with demons, except in those cases where explicit invocation of the demon is in fact present, usually in the love charms of prostitutes, but also in a few cases of learned magic against literate men.[66] Moreover, the most extreme penalty exacted in these trials (whipping and exile) is a moderate one by contemporary European standards.

The fourteenth- and fifteenth-century fusion of concepts of magic, diabolism and heresy into the *crimen exceptum* of witchcraft was at least partially unravelled in these sixteenth-century Italian trials, as the category of 'superstition' was separated out and became the dominant theme in the Catholic campaign against popular magic.[67] Even the efficacy of invoking demons was questioned by Inquisitors and theologians committed to the doctrine of free will, so that persons who did address themselves to the devil were prosecuted for their intent, not for having achieved their goals with his aid. In Eugenia Claveria's abjuration before her exile in 1559, she accepted the court's recommendation that she 'leave off these superstitions through which God is offended; nor do you obtain through such evil means what you desire'.[68] This essentially sceptical attitude towards the efficacy of demonical assistance separates the Italian trials on epistemological grounds from the contemporary witch trials in northern Europe. The distinctive moderation of the Catholic approach to the repression of magical beliefs stems from its de-emphasis of the diabolical source of magical effects, and its treatment of such beliefs in a quasi-sceptical way as characteristic of simple and uneducated people, to whom the church simultaneously offered a wide assortment of orthodox, ecclesiastically administered remedies for the religious relief of everyday misfortune.

# Notes

1. Peter Burk, *Popular Culture in Early Modern Europe* (Harper & Row, New York, 1978), p. 208. Some of these works are reviewed by Natalie Zemon Davis, 'From "Popular Religion" to Religious Cultures', in Steven Ozment (ed.), *Reformation Europe: A Guide to Research* (Center for Reformation Research, St Louis, Mo, 1982), pp. 321-42.

2. The Lutheran parish visitations are studied by Gerald Strauss, *Luther's House of Learning: The Indoctrination of the Young in the German Reformation* (Johns Hopkins University Press, Baltimore, Md, 1978). The varied functions of the consistory in the Scottish Reformation emerge in Christian Larner, *Enemies of God: The Witch-hunt in Scotland* (Johns Hopkins University Press, Baltimore, Md, 1981).

Historical literature on the Catholic Reform movement has been surveyed by John O'Malley, 'Catholic Reform', in Ozment (ed.), *Reformation Europe*, and earlier by Eric Cochrane, 'New Light on Post-Tridentine

Italy: A Note on Recent Counter-Reformation Scholarship', *Catholic Historical Review, 56* (1970), pp. 291-319.

The literature on popular religion is reviewed by Natalie Zemon Davis in 'Some Tasks and Themes in the Study of Popular Religion', in Charles Trinkhaus and Heiko Oberman (eds), *The Pursuit of Holiness in Late Medieval and Renaissance Religion* (E. J. Brill, Leiden, 1974), pp. 307-16, and also in her essay 'From "Popular Religion" to Religious Cultures,' in Ozment (ed.), *Reformation Europe*, pp. 321-42.

3. Jean Delumeau, 'Les réformateurs et la superstition', *Actes du colloque L'Amiral de Coligny et son temps* (Société de l'histoire du Protestantisme Française, Paris, 1974), pp. 451-87. For a survey of the changing historical meanings of this term, see Mary R. O'Neill, 'Superstition', in Mircea Eliade (ed.), *Encyclopedia of Religion* (Macmillan, New York, forthcoming 1986).

4. Gian Matteo Giberti, 'Exhortation to be made by pastors to the people to rid themselves of superstitions', *Constitutiones Gibertinae*, Book IV, Chapter 29, Verona, 1542, in John C. Olin (ed.), *The Catholic Reformation: Savonarola to Ignatius Loyola* (Harper & Row, New York, 1969), pp. 133-48. Council of Trent, Twenty-second session, 'Decree concerning the things to be observed and avoided in the celebration of Mass', in Henry Joseph Schroeder, O.P. (ed.), *Canons and Decrees of the Council of Trent* (B. Herder, St Louis, Mo, 1941), pp. 150-2.

5. Martino de Arles, *Tractatus de superstitionibus* (Vincetium Luchinum, Rome, 1559) p. 354. Thomas Aquinas defined superstition as 'the vice opposed to the virtue of religion by means of excess . . . because it offers divine worship either to whom it ought not, or in a manner it ought not'; *Summa Theologica*, II-II, question 92, article 1 (3 vols, Benziger, New York, 1947), vol. 2, p. 1592. Theologians regarded magical activities as a form of homage to the devil, on the theory that recourse to such presumptively diabolical techniques implied an acknowledgement of the devil's power.

6. The evolution of the orthodox polemic against magic is the subject of Edward Peters, *The Magician, the Witch and the Law* (University of Pennsylvania Press, Philadelphia, 1978). For Renaissance theories of 'natural magic', D.P. Walker, *Spiritual and Demonic Magic from Ficino to Campanella* (Warburg Institute, London, 1958).

The extension of Inquisitorial jurisdiction to cases of magic is discussed by Richard Kieckhefer, *European Witch Trials: Their Foundations in Popular and Learned Culture, 1300-1500* (University of California Press, Berkeley, Calif., 1976), and by Norman Cohn, *Europe's Inner Demons: An Enquiry Inspired by the Great Witch Hunt* (New American Library, New York, 1975). See also the note concerning this issue by Carlo Ginzburg, *The Night Battles: Witchcraft and Agrarian Cults in the Sixteenth and Seventeenth Centuries*, English translation by John and Anne Tedeschi (Johns Hopkins University Press, Baltimore, Md, 1983), p. 177, n. 31.

7. The repression of superstition by the Mediterannean Inquisitions is surveyed by E. William Monter, *Ritual, Myth and Magic in Early Modern Europe* (Ohio University Press, Athens, Ohio, 1984), pp. 61-77. The trials in Modena are studied in Mary R. O'Neil, 'Discerning Superstition: Popular Errors and Orthodox Response in Late Sixteenth Century Italy,' unpublished PhD thesis, Stanford University, 1982.

8. This procedure is described in numerous trials; see for example the trial of April 1601, Contra Sanctam de Ferrariis de Sancto Felice diocesis Mutinensis, dictam la Munchina o la Storta, Archivio di Stato di Modena (hereafter ASM), *Inquisizione*, busta 15.

9. In Spain, the Suprema's centralised control of all Inquisition proceedings and the doubts of some inquisitors about the physical possibility of witchcraft accusations combined to bring a complete halt to witch trials by the early seventeenth century. These developments have been studied by Gustav Henningsen, *The Witch's Advocate: Basque Witchcraft and the Spanish Inquisition, 1609-1614* (University of Nevada Press, Reno, Nev., 1980). As will be seen below, a similar pattern applied in Italy, although because of the dispersal of the Roman Inquisition records, it is less well documented than the Spanish case. See John A. Tedeschi, 'La dispersione degli archivi della Inquisizione romana', *Rivista di storia e litteratura religiosa, 9* (1973), pp. 298-312, and 'Preliminary Observations on Writing a History of the Roman Inquisition', in F. Church and T. George (eds), *Continuity and Discontinuity in Church History* (E.J. Brill, Leiden, 1979), pp. 232-49.

10. Protestant campaigns against 'ecclesiastical magic' in England and Germany are described by Keith Thomas, *Religion and the Decline of Magic* (Scribners, New York, 1971) and by Gerald Strauss, 'Success and failure in the German Reformation', *Past and Present, 67* (1975), pp. 30-63, both of whom stress the tendency of the peasantry to maintain their magical beliefs despite learned Protestant condemnation.

11. William Christian, Jr, *Local Religion in Sixteenth Century Spain* (Princeton University Press, Princeton, NJ, 1981).

12. For the list of the *medicine ecclesiastiche*, see Girolamo Menghi, *Compendio dell'arte essorcista e possibilità delle mirabili e stupdende operatoni delli demoni e dei malefici con i rimedii opportuni all'infirmità maleficiali* (Giovanni Rossi, Bologna, 1578), p. 253.

13. The conflict between orthodox and superstitious remedies is the topic of Mary R. O'Neil, '*Sacerdote ovvero strione*: Ecclesiastical and Superstitious Remedies in Late Sixteenth Century Italy', in Steven L. Kaplan (ed.), *Understanding Popular Culture: Europe from the Middle Ages to the Nineteenth Century* (Mouton, Berlin and New York, 1984), pp. 53-84. This article also considers the impact of Menghi's exorcist writings on the practice of exorcism by the lower clergy.

14. See, for example, the recommendation made in 1577 to the curates of Bologna by the annual congregation of parish priests meeting under episcopal auspices:

> They should seek to collect all the superstitions, incantations, and handwritten prayers or charms, worn or carried on one's person (*brevi da portar adosso*), which contain superstitious words, unapproved names and similar abuses. Even if they do not appear to be evil, they should be collected and notice given of them, for it is planned that a small book warning of these matters should be compiled.

This decree is quoted in Cleto Corraibn and Pier-Luigi Zampini (eds), *Documeni etnografici e folkloristici nei senodi diocesani italiani* (Forni, Bologna, 1970), p. 36.

15. See however on this topic, Carlo Ginzburg, 'Folklore, magia, religione', in *Storia d'Italia*, vol. 1, *I cratteri originali*, ed. Ruggiero Romano and Corrado Vivanti (Einaudi, Turin, 1972), pp. 603-76. A highly effective reconstruction of the assumptions and *mentalité* underlying a Friulian peasant incantation is provided by Luisa Accati, 'Lo spirito della fornicazione: virt' dell'anima e virt' del corpo in Friuli, fra 1600 e 1700', in Carlo Ginzburg (ed.), *Religione delle classi populari*, special number of *Quaderni storici, 41* (1979), pp. 644-72.

16. For example, see the *oratione di Santa Marta*, quoted below (n. 50), which included the following instructions: 'This prayer is to be said kneeling and fasting for nine mornings with nine Pater Nosters, nine Ave Marias, to the praise and reverence of Santa Marta, that she might fulfil what is asked of her.' The printed text of this prayer in included in the trial of a printer's assistant who did the printing at the request of a Modenese prostitute; Contra Thomaso Zanola detto il Cadorino, ASM, *Inquisizione*, busta 10, 1597.

17. Aviso della Santa Inquisizione di Bologna, 4 March 1636, Biblioteca Communale di Bologna (BCB), MS B1891, fo. 119. It is clear from trial testimony referring to similar edicts that they had been issued from at least the 1580s.

18. These statistics are drawn from my PhD thesis, O'Neil 'Discerning Superstition', Table 1, p. 46.

19. However, this success may have been a short-term phenomenon. Trials for superstitious healing decline by the mid-seventeenth century, but the survival of 'signing' techniques in the twentieth century in rural areas around Modena and Bologna indicates that such methods were never totally suppressed.

20. Trial of Fra Girolamo Azzolini, ASM, *Inquisizione,* busta 10, 1599.

21. For these statistics, see my article, *'Sacerdote ovvero strione'*, p. 56.

22. Trial of Antonio Coreggi, ASM, *Inquisizione*, busta 9, 1595. Subsequent quotations are from the same trial.

23. The custom of healing by passing a child through a fissure cut in a tree has been documented in many areas of Europe. See Wayland D. Hand, 'Passing Through: Folk Medical Magic and Symbolism', *Proceedings of the American Philosophical Society, 112* (1968), pp. 379-402.

24. For a similar concept of sin among fourteenth-century French peasants, see E. Le Roy Ladurie, *Montaillou* (Braziller, New York, 1978), pp. 327ff.

25. Sentence of Antonio Coreggi, ASM, *Inquisizione*, busta 9, October 1595.

26. For bibliography on the comparative history of European witch beliefs and witch trials, see H.C. Erik Midelfort, 'Witchcraft, Magic and the Occult', in Ozment (ed.), *Reformation Europe*, pp. 183-210.

27. The centrality of begging in the genesis of English witchcraft accusations has been demonstrated by Thomas, *Religion and the Decline of Magic*, pp. 502-69.

28. Trial of Diamante de Bisa delli Axcari della Mota, ASM, *Inquisizione*, busta 9, 1595. Subsequent quotations are from this same trial.

29. A person's general reputation in a village or neighbourhood (*publica voce et fama*) was admissible as evidence under inquisitorial procedure, but

as Diamante's trial shows, it was not necessarily a decisive factor in the court's deliberations.

30. Sentence of Diamante de Bisa, ASM, *Inquisizione*, busta 9, 9 October 1599.

31. Denunciation of Maria Mariani, ASM, *Inquisizione*, busta 7, 1579.

32. Ibid., testimony of Andreas di Saviolis.

33. Penalties for blasphemy escalated according to the number of times a man had been accused; incorrigible habitual blasphemers were whipped through the streets or in the piazza and in some cases exiled from the city of Modena for a period of years.

34. See for instance the 'Calendar of Witch Trials' for the period 1300 to 1500 in Richard Kieckhefer, *European Witch Trials: Their Foundations in Learned and Popular Culture, 1300-1500* (University of California Press, Berkeley, Calif., 1976), pp. 106-47.

35. Richard A. Horsely, 'Who Were the Witches? The Social Roles of the Accused in the European Witch Trials', *Journal of Interdisciplinary History, 9* (1979), pp. 698-715.

36. Contra Moranda da Fanano, ASM, *Inquisizione*, busta 11, sentence of 3 March 1602.

37. A good example of an inquisitor applying his theological skills on predoctrinal popular beliefs is Bartolomeo da Spina's treatment, in his *Quaestio de strigibus*, of a Modenese myth about the ability of witches to reconstruct cattle they consumed at feasts from the leftover skin and bones; see Maurizio Bertolotti, 'Le ossa e la pelle dei buoi', *Quaderni storici, 41* (1979), pp. 470-99.

38. This is similar to the level of scepticism of the tenth-century *Canon Episcopi*; it denies the possibility of night flying, but condemns as apostates the women who believe they go flying at night with Diana; their real crime is believing 'there is anything of power except the one God'. The *Canon episcopi* is translated in Alan C. Kors and Edward Peters (eds), *Witchcraft in Europe, 1100-1700: A Documentary History* (University of Pennsylvania Press, Philadelphia, 1972), pp. 28-31.

39. Uliva La Grassa testified as follows on 4 January 1594:

I: Whether she believed this superstition could prevent a man from having relations with another woman than herself and whether it was effective.
R: I believed it because I was led to believe it, but the effect did not follow. (Contra Margarita Chiappona et al., ASM. *Inquisizione*, busta 8)

40. Margarita Chiappona, for example, stressed that she used love charms to earn money:

I: Whether she placed faith in the performance of those prayers.
R: I did not believe that the prayer could force either Christ or the Virgin, but I did it out of poverty. (Contra Margarita Chiappona et al., ASM, *Inquisizione*, busta 8, testimony of 22 January, 1594)

41. For example, a prostitute named Teodora Brualdo was accused of having 'done certain things to force Signor Egidio Rangone to come to

her by means of the pignate', a familiar local charm; Contra Margarita Chiappona et al., ASM, *Inquisizione* busta 8, 1593-4, testimony of Caterina Scorana. The Rangone were the most powerful family in Modena, second only to the Este.

42. Contra Camillam Baclaram, ASM, *Inquisizione*, busta 3, 1553.

43. Contra la Burantinazza, ASM, *Inquisizione*, busta 10, testimony of 19 April 1599.

44. Fernando de Rojas's *La Celestina* was published in 1499; Julio Caro Baroja, *The World of the Witches* (University of Chicago Press, Chicago, 1964), pp. 101-2.

45. Moranda da Fanano's accuser, for one, referred to her love magic as *strigarie*, and Margarita Chiappona knew an eclectic assortment of remedies of every sort, not just love magic. However, the focus of the 1593-4 trial against her and other prostitutes was their professional use of love charms.

46. Contra Margarita Chiappona et al., ASM, *Inquisizione*, busta 8, 1593-4. The other women tried were Ludovica de Buzalis, Uliva La Grassa, Pulissena de Bonzelis, Barbara Grafagnina, Pasqua Mutinensa, Francesca Romandila and Lucretia Chardor. A related but separate trial was conducted against another prostitute, Caterina Scorana, in 1594.

47. The *oratione di Santa Marta* was mentioned by many of the prostitutes tried for love magic. The version dictated by Margarita Chiappona to a printer's assistant is preserved in printed form in the trials of Thomas Zanola, il Cadorino, ASM, *Inquisizione*, busta 10, 1597. It is very unusual to find a printed love charm of this sort; the vast majority of those surviving were handwritten or recited from memory during a trial.

48. Contra Moranda da Fanano, ASM, *Inquisizione*, busta ll, 1600.

49. Contra Isabetta, ASM, *Inquisizione*, busta 8, 1594. This is a clear example of a sympathetic magical procedure, where the shoelace represents the person on whom the charm is to work. The general concepts underlying magical beliefs are discussed by Marcel Mauss, *A General Theory of Magic* (Norton, New York, 1972).

50. Contra Camilla Baclara, ASM, *Inquisizione*, busta 3, 1553.

51. Contra Antonia Vignola, ASM, *Inquisizione*, busta 3, 1564, testimony of Magister Pompeo Travis, aurifex.

52. For example, trials were conducted against the Carmelite Alessandro Contines for possession of written incantations in 1583, against Don Gian Batista of Cathedral Church for baptising a magnet in 1584, against the Capuchin Fra Francesco Ippolito for *parole ad amorem* in 1589, and a group trial against Don Pietro de Martinelli, Don Bartolomeo da Bologna and Don Camillo Tondi da Stuffiano for baptising a magnet in 1598; see ASM, *Inquisizione*, busta 8 and 9 for these trials.

53. In his article 'Who Were the Witches?' Richard Horsely accepts the definition of 'good magic' as good from the perspective of the person using it; from the broader perspective of the society within which all witch beliefs operated, the inadequacy of such a definition is clear. However, Horsely is correct to stress the fact that different types of accusations (e.g. magical healing versus love magic) reflect different sociological conditions.

54. Contra Margarita Chiappona et al., ASM, *Inquisizione*, busta 8,

testimony of Francesco Villano, 19 January 1594.

55. The traditional attribution of male impotence to witchcraft was given scholastic approbation by Thomas Aquinas, Quodlibet XI, Quaestio IX, Article X, 'Utrum maleficia impediant matrimonium', *Opera omnia* (26 vols, Petri Ficcadori, Parma, 1859), vol. 9, p. 618. The *locus classicus* on the topic is Heinrich Kramer and Jakob Sprenger, 'Whether witches can hebetate the powers of generation or obstruct the veneral act', *Malleus Maleficarum* (1486), Part I, Question 8 (Dover, New York, 1971), pp. 54-8.

56. Contra Caterina Scorana, ASM, *Inquisizione*, busta 8, 1594.

57. Bronislaw Malinowski's description of magic as embodying the 'sublime folly of hope' is applicable here:

Man, engaged in a series of practical activities, comes to a gap. . . . Forsaken by his knowledge, baffled by his past experience and by his technical skill, he realizes his impotence. Yet his desire grips him only the more strongly. . . . Obsessed by the idea of the desired end, he sees it and feels it. . . . [Thus he] forecasts the images of the wished for results . . . breaking out into words which give vent to desire and anticipate its end. (*Magic, Science and Religion* (Anchor, New York, 1954), pp. 79-80)

58. Contra Moranda de Fanano, ASM, *Inquisizione*, busta 11, 3 March 1603.

59. Contra Magdalena da Ferra, 1552, and Contra Brasilio Brasigella, 1560; ASM, *Inquisizione*, busta 3.

60. Contra Eugenia Claveria, ASM, *Inquisizione*, busta 10, 1599. The subsequent quotation is also from this trial.

61. Upper-class women who dabbled in love magic were sometimes called as witnesses against their clerical and lower-class collaborators, but not tried themselves. Thus Madonna Costanza Superechio, wife of a *cittadino modenese*, testified against the priest whom she had induced to baptise a magnet for her use in thwarting her husband's extramarital affairs; the priest was tried on these charges, but she was not. Contra Don Gian Battista, ASM, *Inquisizione*, busta 8, 1584. .

62. Johann Weyer, *De Praestigiis Daemonum*, Book VI, Chapter 21 (Amsterdam, 1660), passage cited by H.C. Lea, *Materials Towards a History of Witchcraft* (3 vols, Thomas Yoseloff, New York, 1957), vol. 3, pp. 1073-4; Paolo Sarpi, *Historia della Sacra Inquisitione* (Fabbio Albicocco, Serravalle, 1638), p. 63.

63. A summary of the contents of the *Instructio* is given by Lea, *Materials Towards a History of Witchcraft*, vol. 2, pp. 950-66.

64. John A. Tedeschi, 'The Roman Inquisition and Witchcraft: An Early Seventeenth Century *Instruction* on Correct Trial Procedure', *Revue de l'histoire des religions, 200,* fasc. 2 (April-June 1983), p. 185.,

65. The *Instructio* was first published in the 1625 edition of the Inquisitorial manual from which this quotation is taken; Eliseo Masini, *Sacro Arsenale overo Prattica dell'Officio della S. Inquisitione ampliata* (Corbelletti, Rome, 1639), p. 178, Tedeschi, 'Roman Inquisition', discusses the publishing history of the *Instructio* and the controversy surrounding its authorship.

66. For example, the trial of Basilio Brasigella, ASM, *Inquisizione*, busta 3, 1560.

67. The fusion of these concepts is described by Peters, *The Magician, the Witch and the Law*. The attack on popular magic in the Hapsburg lands is discussed by R.J.W. Evans, *The Making of the Hapsburg Monarchy* (Clarendon Press, Oxford, 1979), pp. 381-418.

68. Contra Eugenia Claveria, ASM, *Inquisizione*, busta 10, 1599.

# 6

# Popular Culture and the Shaping of Popular Heresy in Renaissance Venice

*John Martin*

In Reformation studies, social history is altering the landscape of scholarly debate. Until recently, the most familiar markers were confessional, with Catholics attacking and Protestants defending the great reformers. Now, however, with even this most religious of fields largely secularised, the great divide lies between social and intellectual historians. It is not clear which camp holds the higher ground, though both would like to claim it.

In general, the social historians view religion as a collective phenomenon and downplay the importance of cultural and intellectual matters. To them, the Reformation was much more than a reflection of the ideals of its intellectual proponents; far more decisive was the fact that early modern Europe itself was in transition. The new religious ideas took hold, they argue, because individuals and groups stood in new relationships to one another; thus these scholars explore the development of the Reformation in the light of transformations in the workplace, geographic mobility, economic status and family life. To paraphrase Marx, people must find their own salvation but not necessarily under circumstances of their own choosing. Social change underlay the religious revolutions of the sixteenth century.[1]

To intellectual historians, by contrast, it is high culture and grand ideas that were decisive. They too make a convincing case. We need to understand the beliefs and assumptions of the prominent figures of the period, to glean what we can of the character of their dreams and the quality of their inner lives, and to try to comprehend the nature of their education — in sum, to know as much as possible about the interplay of those cultural forces that led them to think about religious issues in new ways. As one Reformation scholar has recently argued, in response to some of the more exaggerated claims of social historians, 'the ideological forces that moved the age of Reformation were also the work of generations of intellectuals and reformers, trained theologians and educated laymen, who spoke to an informed laity unusually sensitive to the societal consequences of religious issues'.[2]

Ironically — despite this debate between social and intellectual historians — both sides are united by their elitism and exclusiveness. With few exceptions, problems of intellectual and cultural history have been explored only in relationship to humanists, preachers and political leaders. Only rarely do they probe the cultural and intellectual worlds of either urban artisans and workers or the peasantry. The loss is enormous. We overlook the inner lives, the dreams, the cultural values and the traditions of the overwhelming majority of those men and women who lived in the age of the Reformation.

This essay is an effort to examine some aspects of the cultural life of artisans and shopkeepers in sixteenth-century Europe. As such, it seeks to contribute to an understanding of the ways popular cultural traditions acted to stimulate and to sustain many of the new religious ideas of Reformation Italy. The artisans in question were Venetians. Even to Renaissance and Reformation scholars, their story is virtually unknown. But it is possible to discover a great deal about them from the records of the Roman Inquisition or *Sant'Uffizio* established in Venice in 1547. As one of Europe's leading entrepôts, with commercial ties not only to the East but also to Germany, France, England and the Lowlands, Venice was especially susceptible — or so it seemed — to heretical ideas. The papacy especially worried that this city might serve as the door through which the Reformation would enter Italy, and its pressure was necessary before Venice, independent by tradition in religious affairs, agreed to co-operate with the pope on even such a grave matter as heresy. None the less, once the Doge and his councillors were convinced that the new religious movements could threaten the stability of the state, they permitted the creation of such a tribunal, though they insisted that three Venetian laymen, chosen from the highest ranks of the nobility, serve as *assistenti* alongside its three clerical judges (the papal nuncio, the local inquisitor and the Venetian patriarch). The intensity of the Inquisition's vigilance varied, as both its personnel and, more decisively, the political climate changed. In comparison with tribunals in other Catholic states, the Venetian Inquisition was not particularly harsh, though (if we include all classes as well as those cases brought to its attention on appeal from the *terra firma* and the city's overseas dominions) it did bring over 1,500 individuals to trial in the second half of the sixteenth century and imposed the death penalty on some two dozen.[3]

Until the mid-1580s, when the preoccupations of the inquisitors shifted to witchcraft and other superstitious practices, the majority of those accused were perceived as proponents of what scholars of the Italian Reformation have called evangelism — a movement with many affinities to the Protestantism of the reformers Luther, Zwingli and Calvin. Evangelism touched all levels of Venetian society, from the very poor to the very rich, though, in absolute numbers, artisans and shopkeepers predominated. But many of the heretics, and these were almost exclusively artisans, were anabaptists, heirs of the religious radicalism generated during the peasant uprisings in the Trentino in the mid-1520s. And, finally, among the heretics were a number of millenarians — again largely shopkeepers and artisans — who, drawing on the apocalyptic writings of the twelfth-century Cistercian Joachim of Fiore, longed for religious unity in a world deeply divided by confessional issues and religious warfare.[4]

Despite this diversity, however, a common thread ran throughout the popular heresies of the city. The artisan heretics were united in their struggle to preserve their dignity in a world that increasingly disparaged and vilified manual workers. The Venetian jeweller and poet Alessandro Caravia, an evangelical, was perhaps the most eloquent spokesman of their common concern. His work was informed by a desire for a simpler and more egalitarian world. What disturbed him most was the excessive pride of those around him. 'Everyone attends to his own good,' he wrote in his *Il sogno dil Caravia*, 'not caring a bit for his neighbour.' He deplored the lack of charity, the unequal distribution of wealth — *le mal partite divitie* — the arrogance of the leaders of the city's great confraternities, the *Scuole Grandi*, the divisions which tore at Christendom from within; and he called for a return to the simplicity of the Gospels, reminding his readers of the humility of Christ, that all had been created equal — a fact of which death was a constant reminder — and in the image of God. This stress on equality in particular served as a critique of the harsh inequalities of Counter Reformation Venice.[5]

Other works echoed Caravia. This was the case with the *Beneficio di Cristo*, the most widely read treatise of the Italian Reform, with a catchism prepared by the Venetian Franciscan and heretic Bartolomeo Fonzio, and, finally, with the writing of Celio Secondo Curione, one of the intellectual leaders of the Italian Reform, a humanist who, taking issue with those who disparaged or vilified the mechanical arts, protested that 'smiths, cobblers, weavers, tailors and cultivators of the land are honourable and useful for the common life'.[6]

Venetian cobblers, silk-weavers, tailors, printers, jewellers and others freely entered into religious discussion. They believed that they could discuss such matters as capably and as deeply as the priests. From the heresy trials we are able to hear their voices. 'God', the silk-weaver Girolamo da Luca insisted, 'has not made one higher than another', adding that it would be best to send the pope and the priests and friars off as galley-slaves.[7] Nor was this a benign anticlericalism, as the testimony of Battista Amai, an itinerant mercer and enameller who spent much of his time at Rialto, Venice's commercial centre, illustrates. Battista made social justice a salient aspect of his emphasis. To a fellow artisan who argued that it was better to be patient with things as they were, he had pointed to the enormous discrepancies in wealth which characterised his society. 'Our lords are dogs!' he protested, adding, 'cardinals have 40,000 to 50,000 ducats of income; they keep mules, dogs, whores; and they do not give alms as they should. The heretics are better, more charitable, because they love one another, and keep things in common.'[8] And the apothecary Piero della Luna was equally emphatic. 'Friars and priests', he argued, 'are like those nobles who deceive their peasants [in an age, it must be remembered, when the poor were likely to eat far coarser cereals than the rich] by telling them that those who eat bread made from wheat will wind up in Hell, for they, too, make what is good appear bad.'[9] Those who refused to pray directly to Christ, the butcher's apprentice Zuane Grison held, failed to see their own merit.[10]

But what was it about the artisans' experience that made it possible for them — in the midst of the Counter Reformation with its stress on hierarchy — to imagine a more egalitarian world? To some degree, there was doubtless a memory of the more egalitarian political arrangements of late medieval Venice. But the heresy trials suggest another dimension. They reveal a rich cultural life which was itself independent, a life which was often focused on the tavern or the inn, which was expressed in games, in rituals, and in Carnival, providing both a refuge from a society in which hierarchy was increasingly valued and a set of structures and expressions which provided alternative ways of seeing the world — resources for developing a critique of 'official' culture and values.

The tavern was a literal haven of unhampered discussion in the Counter Reformation. A meeting place for strangers, it was also a meeting place for ideas. In 1549 an oar-maker named Piero reported a conversation at an inn in Cadore the previous year. Several artisans from Cividale who had business there arrived at the *osteria* and one of them, a certain Prospero, felt the freedom to assert 'that the true body of Christ is not in the consecrated host'.[11] And several years later, the boatman Stefano De Ongari recalled a similar event in the Brianza. Again it was an individual on business, a coal-porter, who had spoken out with a forceful evangelism. 'Christ has suffered for us and has saved us from the hands of the devil', concluding — and this was where the heretical implications of his proclamation lay — that all ceremonies were therefore superfluous to salvation.[12]

The tavern, in part, served as a refuge from the church. It was at once its antipode and its mirror-image. Both the Aquila Nera and the Leon Bianco, inns near the Rialto, were continual sources of preoccupation to the authorities, not only because of their largely German clientele but also because it was precisely within such settings as these that ideas were easily exchanged.[13] One morning in 1549, for example, at the Fosseta Tavern, when a friar urged a group of men who were eating together to come to mass, a boatman refused, asserting, 'what mass could be more beautiful than that of our sharing a meal at this table?' In 1569, a carder — originally from Modena, but who had lived in Venice since the mid-1550s — admitted he maintained contact with Modenese heretics and noted that their conversations had taken place in an *osteria* near the fish market at Rialto.[14] The Bolognese Antonio Canossi, in his testimony before the Modenese inquisitor, left a particularly vivid description of how conversion in a tavern could spill over into religious matters. 'Four years ago in Modena,' he testified

It was summer, I was in a tavern . . . A fellow called messere Cathaldo would come there on feast days. I don't know his surname, but he is a silk-weaver. . . . And once I had come to know this Cathaldo, we came to discuss various matters and finally we began to discuss religion and very soon I realised that this Cathaldo held 'lutheran' opinions and he realised I did, and because of this, we became the closest of friends, and this Cathaldo told me how in this city of Modena there were many good Christians [by which he meant of the 'lutheran' sect] but that they went about with caution and in secret in order to avoid being accused.[15]

Games, too, would provide a structure for encounters among religious allies or between proselytizers and possible converts. In the early 1580s, for example, a vagabond priest disturbed the authorities with his chess games by which — at least from the perspective of his accusers — he was able to lure the unsuspecting into religious conversation.[16] Chess was frequently played in the apothecary at the Due Colombini, a major gathering place for the Venetian evangelicals.[17] And the mere presence of a regular spot for playing chess and cards in the shop of a certain bookman named Vicenzo appears to have raised suspicions. One witness, asked whether Vicenzo held heretical views, asserted, 'I know nothing of his house, but in his shop . . . he has a certain little place where they play chess and various persons go there for tarots.'[18] For in the shop, as in the tavern, artisans could meet together for discussions which were virtually impossible to regulate.

At Carnival, games and the world of the tavern came together. This time was exceedingly important in Venice, and it was marked by activities in which all classes participated in a cycle of festivities ranging from the sophisticated staging of classical and contemporary comedies to the ritual slaughter of a bull and the Rabelaisian celebration of the figure of Carnival himself, acted out by a fat man, with a vat of macaroni at his side. Moreover, despite the increasing efforts of the city's magistracies to repress the excesses of the season and to bring the festivities more and more under the control of the patriciate, Carnival flourished throughout the century. In 1533, one report reads, a group of *popolani* dressed themselves as lords, with some imitating commanders and others trumpeting as though theirs was an official procession.[19] And a heresy trial from 1571 nicely illustrates how popular and patrician dimensions of Carnival could coexist. The case stemmed from a denunciation against a young nobleman and a young lawyer who, wearing clerical vestments, had been overly boisterous in their mocking of Catholic rituals the night of Giovedì Grasso. The testimony from the trial is rich and makes it plain that Venice was filled that night with festive, indeed libidinous and even violent activities, in which the popular classes were fully involved. A certain Antonio di Piero, jeweller at the Papagallo, admitted to having masqueraded as a buffoon, and he was only part of a company that included a carpenter's apprentice, two gunners from the Arsenal, and a merchant — all in costume.[20] The festivity, moreover, with its motifs of social inversion and its mocking of social and religious hierarchy, clearly provided a positive resource for the heretics. Thus, in his poem *Il sogno dil Caravia*, Alessandro Caravia assigned a central role to the Venetian buffoon Zanpolo Liompardi who, in his representations of an intermediary between this world and the next, had been popular with crowds at Carnival throughout the early sixteenth century. In the poem, Caravia has Zanpolo return as an emissary of evangelism, curiously blending the ideas of the moderate reformers with the Carnival tradition.[21]

Finally, the very atmosphere of the artisan's shop, intimate, even secretive, was ideal for religious discussion. And much religious discussion there was. Tomasso Garzoni, for example, in his encyclopaedic *La piazza universale di tutte le professioni del mondo*, first printed in Venice in 1585, observed that cobblers were especially inclined to such discussion. Of these, he noted, 'they are as Christian as anyone else, except when they argue about Scripture — an activity that belongs in the mouth of a cobbler about as much as a cap on the head of an ass'.[22] In a 1548 trial of a sizable group of artisan heretics, for the most part residents of the parish of San Moisè, the gatherings in their shops emerge as a distinguishing feature of their evangelism. Speaking of these heretics, one witness, a butcher, noted that they 'meet now at the shop of maestro Girolamo, now at that of Zuanjacomo the swordsmith'.[23] Another witness was more specific. 'I have seen some of them meet together in the Piazza for discussion and I have seen the turner Jacopo and his son Bernardo meeting at the shop of maestro Girolamo who reads to them from a book.'[24]

The most striking aspect of the culture of the artisan heretics, however, was that it was a literate one — hungrily so. There was an appetite for religious works. The book entered the shop in sixteenth-century Venice. In part, this was the ideal of some of the leading reformers. But the very atmosphere of the shops also encouraged readings, for the artisans of the elite crafts and trades were, by and large, citizens of the *respublica litterarum*. Very few were not literate, in the absolute sense of not being able to read at all.

In general, the Venetian artisans appear to have been much like their contemporaries and counterparts in Lyons, among whom, as the historian Natalie Davis has shown, literacy was not 'distributed evenly'; rather it was, not surprisingly, most diffused among these occupations which required the greatest skills — among apothecaries, for example, printers, musicians, metalworkers.[25] Patterns in which levels of literacy varied from one social group to another were common in early modern Europe, and, indeed, there is some evidence, albeit impressionistic, that this was the case in Venice also.[26] But if literacy was not evenly distributed throughout the population, it is none the less clear that it was on the rise. The Venetian patrician and political philosopher Giovanni Maria Memmo encouraged artisans to learn to read, and in his book of trades Tomasso Garzoni noted that printing itself had made books accessible to the poor.[27] The historian Carlo Cipolla has compiled statistics which seem to prove that this impression of a rapidly growing literacy rate was accurate.[28] In Venice, therefore, as in the French cities of Lyons and Montpellier, the culture of the book could set a man apart from his neighbours, his fellow workers and even his family on religious matters.[29]

But even those few who were unable to read appreciated the nearly magical power of the book. Franceschina, the wife of a silk-weaver, had her husband's apprentice read to her and her spouse from the Bible on Sunday mornings.[30] Alberto da Gesuy, a sword-smith, who resided in Bergamo, when asked by the inquisitors if he could read, responded that he was unable, but added, 'I wish to God that I could!'[31] And the anabaptist Valerio, a Venetian dyer, explained how a friend, upon learning that he could not read, bought him a copy of the *New Testament* and urged him to learn to do so.[32] Thus, those on the margins of literacy hoped to or actually managed to find ways to penetrate the world of books. By contrast, Francesco Cagnolo, an *ormesiner* or silk-weaver, argued that his inability to read was evidence that he was *not* a heretic. When asked if he knew why he had been arrested, he responded that he had no idea, adding, 'I am not a heretic, because I have no letters, if I have said anything, I have said it *semplicemente*, and it will never be shown that I am a heretic.'[33] The problem is thus not simply to establish a correlation between literacy and heresy; rather it is to attempt to grasp the relationship of the book to other aspects of artisan culture. For it is clear that the book did not supplant their traditions and culture but supplemented them. Reading and the discussion of texts was a frequent, almost a distinguishing activity of the heretics. Reading aloud, furthermore, served to bridge the gap between those who could and those who could not make their way through a complex text.

Because the world of the elite artisans of Venice was a literate one, the book did serve as an avenue by which the ideas of such reformers as Luther and Calvin reached them. But the Venetian heretics were by no means the passive recipients of such ideas. In their shops and in their taverns, they enjoyed a cultural life which itself gave shape to their heresies and which sanctified the artisans and their work, blurring the distinction between manual and intellectual labour. Indeed, the activity and beliefs of the heretics repeatedly undermined the distinctions which the Counter Reformation sought to impose. The heretics refused to recognise feast days, fasts, and the authority of priests. They ostentatiously declined to remove their caps when a religious procession passed their shops, mocked those who appealed to saints, and turned their backs to the altar during mass. Holiness, their traditions led them to believe, was to be found with God's people, not in the external arrangements or pomp of a particular society.

In his *Popular Culture in Early Modern Europe*, Peter Burke has observed that Catholic reformers, much like their Protestant counterparts, were preoccupied with the reform of popular culture. Such noted prelates as Gian Matteo Giberti, the bishop of Verona, Gabriele Paleotti, the bishop of Bologna, and Carlo Borromeo, the revered archbishop of Milan, spoke out against the tavern, against a variety of games, and against Carnival. Their reasons for doing so were complex. They believed they saw too many remnants of pagan antiquity in Carnival, for example; and in games and in taverns, they believed there were too few incentives to piety, too many to licence. But the recurrent association of heresy with popular customs and activities in the records of the Venetian *Sant'Uffizio* suggests yet another dimension.[34]

The vitality of popular culture, it seems, appears to have played a role in making it possible for the Venetian artisans — despite the increasingly hierarchical character of sixteenth-century Italian society — to imagine a more egalitarian world. To some degree, such imagination was possible because artisan culture, at its very heart, was one in which experience was of value. Unlike his modern counterpart, the factory worker, the pre-industrial artisan remembered and felt some continuity with his past.[35]

But memory was not enough. The cultural dimensions of the city as expressed in gaming, in Carnival, and in tavern life also made a critique of sixteenth-century institutions and ceremonies possible. These cultural dimensions had quite specific functions. First, each provided a temporal and, at times, even a physical space in which craftsmen and shopkeepers could stand outside the received structures and hierarchies of early modern society. It is precisely by such a suspension of the quotidian and the routine, the anthropologist Victor Turner has argued, that human beings have been able to generate novelty.[36] But there were other functions as well. These dimensions of artisan culture also involved a suspension of status concerns and, in the case of Carnival, led to status- and role-reversals. And, finally, these dimensions provided an opportunity for 'novel' conversations, either by creating an atmosphere of trust among strangers in a tavern or over a board game or card game, or by providing symbols (such as those of Carnival) which invited participants to imagine the world in a new way.

While the evidence from Venice is fragmentary, it none the less suggests that when a sixteenth-century artisan embraced reformed ideas, he did so more easily when the cultural world in which he was most intimately engaged served to call the established order into question. There is little question that literacy (both in the sense of reading and in the sense of the active discussion of texts) was an important factor in leading many Venetian craftsmen to heresy. But it is clear that popular cultural traditions (the games and the rituals, the life of the tavern, and, of course, Carnival) mattered a great deal. As I have shown, such traditions acted to sustain, even to shape the popular urban heresies of the sixteenth century.

Despite the vitality of the popular cultural traditions, however, the heretical movements of Venice never took a firm hold within the fabric of the city. The confident and rather visible conventicles of heretics of mid-century gradually gave way in the 1560s and 1570s to an increasingly fragmented and diffident movement. By the 1580s, most of the heretics brought before the *Sant'Uffizio* were isolated individuals, with no connections to a larger dissident community. At the end of the sixteenth century, heresy no longer constituted a social and political problem. An occasional individual might stray from the teachings of the Roman Catholic Church, and be so denounced, but Venice and the Venetians had reaffirmed Catholicism.

To a large degree, the repressive measures of the Inquisition, preoccupied with heresy for some 40 years, had acted to check and, finally, to uproot the heretical movements in Venice. But there were deeper forces, cultural and political, at work as well. Heresy, after all, had little chance of surviving in a society that, in its political, social and religious life, came to place more and more emphasis on hierarchy. This emphasis was expressed in a myriad of ways, but especially in the growing number of civic processions which punctuated the ritual calendar of the city, in the increasing control by the elites of the larger urban confraternities, and, finally, in the continual assertion of Counter Reformation values from both the pulpit and the press.[37] In the middle years of the sixteenth century, the prevalence of heresy suggests a popular cultural world that was somewhat autonomous. But historians should take care not to exaggerate the autonomy of popular culture. Power shapes cultural as well as social relationships. And in Venice, at least at the end of the sixteenth century, the popular world had been brought under the sway of the Counter Reformation. Lent had triumphed in the city of Carnival.

# Notes

1. Much of the impetus for the social historical study of the Reformation can be traced to the classic essay of Lucien Febvre 'The Origins of the French Reformation: A Badly-Put Question?', in L. Febvre, *A New Kind of History*, ed. Peter Burke and trans. K. Folka (Harper & Row, New York, 1973), pp. 44 to 107 (the essay originally appeared in *Revue historique* in 1929), and, more recently, to Bernd Moeller, 'Imperial Cities and the Reformation', in B. Moeller, *Imperial Cities and the Reformation*, ed. and trans. H.C. Erik Midelfort and Mark U. Edwards, Jr. (Fortress Press, Philadelphia, 1972), pp. 41-114. Representative studies include Robert Scribner, 'Civic Unity and the Reformation in Erfutt', *Past and Present, 66* (1975), pp. 29-60; Gerald Strauss, *Nuremberg in the Sixteenth Century* (Indiana University Press, Bloomington, Ind., 1976); Thomas A. Brady, Jr, *Ruling Class, Regime, and Reformation at Strasbourg, 1520-1550* (E.J. Brill, Leiden, 1978); and Natalie Zemon Davis, *Society and Culture in Early Modern France* (Stanford University Press, Stanford, Calif., 1975). For Italy, Federico Chabod, *Lo stato e la vita religiosa a Milano nell'epoca di Carlo V* (Einaudi, Turin, 1971) is suggestive. The paraphrase is of Marx's assertion that 'men make their own history, but they do not make it just as they please; they do not make it under circumstances chosen by themselves, but under circumstances directly found, given and transmitted from the past', in K. Marx, 'The Eighteenth Brumaire of Louis Bonaparte', in Robert C. Tucker (ed.), *The Marx-Engels Reader* (W.W. Norton, New York, 1972), p. 437.

2. Steven Ozment, 'The Social History of the Reformation: What Can We Learn from Pamphlets', in Hans Joachim Kohler (ed.), *Flugschriften als Massenmedium der Reformationszeit* (Klett-Cotta, Stuttgart, 1981), p. 172. My remarks are by no means meant to detract from the importance of either the traditional intellectual and political histories of the period or the new work of the social historians. Rather they are meant to suggest the necessity of an expansive and inclusive concept of culture for the analysis of religious experience.

3. Two recent works have greatly enhanced our knowledge of the establishment of the *Sant'Uffizio* in Venice: Paul Grendler, *The Roman Inquisition and the Venetian Press* (Princeton University Press, Princeton, NJ, 1977), pp. 35-62, and Brian Pullan, *The Jews of Europe and the Inquisition of Venice* (Basil Blackwell, Oxford, 1983), pp. 3-142. On the relative clemency of the Venetian Inquisition, see the statistical table in Geoffry Parker, 'Some Recent Work on the Inquisition in Spain and Italy',

*Journal of Modern History, 54* (1982), p. 526.

4. The classic work on the Italian heresies remains Delio Cantimori, *Gli eretici italiani* (Sansoni, Florence, 1939). More specialised studies, however, should be consulted. On evangelism, see Eva-Marie Jung, 'On the Nature of Evangelism in Sixteenth Century Italy', *Journal of the History of Ideas, 14* (1953), pp. 511-27, and Karl Benrath, *Geschichte der Reformation in Venedig (Verein für Reformationsgeschichte*, Halle, 1887). On anabaptists in Venice and the Veneto, see Aldo Stella, *Dall'Anabattismo al Socinianismo nel Cinquecento veneto: ricerche storiche* (Liviana Editrice, Padua, 1967), as well as his *Anabattismo e antitrinitarismo in Italia nel XVI secolo: nuove ricerche storiche* (Liviana Editrice, Padua, 1969), and Carlo Ginzburg, *I Costituti di don Peitro Manelfi* (Sansoni, Florence, 1970). On millennarians in sixteenth-century Venice, there is no comprehensive study, but see Carlo Ginzburg, 'Due not sul profetismo cinquecentesco', *Rivista storica italiana, 78* (1966), pp. 184-227.

5. Alessandro Caravia, *Il sogno dil Caravia* Giovanni (Antonio di Nicolini da Sabbio, Venice, 1541), A ii r especially and *passim*.

6. The best modern edition of the *Beneficio di Cristo* is now Salvatore Caponetto (ed.), *Il Beneficio di Cristo con le versioni del secolo XVI documenti e testimonianze* (Sansoni, Florence, 1972). The Catechism of Fonzio, *Istruttione fanciulesca cerca le cose della religione* has been edited by Achille Oliviere, 'Il "Cathecismo" e la "Fidei et doctrine . . . ratio" de Bartolomeo Fonzio, eretico veneziano del Cinquecento', *Studi veneziani, 9* (1979), pp. 360-8. Curione's assertion 'che utili sono et honorevoli alla vita comune, come sono de' sarti, de' agricoltori et de' altri simili' is from his *Della Christiana creanza de figlioli* (Basel, 1545), cited in Cantimore, *Eretici*, p. 105.

7. 'dio no ha fatto un più grande dell'altro', Archivio di Stato di Venezia (hereafter ASVen), *Sant'Uffizio*, busta 17, dossier, 'Girolamo de Luca', testimony of 11 February 1561.

8. ASVen, *Sant'Uffizio*, busta 33, dossier 'C. Prosperum Capellarium et Battista dalle Bambine', testimony of 25 September 1572. On the translation of *lutherano* as heretic, see Elisabeth Gleason, 'Sixteenth Century Italian Interpretation of Luther', *Archiv für Reformationsgeschichte, 60* (1969), p. 167.

9. 'i frati et preti sono alla condition di Nobeli, che ingannono i villani con dir che'l pan de formento dhe'l manzava andeva a Ca del Diavolo cosi anca lor ne mostra che'l ben sia mal', ASVen, *Sant'Uffizio*, busta 40, dossier 'Contra Petrum a luna aromatorium et al', testimony of 13 March 1576.

10. On Zuane, see the testimony of one of the witnesses in ASVen, *Sant'Uffizio*, busta 45, dossier, 'Giovanni Grison', testimony of 16 March 1579.

11. ASVen, *Sant'Uffizio*, busta 7, dossier, 'Prospero Battilana di Belluno', testimony of 6 July 1549.

12. Ibid., busta 12, dossier, 'Stefano De Ongari', testimony of 28 May 1555. The Brianza is a region immediately to the south of Lake Como.

13. On the Aquila Nera and the Leon Bianco, see A. Stella, *Chiesa e Stato nelle relazioni dei nunzi pontifici a Venezia: Ricerche sul giurisdizionalismo veneziano del XVI al XVIII secolo* (Biblioteca Apostolica Vaticana, Vatican, 1964), p. 279.

14. For the assertion of the boatman: 'Lui dissi che piu bella messa è di quella che femo nui qui a tavola,' ASVen, *Sant'Uffizio*, busta 7,

dossier, 'Domenico Canaruol e Antonio da Chioza', testimony of 4 January 1550. On the carder from Modena, ibid., busta 20, dossier 'Paolo Gaiano', testimony of 29 October 1569.

15. Cited in Antonio Rotondò, 'Atteggiamenti della vita morale italiana del Cinquecento. La pratica nicodemitica', *Rivista storica italiana, 79* (1967), p. 1012.

16. ASVen, *Sant'Uffizio*, busta 48, dossier 'Lorenzo Busnardo', denunciation of 9 December 1580.

17. ASVen, *Sant'Uffizio*, busta 20, dossier 'Contra Jo: Baptistam aromatarium duarum columbarum', testimony of 22 May 1565.

18. ASVen, *Sant'Uffizio*, busta 28, dossier 'Vicenzo', testimony of 14 March 1570.

19. Edward Muir, *Civic Ritual in Renaissance Venice* (Princeton University Press, Princeton, NJ, 1980), p. 176. Muir provides an illuminating overview of Carnival festivities, judiciously emphasising the efforts of the state to control the celebrations. See ibid., pp. 156-81.

20. ASVen, *Sant'Uffizio*, busta 30, dossier 'Contra Jacobum Georgium et Zachariam Lombardini', *passim*.

21. Caravia, *Il sogno*. On Zanpolo Liompardi, see Carlo Ginzberg, *The Cheese and the Worms*, trans. John and Anne Tedeschi (Johns Hopkins University Press, Baltimore, Md, 1980), pp. 22-5.

22. Tommaso Garzoni, *La piazza universale di tutte le professioni del mondo* (Gio. Battista Somascho, Venice, 1589), p. 824.

23. ASVen, *Sant'Uffizio*, busta 7, dossier 'Contra denuntiatos pro hereticis de contracta Sancti Moysis', testimony of 14 October 1548.

24. Ibid., also testimony of 14 October 1548.

25. Davis, *Society and Culture*, p. 210.

26. On patterns of literacy in Europe in general, see, for England, Lawrence Stone, 'Literacy and Education in England, 1640-1900', *Past and Present, 42* (1969),m pp. 69-139; for France, François Furet and Wladimir Sachs, 'La croissance de l'alphabétisation en France, XVIIIe et XIXe siècle', *Annales: économies, sociétés, civilisations, 29* (1974), pp. 714-37. On illiteracy among Venetian naval officers and the general suggestion that literacy rates in Venice varied with social status, see Carlo Cipolla, *Literacy and Development in the West* (Penguin Books, Harmondsworth, 1969), pp. 22-3.

27. Giovanni Maria Memmo, *Dialogo . . . nel quale dopo alcune filosofiche dispua un perfetto Prencipe, & una perfetta Republica, e parimente un Senatore, un soldato, et un mercante* (Gabriel Giolito, Venice, 1563), pp. 122-3. Garzoni, *La piazza universale*, p. 833. Garzoni is here drawing directly on a passage of Leonardo Fioravanti's. See L. Fioravanti, *Dello specchio di scientia universale* (Vicenzo Valgrisi, Venice, 1564), p. 61v.

28. Cipolla, *Literacy and Development*, pp. 22-3 and 57-8.

29. For Lyons, Davis, *Society and Culture*, p. 210.

30. ASVen, *Sant'Uffizio*, busta 7, dossier 'Contra Franceschinam uxorem Joannis samitarij', testimony of 18 September 1548.

31. Ibid., busta 15, dossier 'Costituto de Alberto Spader milanese', testimony of 3 December 1560.

32. Ibid., busta 22, dossier 'Odorico Marosells, Valerio Perosin et al.', testimony of 8 March 1567.

33. Ibid., busta 24, dossier 'Contra Francescum Cagnono', testimony of 10 July 1568.

34. Peter Burke, *Popular Culture in Early Modern Europe* (Harper & Row, New York, 1978), pp. 207-22.

35. For an insight and discussion of memory and its role in artisan culture, see Walter Benjamin, 'The Storyteller' and 'On Some Motifs in Baudelavie', *Illuminations*, trans. Harry Zohn (Schocken Books, New York, 1969), pp. 83-109 and 155-94.

36. Victor Turner, *The Ritual Process: Structure and Anti-Structure* (Cornell University Press, Ithaca, NY, 1977), p. vii.

37. On the civic processions and rituals of Venice, see Edward Muir, *Civic Ritual*, as well as his 'Images of Power: Art and Pagentry in Renaissance Venice', *American Historical Review, 84* (1979), pp. 16-52. For the confraternities in Venice and their role in reinforcing hierarchy and protecting Catholic piety, see Brian Pullan, *Rich and Poor in Renaissance Venice: The Social Institutions of a Catholic State* (Harvard University Press, Cambridge, Mass., 1971). For a survey of popular culture in Early Modern Europe, see Burke, *Popular Culture*. Burke's work has the strength of demonstrating the degree to which early modern popular culture was subject to the control of both political elites and privileged reforms — control which was heightened by both the Protestant Reformation and the Tridentine Reforms.

# 7

# The Inquisition and Popular Culture in New Castile

*Jean-Pierre DeDieu*

## A Specialised judicial instrument

The Inquisition was an institution designed especially for the pursuit of heresy. Its judges always represented themselves as defending the purity of the faith against the 'heretical depravity' that had estranged certain individuals from correct doctrine as defined by the Roman Catholic Church; a form of erroneous thinking capable of calling into question and thus endangering the established order of the world. The gravity of the danger dictated the need for the exemplary punishment of the guilty, however little they might have persisted in their heretical activities, by the purifying fire of the stake. It also imposed the adoption of forms of judicial procedure which, without doing excessive violence to the common law of the period, at least pushed to their extremes some of its harshest provisions, such as the secret imprisonment of the accused and, especially, the refusal to identify the witness for the prosecution. It was this latter provision, above all, that was shocking even to contemporary observers because it introduced a radical inequality into the judicial duel by severely handicapping the defence.

We would expect to find, therefore, among the victims of the Spanish Inquisition, representatives of all the heterodox groups that we know existed in the Iberian peninsula at that time: Judaisers, who had been baptised Christian but had become Jews again; Mohammedans, officially baptised but crossing over to Islam; Protestants; representatives of more or less marginal tendencies running through the church from the sixteenth to the eighteenth centuries (e.g. Jansenists, Quietists, Illuminists, etc.), as well as the witches and wizards who were among the favourite victims of the medieval Inquisition. In short, we should find minority groups easy to identify, clearly separated from the church and marginal in some way. These categories, which we call offences of the first order, were

well represented in the activity of the Holy Office during the early
modern period. But they were not the only ones. Taking the survey
that Jaime Contreras carried out for all the cases judged by the Holy
Office in the entire country between 1540 and 1700, these crimes
represent less than 40 per cent of its activity.[1] I myself have carried
out a similar but more detailed study for the tribunal of Toledo
(Table 7.1).[2]

**Table 7.1:** *Inquisition of Toledo, 1483-1700*

|           | Major crimes | Other crimes | Total   |
| --------- | ------------ | ------------ | ------- |
| 1483-1530 | 2,020        | 220          | 2,240   |
|           | 90%          | 10%          | 100%    |
| 1531-1560 | 860          | 3,665        | 4,525   |
|           | 19%          | 81%          | 100%    |
| 1561-1614 | 750          | 1,750        | 2,500   |
|           | 30%          | 70%          | 100%    |
| 1615-1700 | 960          | 1,040        | 2,000   |
|           | 48%          | 52%          | 100%    |
| 1701-1820 | 150          | 450          | 600     |
|           | 25%          | 75%          | 100%    |
| Total     | 4,740        | 7,125        | 11,865  |
|           | 40%          | 60%          | 100%    |

Let us examine more closely these 'other crimes' shown in the
table. Here we are concerned with cases involving blasphemers,
bigamists, astrologers, fortune-tellers, persons who claimed to see
visions, and priests who, during confession, 'solicited' from their
penitents sexual acts forbidden by the sixth commandment. The
Inquisition also found it necessary to repress frivolous statements
about the faith made by ordinary persons who had never dreamed
of cutting themselves off from the church, acts of resistance to the
Holy Office which were more often the expression of rivalry between competitive judicial institutions than any fundamental hostility
to the Inquisition, and the use of Catholic prayers for superstitious
purposes. In addition to these offences, the inquisitors of Barcelona,
Valencia and Zaragoza prosecuted both homosexuality and bestiality. Here we find ourselves far removed from formal heresy, since
these are offences that could be committed by anyone without any
intention of leaving the bosom of the church.

Juan Cabellero a heretic? Let us listen as he explains his situation:

It was said that even though one of my sisters had married

without the family's consent, our mother was going to make her the heir to all her property. I then declared in anger that I would give to the devil the Ave Maria that I would have recited for her after her death. On another occasion, I said that I would as soon believe the Pope as believe my mother-in-law.[3]

The witnesses confirm that there was not much else. At the very most, he had spoken of the Pope in stronger terms than he admitted at the trial.

A heretic, this young doctor, denounced to the Holy Office in that same year of 1567?

One day, I don't remember exactly how long ago, I went out to an inn situated in the plaza de Argamisilla in Alba to visit a patient who had a deep wound in his skull. At the entrance people came to ask how he was getting on; and I told them that according to the usual rules of medicine he should have been dead but that God is all-powerful. Then the sick man's mother, whose name I don't remember except that she is also the owner of the inn, arrived and I said to her 'Be calm, why are you crying now? What more does God have to give than he has already given?'[4]

This was a proverb, said by way of consolation. But in sound doctrine, God could give no greater gift to mankind than his son Jesus, and this gift had already been made.

The inquisitors themselves did not believe that they were dealing with heresy in these cases. Certainly, the prosecuting attorney had no difficulty in demonstrating that these words were not orthodox. He could always find some heretical sect, medieval or modern, which had upheld similar positions, and we can see swarming under under his busy pen Arians, Hussites and Lutherans; but that was his job. He had to make it appear that these people were heretics if he wanted to prosecute them at all, since, officially, heresy was the only crime that the Holy Office could punish. But those involved in the proceedings, frequently including the accused himself, were well aware that it was nothing but a game, a juridical artifice.

The way in which these cases were conducted is sufficient to demonstrate this. First of all, the sentences. Leaving aside cases of homosexuality, bestiality or bigamy, where the penalties were harsh, but in which the Inquisition was content to apply laws already established, the harshest sentences were largely reserved for the major crimes. As evidence, the record of the Toledo tribunal shows that Judaisers, Protestants and Mohammedans, in proportions that varied widely according to the period, were practically the only ones sentenced to the stake. Examples to the contrary are extremely rare and can be attributed to truly exceptional crimes. One such example is the case of one Benito Ferrer who, in the middle of mass, trampled underfoot a consecrated host that he had torn from the hands of the priest moments before. In 1624 he was executed in Madrid on the site where the sacrilege had been committed. The Inquisitor-General himself had followed the case closely and organised a public *auto-de-fe* especially for this accused. That alone should suffice to demonstrate the peculiar character of this case. Equally reserved for the punishment of major crimes was the sentence of reconciliation, involving confiscation of property, a period of imprisonment and service in the galleys, which, after 1560, was systematically applied to Protestants, Mohammedans and bigamists (in accordance with the ordinary criminal code), but very rarely to Judaisers.[5]

For minor offenders, everything could be resolved by the payment of a fine which was rarely very high and generally proportionate to the culprit's resources. If he could not pay he would receive 100 or 200 lashes administered by the public hangman, during which the victim made a tour of the city mounted on an ass. This was combined with a public penance on Sunday at high mass, when the culprit, in shirt-sleeves, would solemnly renounce all forms of heresy before the assembled members of the congregation. Let us be clearly understood: we are by no means dealing here with token punishments, but there is nevertheless a considerable distance between the punishment meted out to minor offenders and that reserved for heretics.

The judicial procedure folowed in these cases (Figure 7.1) is no less novel. The image of the inquisitorial system presented by traditional historiography, of course, is that of a terrible machine designed to pulverise the human spirit, invented in the Middle Ages, perfected by the instructions of Inquisitors-General Torquemada and Valdés, reduced to a formula by legal practitioners and frequently described by historians. All the stages of the trial occurred in an unchanging order but spread over a varying period of time, sometimes years, while the accused languished in gloomy dungeons, isolated from the world. This is a valid image, as far as major crimes are concerned.

On the other hand, let us follow the trials of some minor delinquents, like one Pedro López, a poor shepherd passing through

**Figure 7.1:** *The inquisitorial trial*

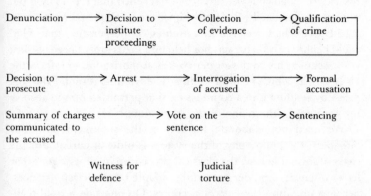

Denunciation ——→ Decision to ——→ Collection ——→ Qualification
institute          of evidence        of crime
proceedings

Decision to ——→ Arrest ——→ Interrogation ——→ Formal
prosecute                    of accused          accusation

Summary of charges ——→ Vote on the ——→ Sentencing
communicated to          sentence
the accused

Witness for        Judicial
defence            torture

Toledo on his way to Madrid. In 1567 he was denounced for having maintained that frequenting houses of prostitution did not constitute a sin. He was arrested the following day and the inquisitors immediately began examining the witnesses in the case. On 29 October, less than two weeks after his incarceration, he was given the formal accusation. On 9 November he was given provisional liberty and he remained free until 10 June 1568, the day when he returned to prison. This can be explained by the fact that there was an *auto-de-fe* scheduled for the thirteenth of June and his appearance at it was expected. A digest of testimony by prosecution witnesses was given to him, and, as expected, the accused, who had already confessed, did not think that it was necessary to present any witnesses for the defence. He participated in the *auto-de-fe*, and on the fourteenth, he was forbidden to reside in Toledo for five years and then released.[6] However, this was a relatively heavy-handed way of dealing with such a case. Pedro de Moratalla, a blind beggar and composer of prayers, declared that he would be prepared to write one, if necessary, against the saints and the Virgin. He was arrested by the *Hermandad* (rural militia), acting of its own accord, and brought to the Inquisition along with his case file. The inquisitors confirmed his arrest and carried on the case until the accusation, and then, without going any further, released the prisoner in June 1670 after giving him a severe reprimand.[7] Another minor offender was Catalina Zapata who came to Inquisitor Soto Salazar, who was carrying out a visitation to the region of Alcalá de Henares in 1564, to denounce herself for having said 'You did not see me in misery in this world and you will not see me suffer in the other' — another proverb with Judaic connotations. She was admonished in the same place and sentenced to fast for two Fridays and recite four rosaries the following week.[8] It even happened that the accused did not appear personally. Believing himself to be on the point of death, José Peñuela had declared in a moment of desperation that 'God could neither pardon his sins nor help him in his urgent need.' Seized with scruples, his confessor demanded authorisation to inform the Holy Office, which he did by letter. The tribunal responded to the priest by sending him a commission that permitted him to absolve his penitent in the name of the inquisitors.[9]

We need not elaborate further on the treatment of minor offenders; the philosophy of the system is quite apparent. For the cases of formal heresy, the classical procedure in all its rigour. For lesser offences, a milder procedure, adapted to the circumstances, perhaps imitating the episcopal courts. On one side a rigid technique that would serve for serious and complicated cases, those that would guarantee the reputation of the tribunal as the terrible and inflexible guardian of the faith. On the other, an extraordinarily subtle juridical instrument which permitted the tribunal to cash in on its prestige and reach the great mass of Castilians by treating, rapidly and effectively, a large number of cases of little real importance in an environment ready to receive its message.

We have to understand that the tribunal's interest in cases of secondary importance was not constant. These cases were largely ignored during the first 50 years of its history and only make a regular appearance around 1530, mainly for financial reasons. Let us return to the example of Toledo. At first this court lived mainly from the property it had confiscated from persons convicted of Judaising. But the *converso* community was skimmed very quickly. The primary material, if I may use the expression, had become depleted. Thus, in order to survive, the Holy Office was forced to hunt in the territory of the episcopal courts and compete with them in trying offences that until then had fallen to them by right: the lesser forms of magic, blasphemy, and unfortunate statements of little gravity concerning the Catholic faith. Furthermore, this reinforcement was quite welcome during a time when the clergy of the region, far in advance of the rest of Europe, discovered the need to take the faithful firmly in hand in accordance with the norms of the church hierarchy.

In the middle of the century, the tribunal lived off a multitude of small fines. But it lived poorly and the financial crisis had become permanent. Moreover, the judges wore themselves out in making tours of inspection because it was necessary to seek out these minor offenders in their villages without waiting for them to come to Toledo. This was what impeded the prosecution of more important crimes. This practice may have appeared dangerous around 1555 when, for the first time in many years, a serious threat to the faith was discovered right in the Iberian peninsula, the Protestants. A middle way needed to be found. This was the work of Inquisitor-General Valdés. On the one hand, he assured the tribunals revenues that were stable and independent of their activity by endowing them with the income from a certain number of canonries. On the other hand, he issued instructions ordering them to reduce the role of cases of secondary importance within their overall activity. In this connection, it is noteworthy that from about 1560-5 the inquisitors were careful to choose from the stream of denunciations those which suited their policy of the moment. The Inquisition was no longer constrained to judge every case in order to survive. It was now a matter of conducting propaganda campaigns on particular points in support of the general interests of the church.[10]

## Blasphemy, sexuality and sorcery

### Blasphemy

The Inquisition of Toledo judged hundreds, perhaps thousands, of blasphemers. It prosecuted them with the same franchise as the episcopal courts or lay tribunals, and without cherishing too many illusions about either the efficacy of its actions or the seriousness of the offence. One inquisitor, who was then judging several dozen such cases every month, wrote to his superiors that 'everyone here seems to be a good christian', while another commented disdainfully on 'some blasphemies and unfortunate words of vile and lowly persons'. The cases were almost always expedited using the most summary procedure, except in the case of hardened offenders like Esteban Gómez who, recently enlisted in the army, terrorised the people with whom he was lodging by studding his conversation with profanity and appeals to the devil. Even so, he was only given a fine and three months of preventive detention.[11]

In the middle of the sixteenth century, blasphemy became the great resource of the tribunal, coming to represent fully one half of its cases. It was also the great victim of the Valdés reforms; its place in the overall activity of the Holy Office declined significantly from 1560. The representatives of other jurisdictions could hardly have appreciated the Inquisition's encroachment on their traditional areas of competence when the accusation of heresy was so difficult to sustain. In Castile, blasphemy was ritualised, stereotyped and the product of very specific circumstances: quarrels, gambling, or violent emotion. In short, it constituted a linguistic custom that did not involve the religious faith of the person who uttered it. Moreover, in its formulation, it presents very particular characteristics that appear to distinguish it from what may be found in the other Mediterranean countries: significantly less scatological, it is more intellectual, centred more on the idea of faith, of belief. We have drawn up a list of the most frequently punished expressions of the sixteenth century: 'I deny God if . . . ', 'I deny the holy oil that was used to baptise me if . . . ', 'I do not believe in God if . . . ', 'I speak more truthfully than God / than the evangelists . . . ' The conditional nature of most of these is noteworthy, as is the fact that the blasphemy most used in Spain today, 'I shit on God / the Holy Sacrament', does not appear in the list. I have not found any mention of it in the papers of the Inquisition until the middle of the seventeenth century, and it only takes on real importance, little by little, during the course of the eighteenth century. I believe that its emergence indicates a profound evolution in religious attitudes.

Finally, it does not appear that the Inquisition exercised a significant influence in this field, nor that it sought to have one. Blasphemy, without doubt, constituted a vein to exploit, hardly more.

## Simple fornication

For a long time, historians have observed that during the second half of the sixteenth century a large part of the activity of the Inquisition of Toledo was occupied by a very special offence: what the judges called 'simple fornication'.[12] In the first place we have to understand that we are dealing with a crime of opinion. In the crown of Castile, acts of this sort were punished, when they could be, by secular (homosexuality) or ecclesiastical (concubinage, incest) tribunals. The Inquisition itself judged bigamists (the majority of those divorced and re-married in our own day would fall into this category), but that is not what concerns us here. In the language of the judges, 'simple fornication' was the opinion that it was not a mortal sin to have sexual relations with a woman other than one's wife, and, many would add, providing that she was paid. In practice, this brings us back to prostitution and this is confirmed by analysing the circumstances in which the majority of these propositions were uttered.

A brief digression is necessary here in order to place this idea in its proper context. The details of popular conceptions of what constituted normal sexual life in central Spain during the middle of the sixteenth century are virtually unknown. Nevertheless, we are in a position to summarise its broad outlines from the masculine point of view. (1) Only heterosexual relations were permitted. (2) A woman did not have the right to have sexual relations with anyone but her husband. If she did, she would seriously compromise her honour and the honour of her family if she was single, and her husband's honour if she was married. Consequently, it was a very serious matter for a man to take her. A young man who, outside of marriage, deflowered a young girl was, at least in principle, liable to be sentenced to serve in the galleys, and, in practice, obliged to marry her or give her a substantial sum by way of compensation, even if everything indicated that the 'victim' had consented. (3) Certain women, however, through their behaviour, departed from the norm and fell into the category of professionals, of prostitutes; from then on, having sexual relations with them no longer called the family honour into question. Now they merely sold a service by a purely commercial contract and the weighty matter was not consorting with them but failing to pay them. (4) Men had the right to satisfy their physiological needs; and not only single men but married men as well under certain circumstances. As a consequence, prostitution, which was recognised as fulfilling a clearly defined social function, was organised and officially tolerated, with houses of prostitution generally belonging to the municipality.

Certainly, prostitution was not considered an honourable profession, but it was neither rejected nor hidden, and consorting with professional prostitutes caused no moral blemish. Travel accounts compared the merits of the different houses of prostitution in exactly the same way as a guidebook of our own day would weigh those of fine restaurants or luxury hotels. A considerable part of the male population of New Castile felt that there was nothing reprehensible in prostitution even in the eyes of God. Moreover, there was a half-serious, half-joking little story in circulation on this subject according to which St Peter went into a tavern to purchase some wine. As he was taking a long time, Christ went in after him and found him making love to the proprietress. 'What are you doing there Peter?', Christ asked. 'Lord, I am multiplying,' Peter called. 'Do it and then come,' Christ replied.[13]

The church deplored this state of affairs but was powerless to do anything about it. After the Council of Trent, a situation like this could not continue. It was precisely from then on that ways were sought to change theory into fact. Moreover, the Holy Fathers at Trent insisted on the necessity of better control of sexual life and marriage, areas which had largely escaped the clergy until that time. Little by little the atmosphere began to change, to the point that in 1623 the King of Spain, Philip IV, decided to close all the illicit houses in the Kingdom. No doubt the measure had little practical effect but it reveals a new sensitivity: from then on prostitution was considered a national scourge.

This is the context in which one has to place the activity of the Holy Office against 'simple fornication'. The analysis of the curves of activity of the Toledo tribunal shows us the evidence. Before 1560, there are only a few isolated cases: when a guilty person was found he was brought to trial, but these cases were not searched out systematically. Then everything changed (Table 7.2). After the period

**Table 7.2:** *'Simple fornication' in the activity of the Inquisition of Toledo*

|  | Number of cases | Percentage of total activity |
| --- | --- | --- |
| 1561–1570 | 94 | 14.4 |
| 1571–1580 | 106 | 22.4 |
| 1581–1590 | 120 | 33.5 |
| 1591–1600 | 26 | 8.1 |
| 1601–1610 | 57 | 16.9 |
| 1611–1620 | 34 | 12.9 |
| 1621–1630 | 9 | 4.0 |
| 1631–1640 | 4 | 1.3 |

of high activity we again get only isolated cases, most often judged according to an extremely summary procedure. Evidently, we are in the presence of a deliberate and organised propaganda campaign. If we are in any doubt, a brief examination of the situation of other tribunals would certainly remove it: the curves are almost parallel. There was even a decision made by the Council of the Inquisition dated 20 November 1574 that ordered (although with a certain delay since the Toledo Inquisition had already become involved in these cases) the generalising of operations against this offence and making it a part of the edict of faith. It would be an interesting but difficult task to be able to judge the results. The curve of cases, which clearly responded to broader inquisitorial concerns, can serve as little more than an indicator to that end. But a sociological analysis of the accused allows us to make some useful observations. Before 1570 and after 1600 there are many foreigners and the majority of those accused are not natives of the region. At the beginning this is understandable because the tribunal, still unsure of the juridical basis of its activity, preferred attacking those living on the fringes of society. At the end these reasons no longer applied, because between 1570 and 1590 it was local people, most often the young but sometimes also well-established members of local society, that suffered the weight of repression. Can we assume that, around 1600, the inquisitors of Toledo had succeeded in convincing the permanent population that fornication outside of marriage was indeed a sin?

A qualitative analysis of the case files allows us seriously to entertain such a hypothesis. At the start of the campaign, it is easy to imagine the atonishment of the accused when they realised that what to them had always seemed acceptable was, in reality, something monstrous, a heresy capable of bringing them before the tribunal responsible for judging the Jews, Moors and Protestants that everyone detested, capable of putting them in the same class with persons that everyone rejected with horror. In those early years, moreover, the future accused believed himself to be in a position of strength. During the following years, the situation was reversed and it was now the delinquent who found himself isolated and subject to a social dynamic that overwhelmed him. Let us listen to a deposition made on 6 June 1575 by Juan Hernández Duque the elder before his village commissioner.

The witness declared that he believed that he had been summoned to tesify about certain statements that García Ruiz had made which seemed to him to run counter to what the parish priest had said in a sermon fifteen or twenty days ago. In effect, he had declared that their Honours the Inquisitors of Toledo had ordered all the parish priests in the district of Santa Olalla to admonish their parishioners in such a way that no one could pretend ignorance that having relations with a woman other than one's own legitimate wife was a mortal sin, and that to maintain the opposite view was heresy. Now on Friday the 14th of May, when García Ruiz and Diego Gómez were shearing their sheep at the witness's house, they spoke with his son, Juan Hernández Duque the younger. García Ruiz said 'Do you know that I had sex with a woman that I met on the road? And then she said,

"Sweetie, would you give me something to eat?" ' And García Ruiz promised her some eggs and fish and gave her a coin because he had made love with her. And he stated that, for a man, it was not a sin to make love to a woman even if she was a prostitute. Then his friends Diego Gómez and Sancho de Rojas the elder who were there, admonished him and told him to shut up because that was heresy. And the other continued to insist that if one paid it was not a sin. Everyone there stared at him and continued to reproach him, saying: 'Shut up: it was a great sin, didn't you hear the priest?' Diego Gómez said, 'May the devil take you. With the wife you have why are you looking for another woman?' And García Ruiz replied, saying 'Leave me in peace, I had a good time with her!' Then he said to this witness's son, 'Don't look so sad, sell one of your father's sheep and find another like her.' At this the said Juan Hernández Duque the younger replied: 'Go to the Devil, you and your filth.'[14]

It was Sancho de Rojas who made the case known to his son, the village priest and commissioner of the Holy Office.

We have not yet referred to a feature frequently mentioned in the testimony: the *auto-de-fe*. As a matter of fact, the inquisitors had systematically taken care to make certain individuals accused of 'simple fornication' appear there. This is what most strongly impressed public opinion, to the extent that one might well ask if the principal goal of the case was, more than the punishment of the accused, the preparation of a 'platform' for the *auto-de-fe*. Whatever it was, it seems that in the villages and towns, at least, under the combined action of the clergy (the case files often mention the action of a confessor) and the Holy Office, 'simple fornication' and heresy were linked. To be sure, one continued visiting prostitutes, but with a less easy conscience and taking the teachings of the church on this matter much more seriously.

## Sorcery

Three or four years ago, one of my daughters was sick. She was suffering from a facial paralysis. Certain women, whose names I no longer remember, advised her to consult Lucía de Toledo, a *morisco* who lived in this village, who would certainly cure her. I called that person, who came to my daughter's house and examined her in my presence. She said that her illness had come upon her because she had angered a spirit, that the spirit had made her ill in revenge and that in order to calm it it was necessary to fumigate the house, that the person who carried this out had to say: 'I was blind not to see you; pardon me so that God will pardon you.'

Item, my son-in-law became ill. His mother and my daughter, thinking that he had been bewitched, decided to send for Lucía de Toledo so that she could examine him. She said that she would do whatever they asked if they paid her, that she would tell what was wrong and that she would cure him. After examining the patient, she said that he had been enchanted and that it was necessary for her to have something that had been in contact with his body. She was given the patient's belt or kerchief. She then fumigated the said Juan López and took away the belt or kerchief. She claimed that in her house she would recite incantations over them. I gave her flour and other things.[15]

This is what Inés Gonzalez, the wife of a wealthy peasant of Damiel in La Mancha, told Inquisitor Yanes in 1538 when he was visiting the town. She was not the only one to denounce Lucía de Toledo. A good 30 witnesses presented themselves to tell how she had cured the impotence of one and menaced the harvest of another; how, using magic, she had reconciled husband and wife, and attracted the lover to the house of his mistress. While reading this case, we also learn that within a radius of 20km there were half a dozen such women who carried on similar activities, and quasi-professionals, and that the clients went from one to the other in accordance with circumstances and moods. Everything suggests that the Damiel region was far from exceptional and that similar occurrences happened everywhere.

During two particular periods, and following a rhythm that we are beginning to become quite accustomed to, the Toledo Inquisition dealt severely with these women and the men (rare) who imitated them. To begin with, during the first half of the sixteenth century, these cases arose as a result of chance discoveries. Lucía de Toledo was first of all prosecuted as a Mohammedan, and the denunciations that we have against her for magic are nothing more than a by-product of this fundamental accusation. Others were arrested on the complaint of dissatisfied clients, so many of them that they seem to have often been prompted to carry out some form of extortion. The penalties were mild: several months of exile, fines and some strokes with the lash. Once again the Inquisition had encroached on an area that was not part of its jurisdiction and there were protests, since traditionally these crimes were the province of the secular and ecclesiastical courts. As a consequence, from the period of the Valdés reforms the Holy Office abandoned this sphere of activity: not only were there practically no cases for 30 years but the text of juridical consultations which has come down to us clearly concluded that the Holy Office should not occupy itself with such cases.

At the very end of the century, however, the great jurist Castillo de Bobadilla held that the Inquisition could judge these cases when there was suspicion of heresy.[16] By the bull *Coeli et terrae* (1585), Pope Sixtus V revived the repression of these practices and sounded the alarm against the inconsidered use of astrology. As in the case of 'simple fornication', the Holy Office mounted a campaign to control public opinion. Cases were considered to fall under suspicion of heresy when there had been an 'explicit or implicit pact with the devil', an elastic concept by grace of the word 'implicit'. The curve of activity rose once again and care was taken to endow the punishment of guilty individuals with a certain gravity. Once again, priests were ordered to preach on this subject and the crime was included in the edict of faith.

In the middle of the seventeenth century, the excitation declined somewhat but until the end, magicians and sorceresses formed an important part of the tribunal's clientele, so much so that Goya, in one of his famous drawings, could leave us visual evidence of the tour of a village on the back of a mule made by one of the last of the condemned. Punishments were as mild as before. It does not appear, judging by the frequency of these cases in the eighteenth century and by the way in which the Inquisition believed it necessary to deal with them, that this approach had very much success. Perhaps — although we lack specialised studies — it succeeded in marginalising these practices and in detaching the elite from them to some extent: at first priests are found rather frequently among the accused. But, even on this point, what we know of the customs of the Spanish royal court at the end of the seventeenth century does not give us much cause for optimism.

It is important to guard against confusing this petty magic, which is in fact a technique for revealing the future, telling fortunes, finding lost objects and attracting lovers, with the grand sorcery of the Sabbath with the appearance and collective adoration of the devil, black mass, orgies and the automatic occurrence of natural disasters. The Spanish language makes plain the difference between *hechicería* (enchantment), the first type, and *brujería* (witchcraft or sorcery), the second. It appears that the latter had been almost unknown outside the northern third of the Iberian peninsula. In fact, in Toledo I have not found more than a half dozen cases all told, all of them situated in the zone that marks the northern limit of the district.[17] It is also worth noting that unlike the medieval Inquisition, the Spanish Inquisition always showed considerable reticence with regard to this offence. It did not deny the theoretical possibility but considered that most of the persons who claimed to have participated in a Sabbath were, in fact, victims of hallucinations. Consequently, it felt that the less one mentioned that subject the better. As to the penalties, naturally it refused to burn the accused because that would mean admitting the reality of the thing of which they were accused. This is an old policy already clearly formulated in the first half of the sixteenth century, even though it was not until the beginning of the seventeenth century that it became official doctrine after an investigation carried out by *licenciado* Salazar y Frías into an epidemic of witchcraft in the Basque region.[18] The Toledo Inquisition completely accepted this line of conduct. Punishment handed down for those accused of *brujería* by the tribunal were similar to those for *hechicería*.

## Conclusion

Every judicial action, every sentence handed down by a court of law, contains a message directed at the wider society. If this is true of all courts it is even more so in the case of the Inquisition. Francisco Peña made this point in his 1578 edition of Nicolau Eymerich's classic *Manuel de los inquisidores* when he said that 'we must remember that the primary goal of the trial and the condemnation to death is not to save the soul of the accused but to contribute to the public good and intimidate the multitude'. One could, therefore, conceive of the institution as a gigantic teaching machine. It would doubtless be an exaggeration to reduce it only to this, but considering it in that way does throw into sharp relief a central aspect of the Inquisition's labours, since by issuing a condemnation it not only sought the punishment of a single individual but aimed at informing, warning and immunising the mass of the faithful. It was communicated by the *auto-de-fe*, where each sentence was an example, and through reading the edict of faith. It was relayed by preaching. It was communicated once again by a simple reference to the Holy

Office on the part of a priest or a private individual: the tribunal enjoyed such immense prestige that everything it marked with its seal acquired enormous consequence.

This message was varied in content and yet limited to a relatively restricted number of themes. I have been able to do no more than examine some of them here: placing the population on guard against the use of magic, instruction on matters of doctrine relating to sexuality. To complete the list I could have spoken of the campaign against the idea that marriage was superior to celibacy, of the way in which Spain was vaccinated against Protestantism, or of the repression directed against bigamy — although as to this last point I am not sure that the repressive aspect did not impose itself over the pedagogic. I could also have concerned myself with the many 'propositions' of little importance that occasioned so many mild sentences, but it would have been difficult for me to have found, running through these, the connecting thread of a coherent message.

In fact, two ideas underlay all this effort at education: that outside of the Roman Catholic Church, its clergy and hierarchy, there could be no salvation and that religion was a serious matter. Faith and confidence in God were not in themselves sufficient: ignorance, negligence in informing oneself, and the refusal to understand the demands of the church, were things worthy of condemnation in the same way as doctrinal error. It is not possible to give any other meaning to cases brought against wretched people for matters that the judges themselves considered trifles.

On each particular issue the results were unequal but, overall, the two fundamental lessons appear to have been well assimilated. But we must not give the credit to the Inquisition alone. Some comments are in order here. From the start we established that the Holy Office was not the only institution that attempted to mould popular thinking. It was no more than a single piece in a much larger apparatus that included preaching, confession, the Catechism, ecclesiastical courts and, to a certain degree, lay tribunals as well. When we come to evaluate the results it is sometimes difficult to know what is attributable to one and what to the other. We must also point out that during the classical period there were 15 inquisitorial tribunals spread throughout Spain. Our study has been based essentially on that of Toledo but not all of them operated on such a grand scale. There were some, such as the one in Valencia, which were so occupied with the more important type of case that they hardly had the leisure to concern themselves with Old Christians. There was also a problem of geography. In order to exert control over the Peninsula, each tribunal covered a district that was anything from 30,000 to 90,000 square km in size and where the population could be more than 1.5 million. How did it disseminate its message? Only a maximum of a few tens of thousands of people could have attended the *autos-de-fe* and these were largely the same people drawn from the population of the chief city of the district where these spectacles were held. And during the eighteenth century these ceremonies became more and more rare. Certainly, the Inquisition could make use of a network of agents to relay its ideas, essentially the commissioners, and to some degree the parish priests. But how did this network function? We must admit that we know virtually nothing about this. Finally, there is the question of chronology; the impact of the Holy Office on the thousands of communities that made up early modern Spain must have varied considerably. For the moment, we are once again compelled to admit our ignorance.

## Notes

1. Jaime Contreras, 'Las causas de fe de la inquisición española, 1540-1700; Análisis de una estadistica', paper presented at the Interdisciplinary Symposium on the Medieval and Modern Inquisition (Copenhagen, 5-9 September 1978).

2. Jean Pierre Dedieu, 'Les causes de foi de l'inquisition de Tolédo, 1483-1820', *Mélanges de la Casa de Velázquez*, 14, (1978), pp. 143-71.

3. Archivo Histórico Nacional (hereafter AHN), *Inquisición*, leg. 202, exp. 6.

4. AHN *Inquisición* leg. 211, exp. 33.

5. Universitäts- und Landesbibliotek Sachsen-Anhalt (Halle), Yc 17-2Ä, Bd 10.

6. AHN, *Inquisición*, leg. 72, exp. 34.

7. Ibid., leg. 42, exp. 11.

8. Ibid., leg. 211, exp. 29.

9. Ibid., leg. 43, exp. 33.

10. In the limited space available I cannot fully demonstrate all of this. I can only summarise briefly the main conclusions of the monograph that I am writing on the subject.

11. AHN, *Inquisición*, leg. 36/21.

12. Henry Charles Lea, 'Die Inquisition von Toledo (1575-1610)', *Zeitschrift für Kirchengeschichte*, 14, (1893), pp. 192-201.

13. An example: AHN, *Inquisición*, leg. 209, exp. 15.

14. Ibid., leg. 74, exp. 22.

15. Ibid., leg. 198, exp. 3. FÄ, 7VÄ-8RÄ.

16. Jeronimo Castillo de Bobadilla, *Política para corregidores* (2nd edn, 2 vols, C. Lasso & F. García, Medina del Campo, 1608), vol. 2, p. 74.

17. AHN, *Inquisición*, leg. 95, exp. 7; leg. 200, exp. 20; leg. 91, exp. 1; etc.

18. Gustav Henningsen, *The Witches' Advocate* (University of Nevada Press, Reno, Nev., 1980).

# 8

# Beatas and the Inquisition in Early Modern Seville

*Mary Elizabeth Perry*

By midnight on 27 February 1627, people began lining the streets of Seville to await a procession of penitents that Inquisition officials would lead the next morning to an *auto-de-fe*. No other seventeenth-century *auto* had attracted such attention in this major port city of early modern Spain. According to one record, so many people crowded the streets that Inquisition officials had 'great difficulty' moving their 14 penitents through the throngs that surged from the prison of the Inquisition to the Convent of San Pablo.[1] Although the ceremony lasted until late afternoon, hundreds of people remained in their places along the streets all day, hoping for one more glimpse of those penanced by the Inquisition. They waited, in particular, to see two penitents: Catalina de Jesús, a *beata* and the leader of a local sect, and Juan de Villapando, the priest who was her foremost disciple.[2]

As a beata, Catalina de Jesús enjoyed a special status. She wore a Carmelite habit, but she did not follow the rule of any religious order. While she had taken a vow of chastity, promising her life to God, she had not vowed obedience or poverty. She taught and wrote, preached and prophesied. Unfortunately, none of her writings can be found, and most of the evidence about her comes through the records of the Holy Office in Seville. Although subject to a certain amount of distortion, these records show how the Inquisition viewed her and others who had adopted the life of the beata.[3]

Most historians have dismissed Catalina de Jesús and other beatas as weak and hysterical women, but archival evidence indicates that they exercised considerable influence in the sixteenth and early seventeenth centuries.[4] A memorial in the Inquisition records reported that nearly 700 people in Seville and thirty nearby villages obeyed the directives of Catalina de Jesús.[5] Her followers believed that God spoke to her in visions and ecstasies. They venerated her life of holiness and gave her the reverential title, 'Madre'. When they met her in a church or on the street, they knelt to kiss her hand. They told stories of her miracles, such as the conversion of a young rake when he merely touched the hem of her garment. Followers distributed relics from her hair and clothing, particularly prizing pieces from a veil that she had worn some 14 years earlier when the Inquisition had first imprisoned her. Many cherished portraits of her that were inscribed 'Santa Catalina'.[6]

The Inquisition became increasingly concerned about the influence of beatas such as Madre Catalina. Table 8.1 shows that the Holy Office in Seville prosecuted only one beata before 1609, but several in the first two decades of the seventeenth century. The trials of these women represent an official attempt to curb popular religious leaders.[7] More than simply the case of an official institution opposing 'the people', however, these proceedings included hundreds of witnesses who gave testimony against beatas as well as in support of them. Some people undoubtedly supported the Inquisition out of fear of a powerful institution, but others gave testimony against beatas that appeared to express class antagonisms.[8]

Sexual ideology provides another explanation for the success of the Inquisition in winning popular support for its prosecution of beatas. In assuming powerful leadership roles, these women had disrupted the traditional pattern of relations between the sexes. If the tumult of the Counter Reformation empowered them for a time, it did not permanently transform gender roles.[9] Their freedom from the customary constraints of gender provoked resentments and fears that prompted some of the witnesses who denounced them before the Holy Office. Prosecution by the Holy Office, therefore, served to reintegrate the beatas into the traditional gender order.

Anthropological theories may help to explain the significance of the clash between beatas and the Inquisition. Religion, according to Clifford Geertz, serves not merely to preserve beliefs and conserve a social order; it also acts as a dynamic cultural system that both motivates and justifies change.[10] People who believed that beatas could directly contact the spiritual source of all meaning infused these women with remarkable power that might have threatened traditional religious authority. Moving to neutralise the beatas, the Church and Inquisition used community rituals that transformed them from a symbol of holiness into one of illusion and deceit.

Four centuries before Catalina de Jesús met the Inquisition, beatas had appeared in historical records that portrayed them as a diverse

**Table 8.1:** *Beatas appearing before the tribunal of the Holy Office, Seville, 1480-1650*

| Year | Beata | Source | Charges and verdict |
| --- | --- | --- | --- |
| 1559 | María de Borborques | AHN, *Inq.* 2075 no. 4 | Lutheran heresy. Relaxed, burned |
| 1609 | Bàrbara Beata, Madre Resident of Seville | AHN, *Inq.* 2075, no. 19 | Led ecstatic prayer meetings of women. Case suspended |
| 1609 | María Beata Resident of Utrera | AHN, *Inq.* 2075, no. 19 | Implicated in religious enthusiasms. Case suspended |
| 1609 | María Ximenez Resident of Moron | AHN, *Inq.* 2075, no. 19 | Implicated with Bàrbara Beata. Case suspended |
| 1609 | Ynes de Jesús Resident of Xerez | AHN, *Inq.* 2075, no. 19 | Prophecies, revelations. Case suspended |
| 1612 | Juana de la Cruz 20 years old Resident of Seville | AHN, *Inq.* 2075, no. 22 | False ecstasies. *Alumbrado* heresies. Recant *de levi*, 4 years reclusion |
| 1612 | Catalina de Jesús, Madre 47 years old Resident of Seville | AHN, *Inq.* 2075, no. 22 | False ecstasies. *Alumbrado* heresies. Case suspended |
| 1622 | As above | AHN, *Inq.* 2962, Letters | Imprisoned for *Alumbrado* heresies. Penanced 1627, 6 years reclusion |
| 1623 | Bárbara de Jesús 30 years old Resident of Cadiz | AHN, *Inq.* 2075, no. 31 | False ecstasies, heresy of Free Spirit. Recant *de levi*, 2 years reclusion |
| 1623 | Catalina de Jesús 30 years old Native of Xerez | AHN, *Inq.* 2075, no. 31 | False visions, heresy of Free Spirit. Recant *de levi*, 2 years reclusion |
| 1623 | Mariana de Jesús, Madre Resident of Seville Native of Aguilar | AHN, *Inq.* 2075, no. 31 | False visions, *Alumbrado* heresies. Recant *de levi*, 4 years reclusion, exile |
| 1624 | Antonio de S. Francisco 30 years old Resident of Xerez | AHN, *Inq.* 2075, no. 31 | False revelations, *Alumbrado* heresies. Public *auto*, warning |
| 1624 | María de Jesús 36 years old Resident of Seville | AMS, Sección Especial, Tomo 20 en folio | False revelations and stigmata. Public *auto* |
| 1645 | María de la Concepción Resident of Mairena | AHN, *Inq.* 2061, no. 12 | False prophecies, creating uproar. Verdict unknown |

*Notes:* AHN = Archivo Histórico Nacional; AMS = Archivo Municipal de Sevilla.

group of women who took a private vow of chastity and dedicated their lives to prayer and good works.[11] They resembled the Third Orders of devout lay people established by Franciscans and Dominicans in the thirteenth century, as well as the beguines and beghards who flourished for a time in the German states, the Low Countries and northern France.[12]

In Seville beatas had lived together 'since time immemorial', as one sixteenth-century historian wrote.[13] They usually wore religious habits and retreated into private houses. Because they did not have chapels, chaplains or choirs, they favoured houses next to parish churches so that they could see the altar directly through a grill and hear mass without leaving the house. Three of these *emparedamientos*, or enclosed houses, remained in the sixteenth century: one attached to the Church of San Miguel, another to the Church of San Ildefonso, and the third to the Church of Santa Catalina.

A variety of women became beatas, according to early records. Some of these women had turned to religious life when they were widowed, while others, lacking a dowry for convent or marriage, became beatas as adolescents. Some beatas lived together, enclosed in the traditional *emparedamientos* or *beaterios*. Others joined a Third Order associated with a Franciscan or Augustinian monastery. Some lived in their own homes and supported family members.

The growing influence of these women appeared to parallel the rise of a larger religious movement in early modern Spain. *Recogimiento*, or looking into the self to seek God, flourished among the Franciscans in the 1480s and persisted through the sixteenth and seventeenth centuries.[14] The emphasis on internal spiritual experience attracted thousands of people who found customary religious observance sterile. Seeking a more meaningful religion, these people believed that human souls could attain union with God through spiritual exercises.

*Recogimiento* supported a certain 'feminisation' of religion during the early modern period. Its focus on the interior self undercut ecclesiastical hierarchies in which males predominated, substituting a form of spiritual egalitarianism in which women as well as men could reach union with God. Its concentration on experience displaced male-dominated theological learning with individual feeling, so that women became renowned for their 'familiar simplicity' in teaching the love of God.[15]

Many people in the movement to revitalise religion looked to women for spiritual inspiration. In the early sixteenth century leaders of the church and kingdom listened to the words of María de Santo Domingo, the 'beata of Piedrahita', who had many visions and ecstasies.[16] Later in the century, Teresa de Jesús demonstrated how one God-loving woman could reform an entire religious order. Perhaps in reaction against male priests who seemed unlikely intermediaries with God, people prayed to Mary, the mother of Jesus. The development of Mariolatry culminated in the early seventeenth century with the proclamation in Spain of the Immaculate Conception of Mary. Exalted as 'the most pure', she had become a symbol of purity which gave her a special status in the heavenly hierarchy.[17]

All beatas made a private vow of chastity, which provided independence from childbearing and could also increase their status as symbols of purity. Many in early modern Spain praised chastity as the highest state for a Christian. One monk who wrote a book about women declared that chastity originated in heaven. He said that God granted the gift of prophecy to the sibyls, virtuous women in the ancient world, as a reward for their chastity. This virtue, in his words, was 'the beauty that is most splendid in woman'.[18] Diego Pérez de Valdivia, a priest who wrote a handbook for beatas, called them 'the brides of Christ', a term often used for nuns.[19] He argued that chastity could strengthen women:

> Zeal for holy chastity and virginity makes a weak young woman or woman of whatever sort stronger than many men, and than the whole world, and than all hell; and when men see such extreme energy and force, they are afraid and jump back dismayed.[20]

The beata's status freed her from many worldly concerns. Because most of these women wore a simple habit, beatas did not have to spend time or money on costume or appearance. Diego Pérez advised them to wear simple, practical shoes, 'very honest, high and broad, not shiny, but all enclosed, so that in no way can part of the foot be seen'.[21] He said that they should wear natural-coloured woollen skirts 'more of necessity than of indulgence'. Of ruffs, gaiters, or hoopskirts, this priestly adviser exclaimed, 'God protect me! Did Jesus Christ our Lord your Spouse or the blessed Virgin wear either the one or the other?' Emphasising practicality, he told them to cut their hair every two months and cover it with a veil because long hair takes time to wash and comb.

Beatas could escape many material restrictions in a world that seemed increasingly conscious of wealth. Their voluntary poverty gave them a special status: it permitted them to devote themselves to the prayer and good works expected of them, and it associated them with a traditional Christian asceticism that many believed necessary to know God.[22] Appearing to be above worldly pride, beatas appealed to those who sought to preserve the tradition of holy poverty. Many of these people were wealthy, themselves, but they requested burial in the simple rough garment of a monk.[23]

Recruitment of beatas was aided by the fact that they did not have to have the dowry that marriage or convent required. As local industry and small-scale agriculture declined, contemporaries noted that economic dislocations made marriage more difficult.[24] Lacking enough wealth to give suitable marriage dowries, some fathers tried to place their daughters in convents. Entering a convent, however, also required a dowry. As money declined in value and as the silk-weaving that supported convents declined in this period, convents had to request larger dowries.[25] One of the reasons that beatas appeared in more Inquisition proceedings in the first two decades of the seventeenth century may simply be that more women became beatas as marriage and convent became less possible for them.

Mysticism provided an escape from many restrictions on the thought and behaviour of these women. Developing a personal relationship with God, beatas could completely avoid the ecclesiastical hierarchy. In contemplation and mental prayer, they could explore an interior world rich in possibilities of meaning and satisfaction. They entered trances, saw visions and received revelations. Sometimes they saw in purgatory people who had already died and wanted the living to pray for them. Others received revelations of divine justice awaiting the living. One beata, for example, allegedly reported seeing in a vision a certain pompous cleric sentenced to blow air through a trumpet eternally as punishment for his vanity.[26]

Religious enthusiasm appeared to justify unconventional behaviour. It explained the assertion of Catalina de Jesús that saying the rosary was nothing more than a ringing of cowbells.[27] Under the cover of religion, beatas could laugh, shriek and cry. They could read aloud from the Gospel in formal groups and interpret its meaning to others. They shared intimate experiences with males and other females, and they hugged and kissed them. One group of beatas danced so vigorously after mass that they lost their veils and fell into a heap with their legs uncovered. Filled with rapture, they sang to the Holy Sacrament, 'Oh, my little fat and round-faced one!'[28] A priest and beata who had neglected their liturgical duties excused themselves as 'drunk with the love of God'.[29] Such enthusiasm resembled that of St Francis and his followers who earlier became known as the 'minstrels of the Good Lord'.[30]

Beatas enjoyed more freedom of movement and expression than most women. The Council of Trent decreed in the later sixteenth century that nuns must live enclosed in convents.[31] Despite official efforts to subject beatas to enclosure or regulation, they did not have to vow obedience to a rule or person. In his book of advice for beatas, Diego Pérez recognised this freedom. He warned them against the dangers of wandering and talkative women, and he urged them to entrust themselves to a 'good master' and accept his counsel for their own mortification and perfection.[32] However, he left to each woman the choice of this master, and he acknowledged the difficulty of finding good masters. Some beatas formed congregations that promised obedience to particular male clerics, but their vow of obedience was voluntary.[33]

After the Council of Trent renewed the rule of enclosure for religious women, beatas provided the supportive and charitable work that became impossible for nuns. Resisting enclosure for a time, some beatas worked actively in the city. They received young girls rescued from procuresses who tried to sell them on the streets. When priests converted so many prostitutes that Magdalene houses had no more space to receive them, they took them to beatas who counselled them, gave them spiritual guidance, and saw that they were safely returned to husbands or parents, or placed as servants in respectable homes.[34]

In the women's prison of Seville beatas filled a salaried position. A Jesuit who worked in the Royal Prison of this city at the end of the sixteenth century wrote of a beata who acted as a warden for the women's prison.[35] The city government paid a salary to the beata who provided spiritual and physical healing in this office. Records show that Augustina de la Cruz, a beata and healer in the prison, was to receive 12,000 *maravedís* in salary in both 1636 and 1639.[36]

Even if they remained enclosed in their houses, beatas were able to carry on charitable work. In the village of Cuellar, for example, beatas administered an institution for poor women established in 1572. According to the terms of the will founding the convent of Franciscan Tertiaries, it was to care for 15 lay women under the direction of five beatas. One beata acted as *madre*, supervising all the women, while another beata, the *ministra*, directed the work and care of the lay women. The will granted an endowment that provided an annual income to support these women.[37]

The charitable and religious activities of beatas remained carefully confined. No document describes beatas out on the streets taking orphans from their adult exploiters, nor do records tell of beatas entering brothels to preach to prostitutes. The church protected the privilege to preach, and priests carefully avoided the word 'preach' by describing the work of the beatas as 'teaching' or giving inspirational talks. One beata observed this restriction so well, according to a Jesuit, that she merely 'indoctrinated' her converts and then called in Jesuits to give the actual homilies.[38] The clergy praised beatas who observed the boundaries of their social work and the restrictions on their power.

Beatas who became charismatic leaders broke these limits and established broader spheres of power. In Weberian terms, these women possessed charisma because they were able to enter states of holy ecstasy. They commanded the respect of people who accepted their claims that they were in direct communion with God. Disciples of Catalina de Jesús, for example, were said to venerate her words as 'oracles from Heaven'.[39] They believed that she was always in the presence of God and did not have to submit to human discipline. In some cases, she was reported to have said that a revelation from God promised punishment for certain people who did not obey her.[40]

Followers of Catalina de Jesús believed that God had sent her to reform the Third Orders of both males and females. Viewed as a spiritual successor to Teresa de Jesús, Catalina was believed to have a divine mission that placed her in authority over men as well as women. In this inversion of the usual gender positions, men listened to Catalina, obeyed her directives, and some even said they would sacrifice their lives for her. They published her revelations, which they said were as holy as those of the recently canonised Teresa.[41]

Catalina's claim that she had the gift of prophecy increased her influence and enabled her to grant power to others. She believed in predestination and asserted that she could look into the interior of people to see whether they would be blessed by God. One whom she identified as predestined to reach the summit of human perfection was Juan de Villapando, a cleric who became second in importance after Catalina herself among Seville's Alumbrados.[42]

Catalina's position of leadership did not shock contemporaries who recognised the long-time tradition that God often worked through common, lowly people, even women. Teresa de Jesús expressed this belief when she referred to herself as 'a dunghill' on which God had 'made a garden of flowers so sweet'.[43] In seventeenth-century Spain the acceptance of the teaching that Mary, the mother of Jesus, had been conceived without original sin revitalised the feeling that women could be the special instruments of God.[44]

Several factors worked to neutralise the influence and independence of beatas, however. A search for security prevented many women from transforming potential power into actual power. It is true that some beatas remained independent of any direction from the ecclesiastical hierarchy, but many others did not. Instead, they subjected themselves to priests and monks whom they believed to be 'good masters'. These women felt vulnerable outside an established hierarchy, and they chose security over independence, tradition over self-assertion.[45]

The economic decline of seventeenth-century Seville also reduced the independence of beatas by making them more vulnerable to economic pressure. Some of these women lived on the income from property they owned. In the sixteenth century a few lived in comparative wealth, such as the beata who purchased a liturgical ornament for 7,480 *maravedís*.[46] However, the economic base of these women crumbled as prices rose, property rents fell, and money became devalued.

Beatas without individual property suffered even greater economic misfortune. The silk-weaving that had sustained many nuns and beatas became so depressed in the seventeenth century that the master of the city's silk guild reported that only 60 of the city's more than 3,000 looms were still in use.[47] Many beatas hoped for payment from the city government for charitable services in the prisons and hospitals, but they had to petition for money. María de la Cruz, the 'barefoot beata', demonstrated the economic dependence of these women when she appealed to the city council, 'I am poor and have an unmarried daughter who is also poor and needy.'[48] Church and municipal officials regarded the poverty of these women as a metaphor for disorder. Their asceticism could be seen as not only a repudiation of the world of material wealth, but also a criticism of it. Catalina de Jesús made this criticism explicit when she declared that people who dressed in fine clothes could not be saved.[49]

Beatas' independence from most formal regulation increased official concern about them. Unless they submitted to a confessor who could impose the discipline of the church upon them, these women could practise religion with very little restraint or guidance. Diego Pérez recognised the dangers of this position when he wrote his book of advice for beatas: 'through the liberty and occasions that they have, and through being fragile by nature, [beatas] need doctrine that teaches modesty, and guards and keeps vigilance in their mode of life'.[50] Part Four of his book, nearly 700 pages, discussed twenty 'dangers' for beatas. In particular, he urged beatas to avoid visions: 'I exhort and admonish the brides of Jesus Christ, and to all people devoted in the name of this same Lord, that they zealously call on him that he not give them visions, nor revelations, nor ecstasies.' He warned that 'spiritual arrogance' brought on false visions by making the Devil into an 'angel of light'.[51] Yet submission to a confessor or spiritual director did not always allay concerns about beatas, for some clerics acted as 'bad masters' for women. Instead of restraining the beatas, the 'bad master' could act so as to enflame their ardour.[52]

Beatas enflamed with their own mystical experiences dared to teach, preach and heal. Diego Pérez warned beatas that preaching to others was 'a very great snare of the Devil'.[53] To preach to others, or to act as spiritual directors for men, inverted the usual gender relations. Earlier the Inquisition had complained that 'nowadays everyone presumes to be theologians, even the women'.[54] Madre Bárbara, one of the beatas discussed in a 1609 report of the Inquisition in Seville, had been denounced for leading prayer meetings of women who entered trance-like states. According to witnesses, this beata not only led the women into undisciplined ecstasies but explained that the Holy Spirit had caused them to grimace and gesture with their arms and 'all the body', and to fall upon the ground.[55]

The only available descriptions of these beatas' visions are Inquisition records, but these official versions can be very instructive in the symbolic language of mysticism in this period.[56] None of the visions reported was experienced collectively, yet several shared striking similarities. God or Jesus Christ or the Virgin Mary spoke directly to the beata as an individual, usually granting the special gift of prophecy or the ability to speak to the souls of people who had died.

With the exception of Catalina de Jesús, all of the beatas' visions included appearances by the Devil or demons. Two of the beatas saw handsome young men whom they recognised to be the Devil when they exposed their genitals. Colour and tactile sensations were reported in Bárbara de Jesús' vision of the Devil dressed in blue and gold with a hat with many feathers, and also in María de Jesús' vision of beating off the Devil who then leaped out as a cinder that burned a hole in her blue mantle.

Spiritual experiences seemed to embolden the beatas denounced to the Inquisition. Earlier, Teresa de Jesús had cautioned that 'We women, and those who are unlearned, ought always to render [God] unceasing thanks — because there are persons who, by labours so great, have attained to the truth, of which we unlearned people are ignorant.'[57] Contrast this humility with the 'spiritual arrogance' of beatas such as Bárbara de Jesús and Maria de Jesús, two women penanced by the Inquisition in 1624. Although they were only in their thirties, these women had assumed positions of authority and treated clerics as 'spiritual sons'. The Inquisition accused Catalina de Jesús of a similar arrogance in presuming to direct men and to release women from obedience to their husbands. In meetings, according to Inquisition records, Catalina de Jesús presided and read from the New Testament, 'pausing a while as if thinking or awaiting God to reveal Himself'. Then she gave 'a formal talk, violating both the words of St Paul: *mulierem docere non permitto nec dominari in virum* and the sacred laws that expressly prohibit it'.[58]

The close association of beatas with the Alumbrado heresy increased official concern about them. Alumbrados emphasised experience over learning and believed that salvation came through grace alone, rather than resulting from good works or external observations of religion. Their focus on internal spiritual truth seemed perilously close to the centuries-old heresy of the Free Spirit, which taught that individuals could attain a state of perfection placing them above all human authority.[59]

A beata, Isabel de la Cruz, acted as the 'true mother and mistress of all the Alumbrados', according to one scholar.[60] In the early sixteenth century, she travelled in the regions around Guadalajara, visiting friends in Franciscan convents and returning frequently to the hospitality of the palace of the Mendoza family. She knew large portions of the Bible in both Spanish and Latin. Critical of traditional convent life, she worked through small groups of people who sought direct religious experience. These conventicles became centres of beliefs that the Inquisition identified in 1525 as heretical.[61] Four years later the Inquisition sentenced Isabel de la Cruz to perpetual prison. The Inquisition continued to find evidence of the Alumbrado heresy, however, and many of the heretical beliefs attributed to the Alumbrados in 1525 appeared in subsequent charges against the beatas of Seville.[62]

A complex power struggle within the religious establishment affected response to Catalina de Jesús and other beatas. In this period, Dominicans dominated the Inquisition and its attempts to ensure religious orthodoxy. Frequently they found themselves in opposition to Jesuits, who developed their own form of mysticism and whom beatas often sought as confessors. In their dispute over orthodoxy, neither side could afford to champion women who moved on the margins of respectability. Jesuits took special pains to distinguish between true and false spiritual gifts, sensitive to a confusion between themselves and Alumbrados.[63] Furthermore, leaders of the reform of religious orders hesitated to associate with beatas, perhaps because the independence of these women and the hints of eroticism in their ecstasies could discredit the reform movement.

The Inquisition countered the influence of beatas by a campaign of repression and misrepresentation. It confiscated their writings, subjected them to interrogation and kept them in isolation. The inquisitors and clerics who recorded testimony in their cases presented their beliefs as errors that were products of feminine weakness. Even those people who respected beatas accepted the generalisation that women without a strong male spiritual director were more vulnerable to the temptations of the Devil.[64] None of the Inquisition records suggests that the Devil actually possessed these women, however. To present them as witches or sorcerers would have acknowledged that they possessed special powers. Instead, official records concluded that they were merely weak and deluded women suffering from mental lapses or victims misled by heretical clerics.[65]

The Inquisition also used the beatas' claims to immunity from normal sexual desires to discredit them. Inquisitors ridiculed Catalina de Jesús' assertion that she had such purity in her body and soul that she could 'deal with all the world' and still remain as pure as an 'angel incarnate'.[66] In the sexual ideology that one anthropologist still finds in Andalucia, female purity without male protection was impossible.[67] Catalina de Jesús' assertion not only contradicted what every reasonable person accepted as the 'natural' order; it also deprived men of the role of protector.[68]

Inquisitors' descriptions of beatas' visions effectively transformed them from ecstatic personal visitations of God into the writhing, troubling appearance of Satan in the form of a snake or a toad or a youth dressed in crimson silk, exposing his private parts.[69] In the case of Catalina de Jesús, the Inquisition further discredited her by attributing any charisma that she possessed to a manipulative self-indulgence. The inquisitors repeatedly described her visions as 'pretended' in order to win some favour, and they wrote that she ate very well and lived with many luxuries, faking reluctance to accept the gifts pressed on her.[70] They reported her 'illness for the love of God' to be mere lazy indulgence. As in the case of so many other beatas, they also accused her of sexual licence. They declared that she had given a cleric a key so that he could visit her at all times of the night and in the very early morning. Although Catalina de Jesús was in her sixties, they insinuated that she had had carnal relations with Juan de Villapando.[71]

Many people outside the Inquisition participated in the proceedings against Catalina de Jesús and Juan de Villapando. First issued on 6 June 1623, the Edict of Grace calling for denunciations of Alumbrados had to be extended on 24 December 1623 because so many came to the Inquisition to denounce themselves or others.[72] A memorial from 1625 stated that 127 individuals had voluntarily denounced themselves within the period of grace.[73] Many of these people undoubtedly implicated Catalina de Jesús and Juan de Villapando in the Alumbrado heresy. Inquisition records do not explain how many witnesses denounced them voluntarily and how many denounced them under torture or intimidation. In the case of Catalina de Jesús, however, the memorial stated that a total of 226 persons testified against her.[74]

The motives of witnesses testifying against Catalina de Jesús were quite varied. Some witnesses must have co-operated with the Inquisition in order to save themselves, their friends and family members from torture, imprisonment and confiscation of property. However, some of the witnesses sincerely believed that Madre Catalina had forfeited her claim to holiness when she became too powerful in directing male followers, dictating which confessors the faithful could see, excusing wives from obedience to their husbands and children from obedience to their parents. Some people felt offended when she presumed to know who was predestined for salvation, particularly when she did not identify them. In the same sense, it is easy to understand the testimony of those for whom she had had revelations promising punishment after they had doubted her holiness or neglected to give her alms. Members of religious orders were offended when she taught that more sinners thrived among them than in the secular clergy. The same could be said of the learned men of the city, whom she was said to have belittled and ridiculed.[75]

Catalina de Jesús did not lie down as a sacrificial victim before the Holy Office. In 1612, during her first trial, she had discredited a witness who denounced her to the Inquisition. Released, she had continued to build up her following. Imprisoned again in 1622, she repudiated her own confession and the testimony against her as fabrications of the inquisitors. Her counter-attack apparently disconcerted two inquisitors who recommended dropping all charges in order to quiet the uproar. However, another inquisitor urged that she be penanced. A letter in the Inquisition records implies that clandestine communication between Catalina de Jesús and other Inquisition prisoners had promoted their resistance to charges against them.[76]

The Inquisition chose punishments for beatas that were designed to emphasise their isolation from the mass of orthodox Catholics. Most were sentenced to be penanced in an *auto-de-fe*, the ceremony in which the community reaffirmed its commitment to the one true faith. Sometimes this ceremony was followed by further public degradation in which the beata had to wear a *sanbenito*, the characteristic penitential costume, and walk through the city streets, or march into exile from the city.[77] These rites effectively demonstrated that beatas had lost their independence and, as everyone else, had to accept the direction of the official church. Through public rituals, they involved the people as a collective of silent witnesses, carefully distinguished from the guilty individuals.

Reclusion in an enclosed house or hospital under the direction of an appointed confessor was the most common punishment given these women. Safely removed from contact with the public, they were instructed to work for their food and shelter. Furthermore, they were forbidden to continue to report prophesies or visions or ecstasies. The Inquisition assigned to each a confessor, who would be able to redirect their spiritual lives into the safe boundaries of official orthodoxy. Beatas were made to disappear from the public life of the city and Inquisition records. Many who had not been penanced by the Inquisition simply joined convents of Tertiaries and faded into obscurity. Catalina de Jesús also disappeared from view, sentenced to six years of reclusion under the direction of an Inquisition-appointed confessor. The Inquisition found that its most effective strategy against this charismatic leader was to reduce her to silence and invisibility.

The contrast in penalties imposed on Catalina de Jesús and Juan de Villapando is striking. While the Inquisition silenced Catalina de Jesús, it required Juan de Villapando to speak publicly 'in a high voice' from a pulpit and publicly retract 22 erroneous propositions.[78] The Holy Office considered his retraction essential for preserving the orthodox faith, but it dismissed into reclusion Catalina de Jesús, who had taught the same propositions. Furthermore, the inquisitors sought to end the beata's popularity by calling for the collection of all relics or portraits or writings of hers that remained in the city. For the woman who had successfully defended herself before the Inquisition in 1612 and defied her inquisitors in 1625, the battle was over. Imposing traditional gender roles on the erring priest and beata, the Holy Office sought to restore the traditional order.

Whether safely confined in legend or prison, beatas never again exercised such power as popular religious leaders. On that February morning in 1627, people in Seville gathered for one more glimpse of Madre Catalina, whom they had not seen since her imprisonment more than four years before. As she appeared now, flanked by bigamists and blasphemers, Judaisers and heretics, her followers must have known that they would never see her again. Perhaps they sensed their own complicity in silencing this woman, their own ambivalence towards this once-sacred symbol. For Catalina de Jesús and the people of this city, power lay not in trials or edicts, but in subtleties of symbols, speech and silence.

# Notes

An earlier version of this paper was presented to the Society for Spanish and Portuguese Historical Studies and also to the Western Association of Women Historians. Of the many people who have contributed suggestions, I should like to thank in particular Elisabeth Gleason, Stephen Haliczer, Stella Menatos, Maria Ramas and John B. Owens. Research for the paper was made possible by a Fulbright-Hays Fellowship and a generous grant from the Del Amo Foundation.

1. 'Relación de un auto de fee que se celebró en el Oficio de la Inquisición de la Ciudad de Sevilla en el Conv tode Sn Pablo . . . el último día del mes Febrero del año de 1627', Biblioteca Capitular (hereafter BC), 74-7-118. See also Archivo Municipal de Sevilla (hereafter AMS), Sección Especial, Papeles del Sʳ Conde de Águila, tomo 4 en folio, no. 47, for another account.

2. 'Memorial de la secta de los alumbrados de Sevilla y de sus doctrinas y delictos y de la complicidad que en ella se ha descubierto', Archivo Histórico Nacional (hereafter AHN), *Inquisición*, leg.

2962, tomo 1. Note that archival sources refer to several women who were called Catalina de Jesús. To my knowledge, this particular woman is the only Catalina referred to as 'madre'. Villapando is sometimes spelled 'Villalpando', as in Henry Charles Lea, *Chapters from the Religious History of Spain Connected with the Inquisition* (Lea Brothers, Philadelphia, 1890), who described Villapando as the leader and Catalina de Jesús as the first disciple. However, this version may have been influenced by his own belief that 'the impressionable female nervous system' suited women to be emotional religious intermediaries, but not leaders to whom people swore obedience. See especially pp. 233, 252, note on 260, 300-8, 360. The memorial in AHN *Inquisición*, leg. 2962, 'And in Seville and its surroundings [the Alumbrados] have for their principal head and spiritual mistress madre Catalina de Jesús, and for their second Villalpando.'

3. Jaime Contreras, *El Santo Oficio de la Inquisición de Galicia (poder, sociedad y cultura)* (Akal, Madrid, 1982), discusses problems of using Inquisition records as evidence, pp. 20-1 and 575. Gustav Henningsen, *The Witches' Advocate: Basque Witchcraft and the Spanish Inquisition (1609-1614)* (University of Nevada Press, Reno, Nev., 1980), emphasises the problem of false confessions made to inquisitors, pp. 20-2.

4. Historians who have dismissed Catalina de Jesús and other beatas include Lea, *Chapters*, pp. 307-8; Marcelino Menéndez y Pelayo, *Historia de los heterodoxos españoles* (2 vols, Biblioteca de Autores Cristianos, Madrid, 1956), vol. 2, pp. 174 and 198-9; and José Deleito y Piñuela, *La vida religiosa bajo el cuarto Felipe: Santos y pecadores* (Espasa-Calpe, Madrid, 1952), p. 300; and Juan Antonio Llorente, *A Critical History of the Inquisition of Spain* (John Lilburne Co., Williamstown, 1967), p. 504. A notable exception to these examples is Claire Guilhem, 'L'Inquisition et la dévaluation des discours féminins,' in Bartolomé Bennassar (ed.), *L'Inquisition Espagnole XV<sup>e</sup>-XIX<sup>e</sup> siècle* (Hachette, Paris, 1979), pp. 197-240.

5. AHN, *Inquisición*, leg. 2962, tomos 1, 15, 17.

6. Ibid. See also AMS, Sección Especial, Papeles del S<sup>r</sup> Conde de Águila, tomo 4 en folio, no. 47. Although the latter report is not an official document of the Inquisition, it should not be seen as independent corroboration of the findings of the Holy Office because the anonymous writer was undoubtedly getting much of his information from the Inquisition.

7. AHN, *Inquisición*, leg. 2075, nos. 19, 22, and 31; leg. 2962; AMS, Sección Especial, Papeles del S<sup>r</sup> Conde de Águila, tomos 4 and 20 en folio. John Bossy, 'The Counter-Reformation and the People of Catholic Europe', *Past and Present*, 47 (1970), p. 52, describes official attempts to impose a 'parochial conformity' on religious observance.

8. Henry Kamen, *The Spanish Inquisition* (New American Library, New York, 1965), p. 58. Ricardo García Cárcel, *Orígines de la inquisición española: El tribunal de Valencia, 1478-1500* (Ediciones Penínsulas, Barcelona, 1976), points out that this popular support could very well have been grounded on fear, pp. 181-2.

9. Natalie Zemon Davis, 'City Women and Religious Change', in her *Society and Culture in Early Modern France* (Stanford University Press, Stanford, Calif., 1977), pp. 65-95 especially.

10. Clifford Geertz, *The Interpretation of Cultures* (Basic Books, New York, 1973), defines religion as a cultural system, 'a cluster of sacred symbols', which can change even as civilisation continues, pp. 90, 129 and 146. His definition of a symbol as a 'vehicle for conception' suggests that its primary function is to give meaning to social and psychological reality, both by adapting itself to reality and by shaping that reality, pp. 91-3.

11. Antonio Ballesteros, *Sevilla en el siglo XIII* (Juan Pérez Torres, Madrid, 1913), p. 147; Alonso Morgado, *Historia de Sevilla* (Andrea Pescioni y Juan de León, Sevilla, 1587), p. 471; Antonio Domínguez Ortiz, *El estamento eclesiástico*, vol. 2 of his *La sociedad española en el siglo XVII* (Consejo Superior de Investigaciones Científicos, Madrid, 1970), pp. 113-14. I am indebted to Professor Julian Bueno for sharing his knowledge of beatas in an earlier period, and to William A. Christian, Jr, for sharing his research on beatas.

12. Vida Dutton Scudder, *The Franciscan Adventure: A Study in the First Hundred Years of the Order of St. Francis of Assisi* (Dent, London, Toronto and New York, 1931), pp. 12-35 especially. For beguines and beghards, see Norman Cohn, *The Pursuit of the Millenium: Revolutionary Messianism in Medieval and Reformation Europe and its Bearing on Modern Totalitarian Movements* (Harper Torchbooks, New York, 1961), pp. 66-7 especially; Lina Eckenstein, *Women under Monasticism: Chapters on Saint-lore and Convent Life Between A.D. 500 and A.D. 1500* (Russell & Russell, New York, 1963), p. 331; Ernest W. McDonnell, *The Beguines and Beghards in Medieval Culture* (Rutgers University Press, New Brunswick, NJ, 1954); Dayton Phillips, *Beguines in Medieval Strasburg: A Study of the Social Aspect of Beguine Life* (Stanford University Press, Stanford, Calif., 1941); and R.W. Southern, *Western Society and the Church in the Middle Ages* (Penguin, Harmondsworth, 1970), 318-25.

13. Morgado, *Historia*, pp. 471-2. See also Ballesteros, *Sevilla*, p. 147; and Domínguez Ortiz, *Estamento*, pp. 113-14.

14. Melquiades Andrés Martín, *Los Recogidos: Nueva visión de la mística española (1500-1700)* (Fundación Universitaria Española, Madrid, 1975), pp. 12-13. See also Íngela Selke, *El Santo Oficio de la Inquisición: Proceso de Fr. Francisco Ortiz (1529-1532)* (Ediciones Guadarrama, Madrid, 1968), pp. 231-9; and M. Bataillon, *Erasmo y España. Estudios sobre la historia espiritual del siglo XVI* (2 edn, 2 vols, Fondo de Cultura Economico, Mexico, 1966), vol. 1, pp. 195-7.

15. Bataillon, *Erasmo*, vol. 1, p. 207. For further discussion of this tradition in Spanish religion, see William A. Christian, Jr, *Apparitions in Late Medieval and Renaissance Spain* (Princeton University Press, Princeton, NJ, 1981), pp. 4-5 and 208-12.

16. Bataillon, *Erasmo*, vol. 1, p. 81; Lea, *Chapters*, pp. 219-21; Menéndez y Pelayo, *Heterodoxos*, II, p. 174.

17. Popular enthusiasm for the Immaculate Conception is recorded in 'Memorias eclesiástics y seculares de la muy noble y muy leal ciudad de Sevilla', BC, 84-7-19, fols 195-7. Antonio Domínguez Ortiz, 'La Congregación de la Granada y la Inquisición de Sevilla (un episodio de la lucha contra los alumbrados)', in Joaquín Pérez Villanueva (ed.), *La inquisición española: Nueva visión, nuevos horizontes* (Siglo Veintiuno de España, Madrid, 1980), discusses the support of alumbrados for the doctrine of the Immaculate Conception, pp. 638-43 especially. For the significance of symbols of purity, see Mary Douglas, *Purity and Danger: An Analysis of Concepts of Pollution and*

*Taboo* (Frederick A. Praeger, New York and Washington, 1966). A broader study of the veneration of Mary and the saints is in William A. Christian, Jr, 'De los Santos a María: Panorama de las devociones a santuarios españoles desde el principio de la Edad Media hasta nuestros días', in María Cátedra Tomás (ed.), *Temas de antropologia española* (Akal, Madrid, 1976).

18. Juan de la Cerda, *Vida política de todos los estados de mugeres: en el qual se dan muy provechosos y Christianos documentos y avisos, para criarse y conservarse devidamente las Mugeres en sus estados* (Juan Gracián, Alcalá de Henares, 1599), pp. 63r-69r.

19. Diego Pérez de Valdivia, *Aviso de gente recogida* (1585), 2nd edn (Universidad Pontificia de Salamanca y Fundación Universitaria Española, Madrid, 1977, p. 221. Mystics often used this term for holy women, according to Lea, *Chapters*, p. 248. See also Selke, *Santo Oficio*, p. 55; and Marina Warner, *Alone of all her Sex: The Myth and the Cult of the Virgin Mary* (Vintage, New York, 1983), p. 128.

20. Diego Pérez, *Aviso*, p. 666. Warner, *Alone of all her Sex*, discusses the long tradition of attributing strength to sexual purity, p. 72. Julian Pitt-Rivers has interpreted female chastity as a major basis for the status of males as well as for the reputation of females, in *The Fate of Shechem, or the Politics of Sex: Essays in the Anthropology of the Mediterranean* (Cambridge University Press, Cambridge, 1977), especially pp. 79-80.

21. Diego Pérez, *Aviso*, p. 754. His discussion of clothing and appearance for beatas is on pp. 753-7.

22. Ibid., pp. 755-7. Cohn, *Pursuit of the Millenium*, p. 162, points out that the poor often gained respectability by assuming voluntary poverty in a religious group.

23. Blanca Morell Peguero, *Contribución etnográfica del Archivo de Protocolos* (Universidad de Sevilla, Seville, 1981), pp. 150-1, discusses such burial requests. Julio Caro Baroja, *Las formas complejas de la vida religiosa (Religión, sociedad y carácter en la España de los siglos XVI y XVII)* (Akal, Madrid, 1978), discusses the conflicts of materialism and religion in this period, pp. 363-87, and the tradition of holy poverty, pp. 445-61.

24. As an example, see Gonzalo Anes Alvarez (ed.), *Memoriales y discursos de Francisco Martínez de Mata* (Moneda y Crédito, Madrid, 1971), p. 129.

25. Mary Elizabeth Perry, *Crime and Society in Early Modern Seville* (University Press of New England, Hanover and London, 1980), pp. 214-15. Economic problems of convents are described in Domínquez Ortiz, *Estamento*, pp. 114-23; and in Teresa de Jesús, *The Letters of Saint Teresa*, trans. and ed. by E. Allison Peers (Burns, Oates & Washbourne, London, 1951), letters 19, 114, and 121.

26. See the vision reported by Ana de los Santos in AHN, *Inquisición*, leg. 2075, exp. 31. Keith Thomas, *Religion and the Decline of Magic* (Charles Scribner's Sons, New York, 1971), p. 138, suggests that another attraction of mysticism for women was that it provided one of the few alternatives that permitted them to be taken seriously.

27. AHN, *Inquisición*, leg. 2962, tomo 2.

28. Ibid., tomo 9.

29. AHN, *Inquisición*, leg. 2075, exp. 31. It should be noted that religious enthusiasm permitted unconventional behaviour for men as well as women. See the case of Fernando Méndez, a cleric in Seville, who fell into trances

and uttered 'terrible roars' during mass, reported in Henry Charles Lea, *A History of the Inquisition of Spain* (4 vols, Macmillan, New York and London, 1922), vol. 4, pp. 29-30.

30. Scudder, *Franciscan Adventure*, p. 50.

31. *Canons and Decrees of the Council of Trent*, trans. H.J. Schroeder, O.P. (Herder Book Co., St Louis and London, 1941), pp. 220-1.

32. Diego Pérez, *Aviso*, pp. 146, 225, and 347-52. The fact that Diego Pérez wrote this book for beatas and included many Latin passages suggests that he believed many beatas were literate. He also advised them to write out their confessions so that they would take up less time with the priest in the confessional, p. 398. Note, however, that he cautioned against too much reading and knowledge as 'a snare of the devil', p. 425.

33. AHN, *Inquisición*, leg. 2962, tomos 6-13 suggest that beatas were under the direction of male clerics, but tomo 1 states that all members of the alumbrado sect in Seville swore obedience to Catalina de Jesús. Padre Méndez, a cleric who directed many beatas, is described in Menéndez y Pelayo, *Heterodoxos*, vol. 2, pp. 195-6.

34. Pedro de León, 'Compendio de algunas experiencias en los ministerios de que vsa la Comp^a de IESVS con q practicamente se muestra con algunos acaecimientos y documentos el buen acierto en ellos', 1619, Biblioteca Universitaria de Granada, Part I, Ch. 4, fols 10-14; Part II, Ch. 25, fols 191r-192. See also Guilhem, 'Inquisition et dévaluation', p. 215.

35. Pedro de León, 'Compendio', Part II, Ch. 12, fols 142-142r.

36. Carlos Caro Petit, *La Cárcel Real de Sevilla*, Archivo Hispalense, Series 2, vol. 12, p. 42; salaries for Augustina de la Cruz are in AMS, Archivo General, Sección 2, Archivo de Contaduría, carpeta 13, no. 148, and carpeta 16, nos. 142 and 206.

37. B. Velasco, 'Fundación del convento de terciarias franciscanas de Santa Isabel en Cuellar', *Archivo Ibero-Americano*, series 2, vol. 31 (1971), 477-81. This study is based on documents in AHN, *Clero*, leg. 6246, del convento de Santa Ana.

38. Pedro de León, 'Compendio', Part I, Ch. 4, fols 11r-12. Diego Pérez, *Aviso*, p. 425, warned that women should avoid preaching, 'which is a very great snare of the devil'.

39. AHN, *Inquisición*, leg. 2962, tomo 2; note that this and the following information report what people said about Catalina de Jesús under inquisitorial questioning and may better reflect the Inquisition's view of her. Max Weber, *Sociology of Religion*, trans. Ephraim Fischoff (Beacon Press, Boston, 1963), discussed charisma, pp. 2-3, 46, and 238, especially.

40. AHN, *Inquisición*, leg. 2962, tomos 1, 13, and 15.

41. Menéndez y Pelayo, *Heterodoxos*, vol. 2, pp. 198-9, 238-40; Bennassar (ed.), *L'Inquisition*, pp. 215-16; AHN, *Inquisición*, leg. 2962, tomo 15. Evidently Catalina wrote, as the Inquisition ordered the confiscation of all her writings, both published and in manuscript form; see AMS, Sección Especial, Papeles del S^r Conde de Águila, tomo 4 en folio, no. 47. To my knowledge, none of these writings has survived.

42. AHN, *Inquisición*, leg. 2962, tomo 17. More information on

Alumbrados is in Andrés Martín, *Recogidos*; Antonio Márquez, *Los Alumbrados: Orígines y filosofía, 1525-1559* (Taurus, Madrid, 1972); Juan Flors (ed.), *Corrientes espirituales de la España del Siglo XVI* (Universidad Pontíficia de Salamanza, Barcelona, 1963); and Selke, *Santo Oficio*.

43. Teresa of Avila, *The Life of St. Teresa of Avila, Including the Relations of her Spiritual State*, trans. David Lewis (Newman Press, Westminster, Md, 1962), p. 66. Caro Baroja, *Formas complejas*, also discusses the tradition of lowly lay-people becoming miracle workers and objects of veneration, pp. 90-91.

44. Bataillon, *Erasmo*, vol. 1, pp. 81-2, and 206-9, discusses women religious leaders; Warner, *Alone of all her Sex*, provides a broader discussion of the impact of this female figure on the status of women, *passim*.

45. Teresa of Jesus, *The Book of Foundations*, vol. 3 in *The Complete Works of Saint Teresa of Jesus*, trans. E.A. Peers (3 vols, Sheed & Ward, London and New York, 1957), pp. xxi and 42, discusses the blessings of obedience.

46. Juan Ignacio Carmona García, *El sistema de hospitalidad pública en la Sevilla del Antiguo Regimen* (Diputación Provincial de Sevilla, Seville, 1979), pp. 287-8.

47. Memorial to the king from the head of the city's silk guild, quoted in the Eighth Discourse of Martínez de Mata, in Ánes Álvarez, *Memoriales*, pp. 194-5.

48. AMS, Sección 3, Escribanías de Cabildo, tomo 7, no. 17.

49. AMS, Sección Especial, Papeles del S$^r$ Conde de Águila, tomo 4 en folio, no. 47.

50. Diego Pérez, *Aviso*, p. 166.

51. Ibid., pp. 389, 470, 566-70.

52. Ibid., p. 334. Caro Baroja, *Formas complejas*, discusses contemporary cases such as those of more than 250 women who became 'possessed' under the leadership of one dominant man in Aragon in this period, pp. 67-8, and that of Padre Méndez in Seville who had women 'swarming' around him like bees, p. 480.

53. Diego Pérez, *Aviso*, p. 425.

54. AHN, *Inquisición*, leg. 4520, no. 4.

55. Ibid., leg. 2075, no. 19.

56. Inquisition records report visions for five beatas examined in Seville between 1612 and 1627, but they report none for the three beatas examined and dismissed in 1609. The five and their records include Juana de la Cruz, AHN, *Inquisición*, leg. 2075, no. 22; Bárbara de Jesús and Catalina de Jesús (not the *madre*), and María de Jesús, all reported in AHN, *Inquisición*, leg. 2075, no. 31, and also in AMS, Sección Especial, Papeles del S$^r$ Conde de Águila, tomo 20 en folio; and Madre Catalina de Jesús, in AHN, *Inquisición*, leg. 2962, tomo 4, as well as AMS, Sección Especial, Papeles del S$^r$ Conde de Águila, tomo 4 en folio, no. 47. Contreras, *Santo Oficio*, discusses methodological problems with Inquisition sources, pp. 571-80 especially. Caro Baroja, *Formas complejas*, presents several women's visions reported in this period, pp. 61-7.

57. Teresa of Avila, *Life*, p. 90.

58. AHN, *Inquisición*, leg. 2962, tomo 17, no. 35. See the descriptions of Bárbara de Jesús and María de Jesús in AMS, Sección Especial, Papeles del S$^r$ Conde de Águila, tomo 20 en folio, addendum to 1624; and the

description of Catalina de Jesús in tomo 4 en folio, no. 47. The term 'spiritual arrogance' is discussed in Diego Pérez, *Aviso*, pp. 475-85.

59. For a more detailed discussion of Alumbrados, see Márquez, *Alumbrados*, and Selke, *Santo Oficio*. The heresy of the Free Spirit is discussed in Cohn, *Pursuit*, pp. 170 and 186-7; and in McDonnell, *Beguines*, pp. 496-8.

60. Márquez, *Alumbrados*, p. 62.

61. AHN, *Inquisición*, leg. 107 and leg. 3716; libro 1299. Isabel de la Cruz is also discussed in Guilhem, 'Inquisition et dévaluation', pp. 196-239.

62. AHN, *Inquisición*, leg. 107, no. 10; leg. 3716, no. 14; and libro 1299, contain the Alumbrado heresies identified in 1525. AHN, *Inquisición*, leg. 2962, and AMS, Sección Especial, Papeles del S$^r$ Conde de Águila, tomo 4 en folio, no. 47, contain the most complete charges against Catalina de Jesús and Juan de Villapando.

63. Pedro de León, 'Compendio', Part III, entitled 'De los confesores de mujeres'. A comprehensive study of the Inquisition in early modern Seville is yet to be made. For Jesuits in Seville, see Antonio Astrain, *Historia de la Compañia de Jesús en la asistencia de España* (Administración de Razón y Fe, Madrid, 1912).

64. Diego Pérez, *Aviso*, pp. 146, 350-8 especially. Gaspar Navarro, quoted in Deleito y Piñuela, *La vida religiosa*, pp. 244-5. See also the quotation of Navarro in Bennassar (ed.), *L'inquisition*, pp. 221-2. Pitt Rivers, *Fate of Shechem*, p. 44 especially, has found a similar belief in twentieth-century Andalucia, although it does not necessarily require belief in the Devil.

65. AHN, *Inquisición*, leg. 2962, tomos 6-13; Menéndez y Pelayo, *Heterodoxos*, vol. 2, p. 195; Guilhem, 'Inquisition et dévaluation', pp. 221-5, especially.

66. AMS, Sección Especial, Papeles del S$^r$ Conde de Águila, tomo 4 en folio, no. 47. This is not to deny that sex was also used to discredit male Alumbrados; see Caro Baroja, *Formas complejas*, p. 470, for a sixteenth-century writer who associated Alumbrados with sodomy.

67. Pitt-Rivers, *Fate of Shechem*, p. 44 especially.

68. Ibid., and also pp. 75-80.

69. See the reports of the visions of Juana de la Cruz and Ana de los Santos, in AHN, *Inquisición*, leg. 2075, exp. 22 and 31.

70. AHN, *Inquisición*, leg. 2962, tomo 4.

71. AMS, Sección Especial, Papeles del S$^r$ Conde de Águila, tomo 4 en folio, no. 47; AHN, *Inquisición*, leg. 2075, exp. 31. I do not mean to imply that all sexual activity attributed to beatas was fabricated by the Inquisition to discredit them. María Helena Sánchez Ortega discusses sexual activity of beatas and other female penitents in the eighteenth century. See her 'Flagelantes licensiosos y beatas consentidoras', *Historia, 16*, no. 41 (Sept. 1979), pp. 37-54.

72. AMS, Sección Especial, Papeles del S$^r$ Conde de Águila, tomo 20 en folio, 'Efemérides', cuaderno 1. See also Menéndez y Pelayo, *Heterodoxos*, vol. 2, pp. 236 and 243; and Perry, *Crime and Society*, pp. 123-4.

73. AHN, *Inquisición*, leg. 2962.

74. Ibid., cartas.

75. All of these charges are contained in the 1625 memorial in AHN, *Inquisición*, leg. 2962. See Bennassar (ed.), *L'inquisition*, pp. 123-40, for a discussion of the factors that resulted in fear of the Inquisition.

76. See especially the letter dated 28 January 1625, in AHN, *Inquisición*,

leg. 2962. Also, see Barnardino Llorca, 'Documentos ineditos interesantes sobre los Alumbrados de Sevilla de 1623-1628', *Estudios Ecclesiásticos, 11* (1932), p. 414.

77. Kamen, *Spanish Inquisition*, pp. 183-9 especially.

78. AMS, Sección Especial, Papeles del S^r Conde de Águila, tomo 4 en folio, no. 47.

# Part III
# The Inquisition and the Control of Thought and Expression

# 9

## Thought Control in Spain

*Virgilio Pinto Crespo*

In his autobiography, José María Blanco White relates a highly
significant event in his life. It was the year 1790 and he was engaged
in performing certain spiritual exercises following the method of
Saint Ignatius Loyola. Finally, he approached a key moment, the
general confession:

> I had to prepare my confession with the aid of a printed question-
> naire that included all the varieties and types of sins as established
> by the casuists. Naturally, reading prohibited books was one of
> the principal articles of the indictment. It was followed by another
> article based on the duty to inform on any person who possessed
> them. I knew very well that the confessor could make no use of
> anything disclosed under the secret of the confessional and that
> it was not necessary for me to reveal the name of the person [a
> friend] who owned [such a] book, but I also knew that I could not
> obtain absolution unless I indicated that he would communicate
> the information to the Inquisition or I committed myself to
> transmitting it. Totally miserable, I told the sub-director [of the
> monastery] whom I had selected as my confessor, about the situa-
> tion and he told me that he could not absolve me unless I agreed
> to accuse my friend. I remember very well with what tremulous
> but resolute courage I told him: 'I would rather go to hell than
> betray him.' The priest was not unaware of the nature and origin
> of such resolution. He put off the decision until the last day of
> the exercises and I believe that he consulted Father Vega, who,
> because he was a man of great insight and probably knew that
> the book in question was not absolutely pernicious, counseled him
> not to insist on forcing me to denounce the owner. They only asked
> me to advise my friend against the possession of a book forbidden
> by the Holy Office, something which I discharged religiously,
> putting an end to my anxiety.[1]

We are at the end of the eighteenth century, at a time when the restraining force of inquisitorial prohibitions regarding books and pamphlets had weakened considerably. Such an incident, however, reveals clearly one of the most decisive, but perhaps least verifiable, consequences of censorship by the Holy Office: the education of the conscience through a process of moral coercion. This is what Antonio Márquez has accurately defined as the 'immanent Inquisition'.[2] But this dimension of inquisitorial censorship, that can be traced through texts such as this one of Blanco White, is difficult to demonstrate with the historiographical techniques presently in use. It is no less real for that and it is necessary to take it as an essential point of reference in any investigations on this theme.

The Inquisition exercised control over ideas, fundamentally, although not entirely, through the censorship of books. But this is, without doubt, one of the most confused and controversial problems in Inquisition historiography. Hundreds of pages have been written on inquisitorial censorship, the majority of which, like most of what has been written about the Inquisition itself, has been marked by the deadly effects of a polemic which has contributed more to complicating the problem than to clarifying it.

The controversy over the influence of the Inquisition on the development of Hispanic thought began in the eighteenth century. The Inquisition came to be seen as an institution opposed to progress, to the development of the Enlightenment. In the eighteenth century, the virulence of this attack was mitigated by the presence and action of the Inquisition itself, but at the end of the nineteenth century this controversy revived, centring around the debate over 'Spanish science'. The detractors of the Inquisition, such as Nuñez de Arce and Revilla y Perojo, felt that one could not even speak of real scientific or philosophical thought in Spain and the main cause of this was the existence of the Inquisition in earlier centuries. Valera, Menéndez y Pelayo and Orti thought exactly the opposite. In early modern Spain, they insisted, there had been philosophers and scientists of great stature. Furthermore, they asserted that the Inquisition itself contributed to the greatness of Hispanic science and culture. In his book *Spanish Science*, Menéndez y Pelayo compiled the best, in his judgement, of Spanish philosophical and scientific thought, while Orti y Lara established a close relationship between the Inquisition and the development of Hispanic science and culture. According to this view, the Inquisition, by saving Spain from heresy, preserved her for the Catholic faith, which for these authors was the driving force behind her spiritual and intellectual dynamism.[3]

This controversy contributed very little to clarifying the problem of the impact of inquisitorial censorship, not so much because of the passions that saturated it but fundamentally because it raised a false, and therefore insoluble problem. Spanish intellectual production was, although not entirely, the consequence of inquisitorial censorship. But we cannot hope to understand its significance without placing the phenomenon of censorship in a specific moment of history. In other words, we want to know how censorship functioned, why it functioned as it did, what its authors attempted to achieve with it, and then, perhaps, we may understand its consequences, including those on the margin of what was desired by the censors themselves. For we must not forget that censorship appeared and developed at a precise historical moment. In saying this we are not attempting to find a false historical justification for it but merely seeking to discover the social conditions that made censorship possible — conditions closely related to the profound institutional transformations, tending towards greater concentration of power, which affected both church and state, and the conflicts and disturbances that they brought with them.

## A century of conflicts

Censorship, and not only that carried out by the Spanish Inquisition, was a phenomenon peculiar to the early modern period. That is not to say that censorship was entirely unknown earlier in the history of European civilisation, but from the middle of the sixteenth century the practice of censorship took on such magnitude that we can affirm that even if we are not being confronted by an entirely new phenomenon, we are having to deal with a phenomenon with a clearly different historical significance.

The early modern period, as a consequence of certain structural transformations that had already begun in the High Middle Ages, witnessed an important process of centralisation of ecclesiastical authority while, at the same time, the consolidation of new forms of demonstrating and exercising political power led to the development of the modern state. The institutional transformation of the church, which some historians of the Middle Ages have characterised as the formation of a papal monarchy, precipitated a series of religious conflicts.[4] The problem of religious dissidence, especially heresy, became a central concern of the jurists and theologians

173

of this period.

As far as the state was concerned, as Maravall has already indicated, ideological uniformity became one of the key objectives in the struggle for institutional consolidation. Since, in the early modern period, political dissent expressed itself as religious dissent and used religious categories, ideological conformity required effective state action against religious non-conformity.[5]

Both church and state, therefore, found themselves confronting a common problem: dissidence. Censorship became one of the chief instruments in their struggle against it. As Alfonso de Castro, the distinguished legal scholar and councillor to the young Prince Philip (later Philip II) noted, the prohibition of heretical books was a task that belonged to both church and state. Curiously enough, as Castro himself pointed out, the authority to prohibit books is derived from human not divine law. This is demonstrated by the fact that violators bring punishment upon themselves not for reading heretical books but by violating the law against reading them.[6] Thus, we have a first element to consider: the relationship between censorship and the institutional transformation to church and state — a relationship made all the more complex by the advent of printing but also by the intellectual ebullition and religious conflicts that characterised western Europe during this period.

From a very early date, the printing industry demonstrated its efficacy in disseminating books and other literary materials. Between 1494 and 1515 Aldo Manuzio, a Venetian publisher with strong ties to the humanists, printed some 120,000 copies of 117 editions of classical works.[7] In the face of this powerful new force church and state began to take their first measure of control by obliging publishers to obtain licences to print. In Spain, these measures first appeared under the Catholic Sovereigns in 1502 and in the Roman Catholic Church after the Lateran Council of 1517. A century later, these first measures had become converted by official censors into a negative view of printing in general. This view was expressed by Francisco Peña, Dominican, judge of the Rota, editor of treatises on inquisitorial law and defender of the Spanish Inquisition in Rome:

> and what I would like to set forth with regard to this question [the prohibition of books] is that it is as impossible to err by being too active in prohibiting works by these moderns, full of a thousand innovations, as it is easy to make a mistake by acting timidly and late. Ever since they began to practise this perverse

excess of printing books the church has been greatly damaged and every day it is confronted by greater and more obvious perils as men exchange the ancient and secure doctrine of the virtuous doctors for the sophisticated and adulterated one of the moderns.[8]

The religious conflicts of the sixteenth century aggravated the situation. The book, 'the silent heretic' as the censors liked to call it, allowed for the propagation of dissident thought. In this sense, even the manuscript book of a previous era had rendered an important service to heretics. The printed book, which could be produced at considerably less cost and with a speed almost infinitely greater than its predecessor, was far more effective.

Furthermore, the religious rebels made imaginative use of printing in order to propagate their ideas so that the Lutheran 'boom' of the early years owed a great deal to the printing revolution. As Teófanes Egido has already noted, between 1517 and 1520 some 300,000 copies of 30 of Luther's writings were sold.[9] Thirty years later, when the religious conflict was revived by the Calvinist offensive, Geneva became the printing capital of Europe and its presses were capable of producing 250,000 books annually. The battle against religious dissidence came to be seen, at least in part, as the battle of the book.[10]

As part of its reaction to the Protestant threat, the Catholic world began to take the measure of this peculiar conflict. In the Low Countries, Charles V published various edicts containing lists of prohibited books and authors and gave the University of Louvain the responsibility for formulating the indexes that were promulgated in 1546 and 1550.[11]

The works contained in Charles V's edicts and in the Louvain Index were also prohibited by the Spanish Inquisition between 1540 and 1551. In that same year, the Inquisition reprinted the Louvain Index of 1550 along with an appendix which contained the Inquisition's earlier prohibitions, coinciding with the prohibitions contained in Charles V's edicts.[12]

For its part, the Sorbonne also entered the lists, beginning in 1521. In that year Francis I decreed the obligatory censorship of works of religion. This censorship had to be carried out by the Sorbonne theology faculty.[13] But the Sorbonne did not confine itself only to prior censorship, it also published its own lists of prohibited books, the most important of which appeared in 1543, 1544, 1546 and 1551.[14] Indices of prohibited books also appeared in other places during the 1540s including Lucca (1545) and Venice (1549).[15] Rome, which had initiated a profound reorganisation of the Roman Inquisition under Paul III, fell behind the others and the first Roman index did not appear until 1559.

These indexes indicated a change in the orientation of religious conflict. On the one hand, they expressed an urgent preoccupation with the problem of dissidence and on the other the need to develop a system of control adequate to the task of identifying and containing heterodoxy.

## Heresy

In fact, from the middle of the sixteenth century, the Spanish Inquisition had created the basis for an apparatus of control upon which an effective system of censorship could be mounted. But in order to understand exactly what this system was we must go beyond its actual functioning, because censorship and its consequences were closely related to the evolution of thought about the problem of heresy among the theologians and jurists of the period. On a theoretical level, scholastics considered the problem of heresy in the many *tractate de fide*. Juan de Torquemada dealt with it in his treatise *de Ecclesia*, an innovative work whose novelty was brought out by jurists writing in the field of inquisition law, while Cano studied it in his *Loci theologici*, a treatise on theological methodology.[16] In fact, the problem fascinated almost all the leading intellectuals of the period, Cano himself, Diego de Simancas, Peña, Bañez and Suarez, to name only the most prominent.

For these writers the problem of heresy had three major foci: the intellectual, or heresy and theological speculation, the religious, or the relationship between heresy and faith and the ecclesiastical, or the relationship between heresy and the church. Following this schema, heresy was first the most extreme and violent way of rejecting the Catholic faith; secondly, the greatest of all sins against the faith and therefore morally punishable; and thirdly, a division in the church not only in terms of dogma but also in concrete reality and, as such, a crime punishable in ordinary law.

The need to confront religious dissidence was the first but not the only consequence of these conclusions. The theologians perceived that it was now of fundamental importance to be able to distinguish between heresy and Catholic orthodoxy. What was contemplated was an attempt to find the point of no return in matters of piety and fix precisely the limits in the search for religious truth beyond which the exercise of freedom of thought was at least ethically punishable.

For their part, those who addressed themselves to issues of inquisitorial law came to other conclusions. For them, confronting heresy became a matter of determining the grades of penal responsibility that heretical beliefs necessarily implied. But, besides this, those writing about heresy sought to exploit the opportunity left by the issue of the ethical consequences of the absolute contradiction between religiosity and heresy. In order to do this they inverted the order of premises. If heresy carried with it an ethical degradation (an absence of religiosity), certain types of conduct which were depraved from an ethical standpoint could be seen as a symptom of heresy. The inevitable result of this mode of thinking was the repression not only of heterodoxy but of all kinds of unorthodox religious practices.

These reflections by jurists and theologians gave a very precise orientation to the war against religious dissidence. The seriousness with which this problem was viewed converted this struggle into a task both rigorous and urgent — one that involved as much a change in the social, cultural and religious climate that would eliminate the basis for the appearance of a successful dissident movement as direct confrontation with the heretics themselves. Inquisitorial censorship was just one of the weapons used in this struggle, and if in the end it was effective, it was not only because it helped arrest the development of dissidence but because it also contributed to changing a cultural climate that had permitted the appearance of heterodoxy.

## Vigilance and control

By the middle of the sixteenth century we can say that the system of control that had begun with the first censorship decrees of the 1520s was fully established and functioning with considerable efficiency.[17] This system continued to function with very few modifications until the Inquisition itself came to an end, since even in the early nineteenth century it was still confiscating and prohibiting books.

The primary object of the investigations carried out by the Inquisition was the book, an object that took on an almost totemic quality as a carrier of depravity. The actions of the system of control, therefore, were extended to all those persons and institutions that had dealings with it and this gave rise to a curious attitude on the part of those responsible for censorship that we will analyse later.

Paradoxically enough, the censors had great difficulty in deciding what kind of books should be the proper subject first of denunciation and investigation and then of prohibition. Of course, from the beginning, books by heretics were the object of prosecution and prohibition. But, with the passage of time, the range of inquisitorial action became so much wider that it would have been difficult for it not to have created suspicion about the book in general, especially among those who, even knowing how to read, belonged to a less educated stratum.[18]

The Inquisition created a series of controls around the book that were derived, in the first place, from a division of functions with the state. By requiring authors to obtain a licence to publish, the Spanish monarchy, through the Council of Castile, reserved for itself the right of prior censorship, while the Inquisition dealt with censorship once the book had been placed in circulation.

This situation was arrived at after a long period of legal ambiguity. A *pragmatica*, issued by the Catholic Sovereigns in 1502, gave the power to issue publication licences to the Chancery courts of Valladolid and Granada, the Archbishops of Toledo and Seville and the Bishops of Burgos, Salamanca and Zamora.[19] Later, the Council of Castile also began to issue these licences. In 1554, the Instructions of La Coruña, through which the Council of Castile was reorganised, gave that institution complete authority in the area of prior censorship. But it was the *pragmatica* of 1558 that clearly defined the Council's jurisdiction and the procedure for obtaining a licence. This *pragmatica* made it clear that obtaining such licences involved two types of control, one of an administrative character and the other ideological. It also established very severe penalties for those who violated the law. This law remained in force until the eighteenth century, when certain administrative reforms were introduced which recognised the fact that the Council of Castile had not only maintained but widened its jurisdiction over licensing.[20]

Meanwhile, the Inquisition, which had issued some licences to publish from 1520, abstained completely after mid-century, reserving for itself *a posteriori* censorship which allowed it greater freedom of action, because it could suspend printing or confiscate books even if they were being printed or circulated with a licence from the Council.[21] This articulation of functions between the Inquisition and the

Council of Castile continued until well into the eighteenth century. In 1768, however, Charles III issued a royal *cedula* which began to limit inquisitorial jurisdiction. This law made it mandatory for the Inquisition to give Catholic authors a hearing when their books were being evaluated for inclusion on the index. At the same time, the Council of Castile assumed the authority to oversee inquisitorial prohibitions; the Inquisition had to submit its edicts of prohibition to the Council before they could be promulgated.[22]

The controls that were established in the first half of the sixteenth century had an impact on the book at almost every stage of its circulation. Books entering or leaving the kingdom, bookshops, libraries, the readers themselves all became the objects of inquisitorial vigilance.

During the second half of the sixteenth century, the Inquisition feared that foreign heretics, aided by some Spaniards, were preparing to subvert the kingdom in order to provoke religious conflicts similar to those in France. As a result, the Inquisition viewed the arrival of 'depraved' or 'heretical' works as a threat to the religious and social peace and alerted its system of control in order to thwart the threat that the Protestant ideological offensive and the activity of heretical Spaniards appeared to present.

In order to prevent the entry of undesirable books the Inquisition's commissioners, who were distributed in the seaports and along the frontiers, carried out a dual function. On the one hand, they were responsible for carefully examining the merchandise carried aboard ships or in carts in order to prevent books from entering the country illegally. On the other hand, they acted to control the legal importation of books. These controls were established by virtue of a royal *cedula* issued in 1558 and, from then on, they were carried out systematically, although at times unevenly. In some areas the control mechanism was late in establishing itself and the commissioners could not carry out the necessary functions, while in others there were abuses or conflicts with royal officials. However it developed, this system gave rise to an important custom: that book importers send lists of their wares to the Suprema. These lists permit us to understand the development of book importing with a considerable degree of precision at least during the seventeenth and eighteenth centuries. Lamentably, this material remains largely unexplored.

In 1558, bookshops were also placed under inquisitorial supervision. Bookshops were inspected at least whenever a new index of prohibited books was promulgated, although normally they were controlled much more systematically. In 1605 there was an attempt to force booksellers to maintain a list of the books that they had sold along with the names of their customers, but this gave rise to considerable protest.

The libraries maintained by individuals or institutions were also subject to inquisitorial control. The examination of libraries was carried out by a process similar to that used for bookshops. A commissioner of the Holy Office, or someone else named specifically for the task, carried out the inspection and removed the suspicious or prohibited books.

Finally, the readers themselves. Here the control was more indirect, exercised by means of warnings or punishment for those who had flouted the prohibitions. From 1559, readers or simply those who possessed books prohibited by the Inquisition, incurred excommunication which only the Inquisitor-General could lift. This had been arrived at by widening the scope of excommunication to include first the readers of Luther (Paul III), then other heretical authors (Julius III) and finally readers of any prohibited books (Paul IV). The development of this legislation was different from the Inquisition than for the church as a whole. In Spain, the scope of excommunication was widened through papal concessions to Inquisitor-Generals Tavera and Valdés while in the rest of the church it was a consequence of the bull *In coena domini* issued by Gregory XIII in 1583 which placed the readers of prohibited books under the ban.[23]

The main object of these controls was to prevent suspicious or prohibited books from circulating but they had other side effects. For one thing, they had a considerable impact on the market for books. Inspections carried out by inquisitorial commissioners at seaports or along the Spanish border damaged books which were frequently shipped without bindings. The promulgation of edicts or indexes of prohibited books meant financial losses to booksellers who were forced to remove the offending volumes from their shelves with no hope of compensation for the investment they had already made in them. Finally, obligating booksellers to maintain lists of the books that they sold as well as the names of their customers must have dissuaded at least some people from purchasing books.

Another side effect of these inquisitorial controls was the apearance of certain stereotypes of intellectual comportment that were impregnated with a kind of cultural xenophobia. The Inquisition's persistent watchfulness over books from abroad contributed to the idea that all evil, all danger and heresy originated with the foreigner and that the Hispanic kingdoms were surrounded by powerful enemies prepared to incite ideological and religious subversion. Traces of this cultural xenophobia can be found in the censorship documents themselves where the censors, in order to sound the alarm about the dangers of a book or to condemn it, frequently used the argument that it was of foreign origin.

## Edicts and catalogues

Edicts prohibiting specific works and the indexes of prohibited books were instruments of censorship that complemented the system of control. It was by means of these that the Inquisition's decisions regarding specific works were promulgated. The ostentatious way in which the edicts and indexes were proclaimed, with sermons at high mass in all the principal churches, contributed powerfully to reinforcing all of these side effects and to creating a rarefied atmosphere around the book and a feeling of estrangement towards it on the part of the common people.

The Inquisition's practice of prohibiting books by using special edicts instead of simply waiting for an updated index to appear dates from the 1520s. The practice was regularised by a *carta acordada* (special order by which the Suprema regulated the provincial courts) issued by the Suprema in 1549, and lasted until the termination of the Holy Office.[24] This was a system which could be activated with relative ease. The Suprema would send a *carta acordada* to the regional tribunals indicating the book which was to be subject to prohibition and they would then post copies of the edict on the doors of the principal churches.

But the edicts themselves were not enough to combat the avalanche of literature that was considered heterodox by the Inquisition. In order to do this, lists or catalogues of prohibited books were made up. The first catalogues issued by the Spanish Inquisition date from the 1550s. In 1551 the Inquisition re-issued the Louvain Index which had come out in 1550 along with an appendix of books prohibited earlier. In 1554, it promulgated an expurgatory index of Latin and Greek editions of the Bible and, in 1559 the so-called Valdés catalogues, which reflected the new politico-religious climate at the end of the 1550s. The Valdés catalogue brought with it important changes in the orientation of censorship, changes that were completed and made systematic by the catalogue of 1583-4. In the seventeenth century, indexes were issued in 1612, 1632 and

1640, and in the eighteenth century in 1717, 1749 and 1790.[25]

Authorship of catalogues has been attributed to noted literary men like Mariana and Pineda but the catalogues were almost always collaborations, fruit of a questionnaire sent to the country's leading intellectuals and the special commissions that were set up after the index of 1612. In the 1540s the Spanish Inquisition learned how to make catalogues from foreigners but it soon became aware of what a powerful weapon they could become and endeavoured to create its own in accordance with certain systematic criteria. As a result, the catalogues are not merely a list of individual prohibitions but may instead be compared to a series of constellations, composed of very specific prohibitions of certain types of books and surrounded by vast but poorly defined ranges of potentially subversive literature.[26]

It is from this that we can see how the influence of the catalogues extended far beyond the specific prohibitions contained within them. As a Jesuit observer commented after the Index of 1583 had appeared:

> Experience shows us that because of the awe in which the inquisitors are held many people, wishing to avoid the confiscation of their books, either burn not only those that have been ordered expurgated or prohibited but even the good and safe ones, or they give them away or sell them at very low prices or they bring them to the officials of the Holy Office in order to have them examined and corrected. But by heaping together an infinite number in this way they are neither examined nor corrected but instead are lost with the passage of time so that no one can make any use of them.[27]

## The book on trial

In light of what has been said, it might appear that the creation of the system of control and its influence contributed to banishing people's love of books and written culture in general and to destroying the intellectual vigour of the central period of the early modern era in Spain. To affirm this, however, would be to oversimplify the problem since what we have described so far is only one aspect of censorship.

Once intercepted or denounced, the book was submitted to a judgement composed of a series of procedures. Let us focus on just one aspect of this process — that of qualification. Qualification was a verdict as to the orthodoxy of a book issued by experts and couched in the specialised terminology in use among theologians. The fact that we are interested in emphasising here is the participation of persons who, in a formal sense, were outside the inquisitorial bureaucracy in the process of qualification.

During the sixteenth century, the collaboration of institutions and groups like the theology faculties of the universities of Alcalá or Salamanca in the preparation of catalogues of prohibited books or in the qualification of certain works was not unusual. This collaboration between the universities and the Inquisition familiarised theologians and professors, more than was perhaps desirable, with the custom of appealing to inquisitorial authority in their intellectual conflicts and gave rise to a number of celebrated and painful disputes like that of the Salamanca Hebraists.

From the seventeenth century, the Inquisition preferred to use a special corps of censors for these tasks. These were mainly recruited from among the members of the religious orders. Before the Inquisition would admit a monk as an official qualifier he had to satisfy a number of conditions such as good moral conduct and a minimum age of 40. There were also educational requirements and, from the beginning of the seventeenth century, the Inquisition insisted that candidates should have read scholastic theology for several years. The Inquisition also attempted to limit the number of qualifiers per tribunal and to divide the available posts equally among the various religious orders.[28]

In practice, however, these conditions were frequently forgotten. Monks from the three great religious orders, Franciscans, Dominicans and Jesuits, predominated among the qualifiers. Men were admitted as qualifiers even though they were under the requisite age and had less than the requisite education. This is not to say that to be a censor for the Holy Office was the equivalent of being an uncultivated person. Thus, for example, when Quevedo became irritated with the qualifier Juan de Pineda and accused him of having a very limited sensitivity to literature (even though Quevedo himself had not been condemned to the author's purgatory of having all his works prohibited), he failed to allow for the fact that Pineda carried out his functions as a theologian and not as a literary critic. The participation of qualifiers and academic institutions in the censorship process assured the Inquisition that its efforts would take root in the social reality in the same way as the speculations of the theoreticians of heresy became rooted in the intellectual and religious actuality of the period.

The Inquisition's collaboration with specific social and intellectual sectors is what permitted censorship and the system of control to survive over the long term. The qualifiers themselves, apparently mere censors, were used to broadcast a series of intellectual and religious attitudes from pulpit and professorship whose contents and limits had been established, at least in part, by the process of censorship itself. Therefore, if the Inquisition made its presence felt through fear it also operated by collaborating with the very institutions and social strata responsible for the production and dissemination of ideology and religion.

## The influence of censorship

The activity of the censors had an unequal impact on Spanish intellectual production. The censors were more concerned with writings of a moral, juridical or theological kind, or with those destined for an academic audience, than with creative literature. Moreover, as Antonio Márquez has already noted, even when it did concern itself with literature the Inquisition was more interested in ideological content than stylistic method.[29]

In selecting collaborators in the task of censorship, the Inquisition practiced a form of intellectual endogamy. It preferred, as we have already said, those who had been trained in scholastic theology. In the mid-seventeenth century there was even an effort to create greater intellectual homogeneity among the qualifiers one sign of which was the relative success of Alberghini's *Manual de Calificadores*.[30] In this way the Inquisition strengthened a certain kind of thinking and sought to shape the work of the qualifiers by encouraging them to assimilate the work of the jurists and theologians who had dealt with questions of heresy and inquisitorial law. All of this served to fix a certain intellectual structure among the censors, a structure that became more and more closed to outside influences. This became especially noticeable in the seventeenth century when this structure had crystallised and doctrinal disputes among the Inquisition's collaborators owed more to a desire to affirm their connection to a specific religious order than to any serious intellectual disagreements. This development within the system of control had some important consequences.

In the first place, the actual functioning of the censorship mechanism itself was affected by it. The increased autonomy of the system of control explains the seventeenth-century re-evaluation of works that had circulated for decades without any difficulties. It also accounts for the fact that the indexes of the seventeenth century listed books by the great masters of the sixteenth — including some by censors — because of isolated propositions that could have been dealt with by a simple clarification or academic refutation.

Intellectual fossilisation and autonomy also explain the lack of versatility displayed by the system of control which was feeding on itself and more and more removed from reality. As a consequence, periods like the second half of the eighteenth century when there could have been a convergence between censors and leading Enlightenment figures over the suppression of popular theatre, instead produced the strongest tensions between royal power and the Inquisition over censorship. At the same time, the censorship mechanism had ceased to be useful to the state and no longer served as an effective bulwark for the defence of orthodoxy.

Normally the existence of censorship has been linked to a legal and institutional famework characterised by an absence of freedom of expression. This terminology, which was clear to the liberals of the past century, raises what is, to some degree, a false issue. In the context of sixteenth- and seventeenth-century thought, cultural and intellectual development was not linked to freedom of expression. If by chance there was a certain critical freedom, its principal objective was to restore the authentic thought of the ancient masters.[31] It is precisely at this point that the system of control erected by the Inquisition drained away the basis for intellectual endeavour. It gravely weakened the principle of academic authority and strengthened official, institutional authority as the sole criterion of truth. As a consequence, the censors' successive confrontations with the most innovative schools of thought of the period such as mysticism, humanism, philological criticism, Erasmianism, Hebraism, rationalism, the Enlightenment or the first manifestations of bourgeois liberalism, were carried out not from the perspective of an intellectual struggle but from a dogmatic position supported by a powerful judicial institution. Furthermore, censorship definitely contributed to the fossilising of the Spanish academy. As a consequence there existed for a long period, throughout the life of inquisitorial censorship itself, a fossilised academic culture with pretensions to setting standards and exerting control over all forms of thinking and a considerable degree of free criticism at the margins of the academy outside the circle of polite culture.

This can be seen with a certain clarity in the revised opinion concerning the works of Benito Arias Montano (royal chaplain and leading sixteenth-century scholastic theologian) that was handed down by the junta of censors called together in 1633 to revise the index of the previous year.

And having conferred for a long time they agreed to remove the expurgatory preface [mandated] in 1633. And because it is important that everyone understand that this author is not an accomplished theologian and that he learned more than his level of education really permitted, carried forward by his knowledge of latin and utilising unusual methods not now in use in the schools, a warning should be placed in the appendix as well as at the beginning of all of his works in order to put the reader on his guard and with this they may be permitted.[32]

Therefore, regardless of what Arias Montano said, the censorship of his work was based on the fact that he did not belong to the academic guild and utilised new forms of language. We can see from this that the censor's function was not only to preserve the secrets of power (civil or religious), as Ginzburg likes to observe,[33] but to close the doors of the academy to innovative thinking and preserve the monopoly of the school over all forms of learning.

## Notes

1. J.M. Blanco White, *Obra inglesa* (Seix Barral, Barcelona, 1974), p. 127. This is taken from his autobiography, *The Life of the Rev. Joseph Blanco White, Written by Himself with Portions of his Correspondence* (John Chapman, London, 1845).

2. A. Márquez, *Literatura e Inquisición en España, 1478-1834* (Taurus, Madrid, 1980), p. 164.

3. E. García Camarero, *La polémica de la ciencia española* (Alianza, Madrid, 1970); J.M. Orti y Lara, *La Inquisición* (Aguado, Madrid, 1877), p. 299.

4. F. Rapp, *L'Eglise et la vie religieuse en occident à la fin du Moyen Age* (PUF, Paris, 1971), p. 47.

5. J.A. Maravall, *Estado moderno y mentalidad social* (2 vols, Revista de Occidente, Madrid, 1972), vol. 1, p. 236.

6. A. de Castro, *De iusta haereticorum punitione* (Ad signum spei, Venetiis, 1549), p. 227.

7. M. Lowry, *The World of Aldus Manutius. Business and Scholarship in Renaissance Venice* (Basil Blackwell, Oxford, 1979).

8. Archivo Histórico Nacional (hereafter AHN), *Inquisición*, leg. 4517, exp. 2.

9. M. Lutero, *Obras*, ed. de Teófanes Egido (Sigueme, Salamanca, 1977), p. 15.

10. G. Rupp, 'The battle of the books: The ferment of ideas and the beginning of the Reformation'. in J.R. Brooks (ed.), *Reformation Principle and Practice* (Scolar Press, London, 1981),pp. 1-20.

11. H. Reusch, *Die Indices Librorum Prohibitorum des Sechzehnten Jahrhuderts* (Laupp, Täbingen, 1887), pp. 23-5.

12. I.S. Revah, 'Un index espagnol inconnu: celui édité par l'inquisition de Séville en novembre 1551'. in *Homenaje a Dámaso Alonso* (4 vols, Gredos, Madrid, 1963), vol. 3, pp. 131-50; p. 11. V. Pinto, 'Nuevas perspectivas sobre el contenido de los índices hispanos del siglo XVI', *Hispania Sacra, 83* (1981), pp. 597-602.

13. Francis M. Higman, *Censorship and the Sorbonne* (Droz, Geneva, 1979), p. 83.

14. Ibid., pp. 107-61.

15. Reusch, *Die Indices*, pp. 44, 86; P. Grendler, *The Roman Inquisition and the Venetian Press* (Princeton University Press, Princeton, NJ, 1977), pp. 20ff.

16. J. de Torquemada, *Summa de Ecclesia* (Andreae & Portonarijs, Salmanticae, 1560), pp. 561-78; M. Cano, *De locis theologicis* (Mathias Gastius, Salmanticae, 1563), pp. 185-215.

17. V. Pinto. *Inquisición y control ideologico en el siglo XVI* (Taurus, Madrid, 1983), pp. 149ff.

18. Ibid., pp. 261-72.

19. A. Sierra Corella, *La censura de libros y papeles en España* (Cuerpo Facultativo de Archiveros, Bibliotecarios, y Arqueólogos, Madrid, 1947), p. 80.

20. J. Eguizabal, *Apuntes para una historia de la legislación española sobre imprenta* (Imprenta de la Revista de legislación, Madrid, 1877), pp. 88-90; cf Pinto, *Inquisición y Control*, pp. 88-90.

21. Eguizabal, *Apuntes*, pp. 91-3.

22. M. Defourneaux, *Inquisición y censura de libros en la España del siglo XVIII* (Taurus, Madrid, 1973), pp. 80-5.

23. For an analysis of the apparatus of control see Pinto, *Inquisición y control*, pp. 97-146. For the development of the bull *In coena domini*, cf. G.H. Putnam, *The Censorship of the Church of Rome* (2 vols, G.P. Putnam's Sons, New York, 1906), vol. 1, pp. 112-14; cf. also Toledo, *Summa de instructione sacerdotum libri septem* (Horatium Cardon, Lugduni, 1599), p. 1037.

24. AHN, *Inquisición*, lib. 574, fol. 201.

25. Defourneaux, *Inquisición y censura*, pp. 30-5.

26. V. Pinto. 'Los indices de libros prohibidos', *Hispania Sacra, 35* (1983), pp. 161-91.

27. AHN, *Inquisición*, leg. 4435. exp. 5.

28. Pinto, *Inquisición y control*, pp. 48-59.

29. Márquez, *Literatura y Inquisición*, p. 226.

30. I. Alberghini, *Manuale qualificatorum* (A. Verges, Caesaraugustae, 1671).

31. It makes more sense to discuss the problem of free expression with regard to the eighteenth century than with respect to earlier periods as has been done recently. L. Domergue, *Censure et lumières dans l'Espagne de Charles III*

(CNRS, Paris, 1982), pp. 1-9.

    32. AHN, *Inquisición*, leg. 4435, exp. 7.

    33. C. Ginzburg, 'High and low: the theme of forbidden knowledge in the sixteenth and seventeenth centuries', *Past and Present*, 73 (1976), pp. 28-41.

# Index